Anti-Spam Techniques Based on Artificial Immune System

Anti-Spam Techniques Based on Artificial Immune System

YING TAN

CRC Press
Taylor & Francis Group
Boca Raton   London   New York

CRC Press is an imprint of the
Taylor & Francis Group, an **informa** business

CRC Press
Taylor & Francis Group
6000 Broken Sound Parkway NW, Suite 300
Boca Raton, FL 33487-2742

© 2016 by Taylor & Francis Group, LLC
CRC Press is an imprint of Taylor & Francis Group, an Informa business

No claim to original U.S. Government works

Printed on acid-free paper
Version Date: 20151013

International Standard Book Number-13: 978-1-4987-2518-7 (Hardback)

Visit the Taylor & Francis Web site at
http://www.taylorandfrancis.com

and the CRC Press Web site at
http://www.crcpress.com

Contents

List of Figures

List of Tables

List of Symbols

DS_l Legitimate detector set
DS_s Spam detector set
LC_i Legitimate concentration of the *ith* local region
SC_i Spam concentration of the *ith* local region
$tendency(t_j)$ Tendency of term t_i occurring in e-mails of a certain class
TD_h Ham term density
TD_s Spam term density
TR_h Ham term ratio
TR_s Spam term ratio

Preface

With the rapid development of the Internet and mobile Internet, e-mails and instant messages have become the most common and convenient media for our daily communication. However, spam, usually defined as unsolicited commercial or bulk e-mails, has been considered as an increasingly serious challenge to the infrastructure of the Internet and has severely affected people's normal communication both at the workplace and in personal life. According to the statistics from the International Telecommunication Union (ITU), about 70% to 85% of the present e-mails on the Internet are spam. Numerous spam e-mails not only occupy valuable communications bandwidth and storage space but also threaten the security of networking computer systems when used as a carrier of viruses and malicious codes. Detecting and tackling spam is highly time consuming, which decreases productivity tremendously.

Many solutions have been put forth to filter spam off; they can be grouped into three categories: simple approaches, intelligent approaches, and hybrid approaches. Simple approaches such as munging, listing, aliasing, and challenging can be easily implemented, but they are prone to be deceived by the tricks of spammers. Intelligent approaches have been playing an increasingly important role in anti-spam in recent years due to their self-learning ability and good performance. However, a single anti-spam shield with one technique alone can be easily intruded in practice. Consequently, hybrid approaches, combining two or more techniques, are proposed to improve overall performance that can overcome the limitations of a single technique.

Among the varieties of anti-spam techniques, the artificial immune system (AIS), inspired by the biological immune system (BIS), shows its excellence in performance and is increasingly becoming one of the most important methods to filter spam.

The BIS is a dynamically adjusting system that is characterized by the abilities of learning, memory, recognition, and cognition, which make it good at recognizing and removing antigens effectively for the purpose of protecting an organism. Generally, the AIS is an adaptive system inspired by theoretical immunology and observed immune functions, principles, and models for problem solving and is a dynamic, adaptive, robust, and distributed learning system. AIS has been developed mimicking BIS's mechanisms and functions and is now widely used in time-varying unknown environments for anomaly detection, fault detection, pattern recognition, optimization, learning, spam filtering, and so on.

AIS features are just what an information security system such as a spam filtering system needs, while the functions of BIS and information security system are very similar to some extent. Therefore, biological immune principles provide effective solutions to computer security issues. The development of AIS-based information security systems, especially AIS-based anti-spam systems, is increasingly receiving extensive attention. The application of immune principles and mechanisms can protect our computer and Internet network environments greatly.

Filtering spam from e-mail traffic is essentially a typical pattern recognition problem. To address the problem, many approaches have been proposed. In most cases, spam filtering involves three stages: term selection, feature extraction, and classifier design. This book presents these stages in detail. Specifically, for term selection, this book presents a term space partition (TSP) approach AND then a novel feature construction approach based on TSP, for the purpose of establishing a mechanism to make terms play more sufficient and rational roles in e-mail categorization. As for feature construction, this book emphasizes on AIS-based feature construction methods that contain several feature construction approaches based on a variety of immune concentrations. As for classifier design, this book shows that the mechanisms of danger theory are effective in combining classifiers. Finally, online implementation strategies of an immune-based intelligent e-mail server are developed under the Linux operating system environment.

This book consists of 13 chapters. Chapters 1 and 2 briefly introduce anti-spam techniques and artificial immune systems, respectively. From Chapters 3 through 9, immune-inspired feature extraction methods from a variety of immune principles are elaborated, which include the feature extraction or construction approaches based on term space partition, global concentration, local concentration, multi-resolution concentration, adaptive concentration selection, variable length concentration, and parameter optimization of concentrations. Chapters 10 and 11 address two kinds of classifiers based on immune danger theory: immune danger theory–based ensemble method and immune danger zone principle–based dynamic learning method. Finally, Chapters 12 and 13 describe immune-based dynamic updating algorithm and AIS-based spam filtering systems and their implementation.

All the material in this book is the result of our research work and the academic papers published by me and my guided PhD and master's students over the past decade. This book gives a panoramic image of spam filtering based on artificial immune system, which applies immune principles to feature attraction, classifier combination, and classifier updating, as well as online implementation for the purpose of demonstrating the rationality of AIS methods for spam filtering.

In addition, the author presents AIS-based anti-spam techniques using a didactic approach with detailed material and shows their excellent performance through a number of experiments and comparisons with the state-of-the-art anti-spam techniques.

Furthermore, a collection of references and resources can be found in the website of Computational Intelligence Laboratory of Peking University: http://www.cil.pku.edu.cn/resources/ and http://www.cil.pku.edu.cn/publications/.

Nevertheless, there is still a long way to go for us to apply immune-based anti-spam techniques to real-world mail filtering systems for their advancement.

The aim of this book is to provide a single source for all our models and algorithms of anti-spam based on artificial immune systems proposed in the past decade, which are scattered in a variety of academic journal papers and international conference papers, for academia, researchers, and practitioners interested in AIS-based solutions to spam filtering.

This book is intended for those who wish to learn about state-of-the-art AIS-based anti-spam techniques. In order to understand the contents of this book comprehensively, readers should have some fundamental knowledge in computer architecture and software, computer security and spam filtering, artificial intelligence, computational intelligence, pattern recognition, and machine learning.

A few errors, typos, and inconsistencies may remain in this book due to my limited specialty knowledge and capability. Critical comments and valuable suggestions are always welcome. All comments and suggestions can be sent to ytan@pku.edu.cn.

Finally, I express my heartfelt thanks to all who have helped and will help in improving the quality of this book.

Ying Tan
Beijing, China

Acknowledgments

I thank my colleagues and students who assisted me greatly during my research on such an amazing topic. I am grateful to my PhD/master's students who took part in the research project entitled "Anti-spam Techniques Based on Artificial Immune System" under my guidance in the Computational Intelligence Laboratory at Peking University (CIL@PKU).

The entire material in this book is excerpted from the research work conducted by, or from academic papers published by, me and my supervised PhD students, master's students, and postdoctoral fellows, including Dr. Guangchen RUAN, Dr. Yuanchun ZHU, Dr. Pengtao ZHANG, Dr. Junqi ZHANG, Dr. Andreas Janecek, Mr. Zhongming XIAO, Ms. Wenrui HE, and my current graduate students Mr. Guyue MI and Mr. Yang GAO. My special thanks to all of them. Without their hard work, it would have been impossible for me to make this book a reality.

In addition, Guiyue MI and Yang GAO assisted me in the preparation of the manuscript. It was through our cooperative effort and hard work that we were able to bring the AIS-based anti-spam filtering research work scattered in a variety of academic journal papers and international conference papers together into this single book, which is organized to be user-friendly.

I thank Mr. Ruijun He, editor of CRC Press, and Mr. Joselyn Banks-Kyle, project coordinator, Editorial Project Development of CRC Press, for their kind coordination and help in reviewing the manuscript. I also thank CRC Press and Taylor & Francis Group, LLC, for their commitment to publish and stimulate innovative ideas and for giving me this opportunity to publish this book so quickly.

While working on the topics of this book, I was supported by the National High Technology Research and Development Program of China (863 Program) under grant no. 2007AA01Z453; by the Natural Science Foundation of China (NSFC) under grants no. 61170057, 60673020, 60273100, 61375119, and 60875080; and partially supported by the National Key Basic Research Development Plan (973 Plan) Project of China under grant no. 2015CB352302.

Author

Dr. Ying Tan is a full professor and PhD advisor in the School of Electronics Engineering and Computer Science at Peking University, and director of Computational Intelligence Laboratory at Peking University, Haidian, Beijing, China (CIL@PKU: http://www.cil.pku.edu.cn). He received his BEng from the Electronic Engineering Institute, MSc from Xidian University, Xi'an, Shaanxi, China, and PhD from Southeast University, Dhaka, Bangladesh, in 1985, 1988, and 1997, respectively.

His research interests include computational intelligence, swarm intelligence, data mining, machine learning, intelligent information processing for information security, fireworks algorithm, etc. He has published more than 280 papers, authored/coauthored 6 books and more than 10 book chapters, and holds 3 invention patents.

He serves as the editor-in-chief of *International Journal of Computational Intelligence and Pattern Recognition* (IJCIPR), an associate editor of *IEEE Transactions on Cybernetics* (Cyb) and *IEEE Transactions on Neural Networks and Learning Systems* (TNNLS), etc. He also served as an editor of Springer's Lecture Notes on Computer Science (LNCS) for more than 15 volumes and as guest editor of several refereed journals, including *Information Science, Softcomputing, Neurocomputing, IEEE/ACM Transactions on Computational Biology and Bioinformatics, Natural Computing,* etc. He is the general chair of the ICSI-CCI 2015 joint conference, was the founding general chair of the series International Conference on Swarm Intelligence (ICSI 2010–2014), program committee co-chair of IEEE WCCI'2014, etc. He is a senior member of the IEEE.

Chapter 1

Anti-Spam Technologies

Huge amount of spam not only wastes resources but also brings severe threats to computer system security. To cope with these problems, researchers have conducted extensive researches on anti-spam technologies. This chapter presents the history, current situation, and latest advances in researches on anti-spam technologies in detail. First, this chapter describes and discusses current anti-spam techniques, including legal means, e-mail protocol methods, simple techniques, and intelligent approaches. Then, intelligent anti-spam techniques, which are the most widely used and researched recently, are introduced and analyzed from two aspects: feature extraction approaches and classification methods. After that, performance evaluation methods and benchmark corpora for spam filtering are given. Finally, this chapter summarizes the current anti-spam techniques, and points out the directions of anti-spam researches in the future.

1.1 Spam Problem

With the development of information technology and the popularity of the Internet, e-mail has been one of the most important communication tools. At the same time, the sending of numerous spam has caused much trouble in e-mail communication, because these bulk e-mails not only waste communication bandwidth and storage but also cost large resources of capital and time. Consequently, anti-spam is an urgent measure and becomes a hot research issue in the fields of computer and information security [199].

1.1.1 Definition of Spam

In 1978, e-mail spam first appeared in Arpanet, bringing minor annoyance to the Arpanet users [32]. Today e-mail has gradually developed into a major means of communication among people, while the number of spam e-mails is increasingly expanding and the impact on people's daily life becomes more and more serious. Although the e-mail has diversity in form and content, there is a clear distinction between junk e-mail and regular e-mail. From e-mail users' (recipients') point of view, the normal daily e-mails contain useful communication information, while junk e-mails comprise meaningless information that users are not interested in. Unlike the daily communication use of normal e-mails, the goals of sending a large number of junk e-mails are usually business promotion, marketing, advertisement, and others. In order to achieve real effectiveness of propaganda, the sending frequency of the same e-mail is very high and in huge scales.

Researchers usually define spam from the previous three general characteristics [174]. The classic definition of spam [47] is "unsolicited bulk e-mail (UBE)," or "unsolicited commercial e-mail (UCE)" by taking the business purpose of spam into account. Reference [67] defines spam as those e-mails which users are not interested in, and spam can be regarded as the electronic version of traditional paper junk mail. Reference [7] gives the definition of spam from the perspectives of both sending behavior and content and says spam are e-mails that are sent and spread in large numbers but without permission of the recipients. Reference [178] points out that spam has the following three characteristics: (1) the e-mail is not associated with a specific user, and the user's identity has no relationship with the content of the e-mail; (2) the recipient does not expressly consent to receive the e-mail; and (3) the content of the e-mail does not make any sense to the recipient, and the recipient is also not interested in the e-mail. Although there are some differences between these definitions, they all take users' experience into account during formulating features of spam. Spam is and will be only a burden to e-mail users.

1.1.2 Scale and Influence of Spam

Compared with the traditional mail, e-mail brings great convenience to our daily communication, for both reducing the communication cost and enhancing the communication efficiency. However, the features of low cost and fast speed of mail also make it convenient for spam senders to spread commercial advertising, bad information, and even computer viruses. Symantec report gives the statistics of the number and type of global spam e-mail and analyzes the current status of spam e-mail [177]. Spam made up 67.7% of total e-mails in December 2011. This ratio rose to 69% in January 2012, for the spam senders' mailing of large number of commercials during the New Year period. As can be seen, the number of spam is very large, and spam has occupied a major portion of the e-mail traffic. The contents of spam are mainly related to pharmaceutical, watch, adult dating, weight loss, etc., where the number of spam that are related to pharmaceutical advertising is the most and makes up 38% of the overall spam. In addition to advertising, a small amount of spam involves malicious software, such as e-mail virus and Trojans.

Commtouch Internet threats report [44] makes a statistical analysis of spam in the first quarter of 2012, pointing out that the number of spam has declined when compared to the same period in 2011, but the average daily sending amount of spam is still up to 94 billion. Among all types of spam, the ratio of spam associated with pharmaceutical advertising has risen over that of the same period in 2011, accounting for the overall proportion of 38.5%. The report also analyzes the domains of spam's header information and concludes that the spam senders generally forge the header information of e-mails, and the use of domain "gmail.com" gets the highest proportion when counterfeiting domain names.

Sophos security report [172] points out that spam senders often use viruses, worms, Trojan horses, and other malicious programs to infect and damage others' computer systems and steal their user names and passwords, and even send spam by controlling those infected computers. Those infected computers essentially constitute a huge spam-sending network, called "botnet" by the researchers. This method is one of the primary means of sending spam e-mails, and botnets often contain a lot of junk e-mails. The botnet Rustock, which was closed in 2011, could send more that 30 billion spam in a day. When the botnet Rustock was closed, the global number of spam instantly noticeably declined. Sophos security report also analyzes the regional distribution of spam. According to the country-wise statistics, the United States, India, and Korea are the top three in the number of spams sent. According to the statistics based on continents, Asia has the largest number of spams sent, accounting for 45.04%.

With the growth of sending scale, the impact caused by spam has become more and more serious [174]. Ferris research group [153] points out that spam not only wastes network resources and affects network performance, what's more important, it also wastes a lot of users' valuable time to review and delete spam, resulting in low productivity. They estimate that the waste of resources caused by spam worldwide in a year is up to $130 billion. In addition, some spam comes with viruses, Trojans, worms, and other malicious software, threatening the network security and user privacy. Symantec report [177] shows that there is one e-mail containing the malicious software among every 295 spam and one phishing e-mail among every 370 spam.

1.2 Prevalent Anti-Spam Technologies

1.2.1 Legal Means

To deal with the massive losses resulting from spam, some countries have worked out corresponding acts to regulate the e-mail sending field, attempting to narrow down the stream of spam. The United States has, in 2003, formulated the Anti-Spam Act—Controlling the Assault of Non-Solicited Pornography and Marketing (CAN-SPAM) Act. Actions like forgery of mail header information, mail address fraudulence, and mail address attacks are explicitly prohibited in this act. At the same time, business e-mails are required to be linked with the unsubscribed button or website. This rule in the act, however, as the document [74,81] points out, has not had the clear effect on spam control, but has provided a way for the spam creators to conform to the authentic or say effective mail addresses.

The 107th article of the Telecom Act of Australia has different requirements for individuals and companies [74,142]. For individuals, only under the allowance of the recipient can spam producers send e-mails to them (including business e-mails and e-mails to over 50 people). The requirements are relatively loose for companies, and spams consisting of the unsubscribed links have their access to the business.

The European Assembly passed in June 2002 the law and regulation on the privacy and electronic communication [25], which banned the sender to send spam without the permission of the recipient.

The formulation and implementation of these laws and articles have tackled some spam problems to an extent. These laws and regulations alone, however, can by no means completely eradicate spam. Therefore, the combination of laws and regulations with other technical approaches are supposed to be the best way to better filter spam and guarantee the effectiveness of e-mail communications.

1.2.2 E-Mail Protocol Methods

E-mail protocols control the delivery of e-mail between the sender and recipient, including SMTP protocol (Simple Mail Transfer Protocol), POP protocol (Post Office Protocol), and IMAP protocol (Internet Message Access Protocol). SMTP protocol is used to control the delivery of e-mail between MUA (Mail User Agent) and MTA (Mail Transfer Agent), and the delivery between two MTAs [110,145]. POP protocol controls how to receive e-mails from MTA and put them into the local MUA [136]. According to the IMAP protocol, users can directly access remote MTA and read e-mails on the e-mail server, instead of downloading e-mails to a local MUA [48].

Among these protocols, SMTP protocol is mainly used to control the sending and delivery of e-mails. Under this protocol, users can easily and conveniently interact with others via e-mails. However, since the control strategy of this protocol is very simple, it creates an opportunity for spam senders. To effectively control sending spam, there are two aspects of the SMTP protocol that need to be improved [126]: On the one hand, during the delivery of e-mails, the unread e-mails are stored on the recipients' MTA, a price for which the recipients would pay. Due to this strategy, the cost of sending spam is very low, which is one of the main reasons for the massive flooding of junk e-mails. On the other hand, the SMTP protocol does not provide a valid sender authentication mechanism. According to the SMTP protocol, the e-mail header information is the basic text information and can be filled in by e-mail senders at will, while the protocol does not provide verification mechanism. This makes it possible for spam senders to easily forge the e-mail header information and successfully evade the filtering of those techniques based on header information.

To transfer the cost of sending spam to the e-mail senders, Reference [20] proposes a method to improve the way of e-mail delivery: during the delivery process, e-mails are always stored on the senders' MTA until the recipients successfully finish receiving the e-mails. Reference [68] proposes a protocol in which the recipients could control the sending process of e-mails. When sent from strangers, the e-mails are first stored on the senders' MTA and the e-mail summaries (or envelopes) are delivered to the recipients, and only when the recipients are interested in the e-mails, the e-mails are sent successfully. Reference [101] proposes a protocol where the e-mail addresses are encapsulated. Under this protocol, when users publish their e-mail addresses on the Internet, information for restricting the use of the e-mail addresses are encapsulated into the e-mail addresses at the same time. When sent to these addresses, e-mails are verified if the information encapsulated is according to the limit and sent successfully only if they meet the limitation. This strategy could avoid the malicious use of e-mail addresses. These methods for protocol improvement could theoretically achieve good effect as they control the mails from the source. However, it is too complicated to implement the improved protocols since it needs to upgrade the existing mail delivery facilities completely.

1.2.3 Simple Techniques

In the early days of the process of anti-spam studies, people created some simple countermeasures through observation of the basic features of spam and the cardinal methods of sending them. These simple ways of handling spam have been extremely effective.

1.2.3.1 Address Protection

Reference [93] mentioned a comparatively easier way in dealing with spam, which is to keep spam away by changing the open e-mail addresses. For example, converting the e-mail address "usernamedomain.com" into "username#domain.com" or "username AT domain.com." And sometimes changing the "." into "DOT" can also work. By doing so, we can prevent the spam senders from getting the e-mail addresses on websites through creeper skills. Nevertheless, the protective ability of this technology is too weak. The spam senders can still extract the real e-mail addresses by simply adding some simple identification code when collecting e-mail addresses. By now, through the dictionary attacks, the e-mail address collection program can examine the ID number of the mail servers, as well as extract e-mail addresses of the non-page documents (like DOCJPEGPDFXLSRTFPPT) on the Internet.

1.2.3.2 Keywords Filtering

Keywords filtering technology [45] is a way of judging the types of e-mails by testing whether or not there exist the words among the predefined ones, such as "invoice," "sales promotion," "Viagra," etc. At first, we use a complete match method. For example, "Viagra" can only match with "Viagra", and not applicable for "Viiaagra". But this method can be easily avoided by spam makers by making some small changes in the words. Later on, a so-called regular expression method is gradually accepted by many approaches. The particular mode of "V*i*a*g*r*a" can be matched with "V-i-agra", "Viiaagra", and "Viagra". This mode-match method can effectively decrease the sphere of the keywords and can be applied to the small changes of spam in some degree.

1.2.3.3 Black List and White-List

Both the methods are based on the simple recognition of the senders' identity. When information about identity is found to be forged, these two methods will lose their effect [159]. Black list method is a way of filtering the spam by rejecting e-mails from specific IP addresses, TCP links, or domain names. But sometimes some information contained in the head of the e-mail may be fabricated by the spam makers into other addresses. Thus the result is some innocent people's e-mails may be filtered altogether [92]. White-list method refers to a way of rejecting all the e-mail resources, only allowing e-mails from the specific IP addresses, TCP links, or domain names. This is not a very convenient method to be used as it requires the two parties to send e-mails to each other for identity conformation.

1.2.3.4 Gray List and Challenge-Response

Gray list method will respond to those e-mails which are not within the list of the server as the e-mail is temporarily failing to be sent [224]. For those normal e-mails, the MTA will resend the e-mail when it senses the response, that is, the server will resend it successfully on receiving the e-mail. But for spam, e-mails tend to be sent through open relay, unable to be resent for wrong responses, as a result the e-mail cannot be reached by the recipients. The disadvantage of this method is that there will be some delay in sending normal e-mails.

Challenge-response has added the challenge-response strategy on the basis of the white-list [208]. Likewise, this method has a white-list. E-mail addresses from the white-list will be successfully received. But when the addresses are the ones out of the list, the server will send to the sender a "Turing test." The e-mail will reach the receiver on the condition that the sender has passed the test, and the corresponding sender's e-mail address will be added to the original white-list. Spam makers will usually adopt the forged senders' addresses to avoid the backward traces and are not expected to receive any returned tests.

On one hand, these two methods are responses made on the premise of the normal e-mails and spam, which takes advantage of the fact that spam cannot respond accordingly and be able to judge the types of e-mails. On the other hand, the process of making responses means delay and occupying the bandwidth of the Internet.

1.2.4 Intelligent Spam Detection Approaches

Intelligent spam detection approaches are the most effective and widely used technologies in the field. On one hand, intelligent detection approaches are highly automated and do not need much human intervention. But, on the other hand, intelligent detection approaches are characterized by high accuracy, robustness, and strong noise tolerance and can adapt to the dynamic changes of the e-mails' content and users' interests.

In view of the intelligent approaches, spam detection is a typical classification problem, which could be solved by the supervised machine-learning methods. Commonly, supervised machine-learning methods extract discriminative information as features from the training sets and construct classifiers based on the features extracted according to the corresponding learning principles to classify newly in coming e-mail samples. Except for some human involvement during the process of training set generation, the learning and classification processes are completely automated. Meanwhile, the learning model can adapt to the dynamic changes of e-mails' content and users' interests through adjusting the training sets and updating the classifiers [98,197]. A lot of classical machine-learning methods have been successfully applied in spam detection [32,45,113], including Naive Bayes (NB) [40,156,168], Support Vector Machine (SVM) [22,67,108,196], *k*-Nearest Neighbor (*k*-NN) [12,83,84,157], Artificial Neural Network (ANN) [41,198,228], and Boosting [33,90]. These methods have completed theoretical analysis and can achieve high performance in spam detection, which endows them with good prospects of development. The following sections will concentrate on the intelligent spam detection approaches from two aspects: feature extraction and classification.

1.3 E-Mail Feature Extraction Approaches

The feature extraction of an e-mail is an essential part in a spam detection system. The accuracy, distinctiveness, robustness, and adaptability of the feature extraction approach can affect the overall classification results and performance directly. According to the report by Chinese Internet Association in the fourth quarter of 2008 [173], the format of spam are mainly divided into three categories: text + image, text only, and image only. This section reviews the classical feature extraction approaches based on text, image, and behavior, respectively.

Before introducing the feature extraction approaches, let's talk about the term selection strategies (feature selection strategies) at first, which are indispensable and widely used in the process of feature extraction. Term selection strategies are used to evaluate the importance of a term or feature, or the quantity of information that a term or feature has, for the classification task to reduce the computational complexity and the possible effects from the noisy terms or features.

1.3.1 Term Selection Strategies

1. *Information gain (IG)*: In information theory, the entropy is also known as Kullback–Leibler distance [231]. It can measure the distance of the sum of two probability distributions. In the studies on spam detection, it is used to measure the goodness of terms or features (discrimination). According to this strategy, when knowing whether a given term appears in an e-mail, we can calculate the amount of information about the types of the receiving e-mails

$$I(t_i) = \sum_{C \in \{c_s, c_l\}} \left\{ \sum_{T \in \{t_i, \bar{t}_i\}} P(T, C) \log \frac{P(T, C)}{P(T)P(C)} \right\} \qquad (1.1)$$

where
  C represents the mail type

  c_s and c_l indicate that the mail types of spam and legitimate e-mail, respectively

  t_i means the term appears in the e-mail

  $\bar{t}_i$ shows the term t_i is not in the e-mail

According to this formula, the information entropy of each term will be calculated and the larger one will be selected to enter the next stage.

2. *Term frequency variance (TFV)*: Koprinska et al. [112] develops the term frequency variance (TFV) method to select the terms with large term frequency variance. They think that terms with large term frequency variance contain more information. According to this strategy, these terms tending to appear in the same e-mail type (spam or normal e-mail) will be chosen while those with equivalent term frequency in the two types will be removed. In research of spam detection, term frequency variance is defined as follows:

$$T(t_i) = \sum_{C \in \{c_s, c_l\}} [T_f(t_i, C) - T_f^{\mu}(t_i)]^2 \qquad (1.2)$$

where
  $T_f(t_i, C)$ is the occurrence frequency of term t_i

  $T_f^{\mu}(t_i)$ is the average occurrence frequency of term t_i in both types of e-mails

Reference [112] shows that the performance of TFV is better than IG in most cases. The top 100 terms of TFV and IG display that these terms have two characteristics: (1) frequently appearing in linguistics-related e-mails and (2) appearing frequently in spam but rarely appearing in legitimate e-mails.

3. *Document frequency (DF)*: Document frequency is the total number of a specific term t_i over the whole training set [232]. According to this strategy, the term whose DF is larger than a threshold will be chosen. The definition of DF of term t_i is as fellows:

$$D(t_i) = |\{m_j | m_j \in M \text{ and } t_i \in m_j\}| \quad (1.3)$$

where

M represents the whole training sets

m_j represents a single e-mail in M

DF indicates that the low-frequency terms have little information, so it will make no difference when these terms are removed. Reference [232] shows that when 90% of the low-frequency terms are removed, the performances of DF and IG are similar. The advantages of DF are its low computational complexity and linear proportional increase.

4. *Other term selection strategies*: Term selection strategy plays an important role in the spam detection system [77,132,133]. In order to further understand term selection, three functions are listed as follows [25,87,232].

$$\text{CHI: } \chi^2(t_i, c) = \frac{|M|(P(t_i, c)P(\bar{t}_i, \bar{c}) - P(\bar{t}_i, c)P(t_i, \bar{c}))^2}{P(t_i)P(\bar{t}_i)P(c)P(\bar{c})}$$

$$\text{Odds ratio: } \tau(t_i, c) = \frac{P(t_i|c)}{1 - P(t_i|c)} \frac{1 - P(t_i|\bar{c})}{P(t_i|\bar{c})}$$

$$\text{Term strength: } S(t_i) = P(t_i \in y | t_i \in x)$$

In these formulas, $C \in \{c_s, c_l\}$ are the types of e-mails and x and y represent two different kinds of e-mails in the training set, respectively.

1.3.2 Text-Based Feature Extraction Approaches

The e-mail feature extraction based on text usually contains two steps: (1) Term selection. According to the importance of terms, distinctive terms are chosen to enter the next stage, as has been introduced earlier; and (2) Feature extraction and display. The features of e-mails are extracted and displayed, which are expressed in a unified form.

1. *Bag-of-words (BoW)*: This approach is also called vector space model, which is one of the most widely used feature extraction approaches in spam detection [9,10,82,87,102]. It converts each e-mail into a n-dimension feature vector $\langle x_1, x_2, \ldots, x_n \rangle$ through observing whether the term occurs in the e-mail. In this approach, the value x_i of each X_i is the function of the term t_i. And there are usually two types of representation for x_i: Boolean type and frequency type [13]. In the Boolean type, x_i is assigned as this mode: if t_i occurs in the e-mail, then x_i is 1 and otherwise, x_i is 0. In the frequency type, x_i is the frequency of term t_i. In the experiments by Schneider, performance of the two representation types is similar [164].

2. *Sparse binary polynomial hashing (SBPH)*: This method uses a sliding window to extract different features from e-mails [170,234]. The N-term-length sliding window slides the e-mail and in each step it moves a term. In each sliding of the window, we extract $2N - 1$ features: the fresh terms into the window are reserved and other terms are reserved or deleted. And there are $2N - 1$ choices for the $N - 1$ terms in the window, so we can obtain $2N - 1$ features. Then each feature is converted into a specific Hash value. After the extraction of features, the method will choose terms by the previous terms selection methods, which has a high precision but also a high computational complexity.

3. *Orthogonal sparse bigrams (OSB)*: In order to reduce the redundancy and complexity of SBPH, Siefkes [170] proposed orthogonal sparse bigrams (OSB) to extract a smaller feature set, which uses a N-term-length sliding window. What is different from SPBH is that only the common terms are extracted by OSB. For each window, the fresh term will be reserved for the common term and another $N - 1$ term will be chosen to match it. As a result, each window can construct $N - 1$ pairs of terms to reflect $N - 1$ features. Compared with PSBH, it can reduce the number of features. Reference [170] shows that the performance of OSB is better than SBPH.

4. *Artificial immune system (AIS)*: Oda and White [139] designed an anti-spam immune system, which takes advantage of regular expression to construct antibody (detector). The application of regular expression makes every antibody match massive antigen (spam), which can reduce the features effectively. Biological immune system (BIS) gives weights to each antibody. In the beginning of the algorithm, the entire antibody is initialized as default values. After a period of running, the weights of antibody matching more spam will increase and those matching legitimate e-mails will reduce. When the weights of antibody are less than the preset threshold, the antibody will be removed from the model.

More advances in research of AIS-based spam filtering will be introduced in Chapter 2.

1.3.3 Image-Based Feature Extraction Approaches

Besides text content, e-mails sometimes contain image information. In normal e-mails, attached images are generally daily life photos about portraits, landscapes, architectures, and others for daily communication in life and work; While in spam, images always contain advertising text information for the purpose of advertising and marketing [25,75]. There are apparent differences between the spam images and normal images on the aspects of image attributes, colors, text, background, etc., and a number of image-based feature extraction approaches have been proposed according to the significant differences between these two categories of images [16,24].

1.3.3.1 Property Features of Image

Since spam is sent in huge quantities, spam senders usually control the size of the spam image by taking the network bandwidth and transmission efficiency into account. This makes the attributes of a spam image significantly different from that of a normal image. Reference [65] extracts the attribute information of images as feature vectors, including storage size, image length, image width, image compression formats, and other information. Similar to the earlier work, Uemura and Tabata use the image name, storage size as features and meanwhile add the image compression rate information [207]. They point out that the spam image generally has a higher compression ratio than that of a normal image because the content of a spam image is relatively simple. Reference [114] employs similar attribute information as image features and analyzes the quantity of information that each attribute feature has by defining and calculating the noise ratio, which is associated with the e-mail category information, of each attribute feature.

Reference [229] points out that the aspect ratio of a spam image is quite different from that of a normal image. There exist a large number of banners among the spam images and the difference between the length and width of a banner image is obvious. They take the number of banner images as an individual feature to construct the feature vector together with other features. He et al. compare images from the attributes like storage size, height, width, aspect ratio, etc., which are taken as preliminary features [91]. When it is difficult to determine the type of the e-mail based on the earlier preliminary features, the color and histogram information are further extracted.

1.3.3.2 Color and Texture Features of Image

Byun et al. have noted that normal images have significantly different color features from spam images [31]. There are discriminations between the spam images and normal images in the aspects of color distribution, color intensity, etc., according to the histograms. The regional similarity of a spam image is high, while the spam images have color heterogeneity. The color saturation of spam images differs from that of the normal images [83]. This method divides the images into multiple categories by extracting these color features, where five types of spam images are included, like synthetic image, complex background image, etc., as well as three types of normal images: photograph, map, and comic. Reference [130] pointed out that the smoothness of color distribution of spam images is not as good as normal images, because the spam images are generally synthetic and contain clear and sharp objects.

Wang et al. construct feature vectors by extracting the color histogram, direction histogram, and coefficients of Haar wavelet transform and detect spam images with similarity comparison [222]. Since the number of spam e-mails sent is very large, spam images sent in the same batch generally have great similarities. In the training phase, similarity distances between the spam images and normal images are calculated and the minimum similarity distance is made threshold value. In the classification phase, similarities between the feature vectors of newly coming images and the vectors in the feature library are calculated, and categories of new images are achieved by weighted voting. Wu et al. [229] extract the vertical, horizontal, and diagonal texture features of images by using wavelet transform. Reference [76] points out that spam images mostly contain advertising information and are generally artificially generated, which result in that the spam images have different color and texture features from normal images. They extract features through global color histogram and gradient direction histogram, and classify the e-mails by using boosting methods.

Reference [214] incorporates the property information with color and texture information together to form the features of each image. The property information used in this method includes: image length and width, aspect ratio, image size, compression ratio, and format information; the number of colors, primary colors, color saturation, etc. are used as color features; texture features are calculated by using the histogram method. Support vector machine (SVM) is utilized for classification after the feature extraction [194,195]. Experimental results show that the hybrid types of features have better distinguishability than a single type of features. Huamin et al. [97] achieve higher accuracy by combining the text features, image property features, and histogram features and integrating the multiple classifiers that are built. Li et al. [118] points out that global features and local features can reflect different sides of the image. They use the scale invariant feature extraction algorithm to extract the local features, then combine the local information with the global color and texture features and execute weighted classification according to the posterior probability.

1.3.3.3 Character Edge Features

On the basis of extracting edge of character vertically, Aradhye et al. [15] divide the image into text area and non-text area by calculating the similarity of character edge in each region and merging the similar regions. After the division, features of each image are constructed by calculating the size of text area in each image as well as the corresponding color saturation and color unevenness in text and non-text areas, respectively. Finally, the feature vector of an e-mail is achieved by calculating the weighted sum of related features of all images included in the e-mail according to the acreage of each image and support vector machine (SVM) [195] is employed for classification.

Wu et al. [229] give an effective method for detecting the text area. Firstly, three feature pattern sets are established: local edge pattern, local edge concentration, and global edge concentration. Boosting algorithm is used for generating detectors by training on the feature pattern sets to detect the text areas in images. Wan et al. [213] extract edge features by using color-based edge detection method and corner information of character edge is also extracted in their work. Edges of characters and other objects are distinguished according to the corner information and width and height of the edges. Liu et al. [122] detect spam images through combining the text area features, which are edge information and corner information, and the color features.

1.3.3.4 OCR-Based Features

Fumera et al. [72] extract the text information in images by using Optical Character Recognition (OCR), and the text information is further processed by adopting the text-based approaches. Considering the high computational complexity of the OCR technology, they also point out this method should be combined with others and only applied to the e-mails that are hard to classify. However, they do not consider the influence of noise in spam images on the OCR technology as there hardly exists noise in spam images at that time. Biggio et al. [23] point out that the OCR-based feature extraction approach could achieve good performance only when noise does not exist in the spam images.

To fight against the OCR-based detection method, spammers add noise information into the spam images, such as mixed fonts, background blur, text distortions, and so on. However, these noise information has become the features distinguishing spam images from normal images. Biggio et al. [23] analyze the main principle of fuzzy techniques for spam images as well as the major impact of these techniques on fuzzy OCR process, and further extract the noise features by detecting abnormal in OCR processing steps. They propose a method to detect the noise in which the image is converted into a binary image and the vision complexity is calculated. Since the vision complexity of the normal image is located in a different range of values from that of the spam image with noise, we can extract noise features of character pieces and the background by utilizing this metric.

1.3.4 Behavior-Based Feature Extraction Approaches

There are significant differences between spam and normal e-mails not only on the content, but also on the sending purpose, transmission method, interaction range, etc. In addition, spammers usually take certain measures to protect themselves to evade the spam filters. Thus, we can distinguish spam and normal e-mails by extracting different behavior features in the sending process of e-mails.

1.3.4.1 Behavior Features of Spammers

In the sending process, spammers forge the header information of e-mails to hide their identity. This makes the header information of spam have significant difference from that of normal e-mails, and the corresponding behavior features of forgery could be extracted by analyzing the header information of e-mails [206,233]. Yeh et al. [233] extract 17 behavior features for spam detection by analyzing the abnormality of single entries and the effectiveness and consistency of cross entries, and obtain the 113-dimensional feature vector by sparse coding. Abnormality of single entry is discriminated by checking whether "From," "To," "Delivered-To," "Return-Path," "Date," and other information is abnormal, such as format correctness, whether it is empty, the time rationality, and so on. Features of cross entries are obtained by checking the effectiveness and consistency of corresponding entries on type and format. Wu [228] adds the comparison of header information and system log on the basis of the earlier, and tells whether there is forgery by checking the consistency of the corresponding entry. Good performance is achieved by extracting the 26-dimensional behavior feature vectors and applying a hybrid model of rule processing and back-propagation neural network for classification, which further confirms the validity of such behavior features. In Reference [6], information of the sending process is taken as behavior features, including the number of servers involved in mail delivery, mail transmission time, and sending the existence of domain names and others. Experiments show that adding these sending process information can effectively enhance the performance of the original behavior feature extraction methods.

Since the sending purposes of spam are similar and the sending behaviors have some similarities, some studies can filter spam by group from the perspective of similarity. Reference [117] studies the similarity of spam sending behaviors (e.g., containing the same URL link), and filters spam by group according to the similarity. Through analyzing the characteristics of e-mails, it is found that there is a higher possibility for the spammers who appear in more than one group to send spam again. Ramachandran et al. [151] study the similarity of e-mail sending mode. They define sending modes according to the sending frequency of an IP address to d different domains in the period t and adopt a clustering analysis on behaviors according to the sending modes. Reference [8] analyzes the URL links in e-mails and clusters e-mails by tracking the located servers of the linked websites. They point out that one server usually provides service to a number of linked websites of spam, allowing clustering e-mails according to the server information.

1.3.4.2 Network Behavior Features of Spam

Network features of spam and normal e-mails are quite different [152], and researches have extracted the related behavior features from the perspective of IP address, that is, sending server, sending time, persistence, etc. Reference [230] analyzes the login information of mailbox and changes in the login IP and concludes that most of the e-mails sent from dynamic IP addresses are spam, while nearly half of the Hotmail spam are sent from dynamic IP addresses, so it should be paid extensive attention to the dynamic characteristics when to extract the IP address related features. West et al. [226] find through analysis that there is a spatial similarity between spam addresses, and they are always located in adjacent spaces though the spam-sending addresses dynamically changed. In addition, they found that the historical data in blacklist have a good reference value in the forecast. They propose a space-time evaluation method by combining spatial characteristics and historical data, whose error rate is half lower than that of traditional IP blacklist filtering.

Ramachandran and Feamster [150] study the characteristics of network behavior during the sending process of spam, and they specifically analyze the distribution of IP addresses that send spam, situation of BGP (Border Gateway Protocol) routing hijack, persistency of spam sending hosts and characteristics of spam botnets. Through analysis, they obtain that the majority of spam comes from a small range of IP addresses (e.g., $60.^* - 70.^*$), and the spam-sending process of botnet is not persistent. They point out that these network related features should be concerned about during spam filtering and pay attention to identify botnets. Reference [111] analyze the spam datasets from 2005 to 2009, and find that the distribution of IP addresses of botnets becomes more widespread in 2009 compared with that in 2006. This change will lead to a decline on the performance of IP address–based filtering methods and makes it more difficult to control the botnets.

In Reference [152], the network behavior features of spam are comprehensively analyzed, which includes the range of IP addresses, type of operating systems, geographical characteristics, sending modes, etc. Three unsupervised methods are utilized to analyze the association characteristics of the spam-sending process. Duan et al. [69] systematically analyze the behavior characteristics of spammers from the perspective of the mail server and the network layer, such as the distribution of mail servers, the proportion of spam, the active time of spammers, and so on. They point out that new methods on sender authentication mechanism and e-mail sending control should be studied in order to effectively reduce spam.

1.3.4.3 Social Network–Based Behavior Features

The sending and receiving networks of normal e-mails and spam are significantly different. Normal e-mails are generally used for interaction between friends, colleagues, and relatives, forming normal social network features, while the spammer always needs to extract a large number of e-mail addresses from web pages to send spam, forming abnormal interaction networks [27]. In Reference [27], each e-mail account is taken as a node and the edges between nodes are constructed in accordance with the sending and reception of e-mails. For the sending network of spam, the number of nodes in the network is large while the relation between adjacent nodes is relatively simple. The clustering coefficient calculation methods are given to distinguish normal e-mail sending networks and spam sending networks according to interconnection of nodes and situation of shared nodes between adjacent nodes.

Based on Reference [27], Lam and Yeung [115] construct social networks by extracting information from the interaction logs of e-mails to determine whether an e-mail address is used to send spam according to the characteristics of the social networks. This method extracts a seven-dimensional vector to express the social network characteristics of each e-mail account, including the number of e-mail accounts that have sending–receiving relations with this e-mail account, the interaction frequency of this e-mail account with others, etc. For a spammer account, the number of e-mails sent by this account will be very large while the number of e-mails received is very small, which makes it significantly different from the interaction process of normal e-mails. Debarr and Wechsler [63] take the space distance into consideration when constructing the social network features, which is defined as the number of transit between two e-mail accounts during the sending process of e-mail.

Li and Shen [120] consider not only the connection relationship between e-mail accounts but also the metrics of intimacy of social relations and user interest in the process of constructing social networks. This algorithm requires user involvement and encourages users to provide their social information, such as hobbies, occupation, religion, family relationships, and so on. Social relationship and closeness between e-mail accounts are measured through these information. For e-mail interactions between distant nodes, the algorithm performs more stringent checks. At the same time, this algorithm extracts user preference from user information and provides personalized spam filtering policies based on user preferences. In addition, the link weights between nodes are dynamically adjusted to avoid hijacking attacks of e-mail accounts.

1.3.4.4 Immune-Based Behavior Feature Extraction Approaches

Yue et al. [235] extract character information from IP addresses, SMTP marks, URL links and reply addresses, and computes the corresponding "spam score" of each part according to the character information and the designed feature calculation formula. These spam scores are combined to generate antibodies. On basis of this, the initial set of antibodies are adjusted by using the artificial immune network theory, and antibodies with high affinity are cloned and mutated by adopting the clonal selection algorithm, where the number of antibodies with low affinity are suppressed.

Eventually, the antibodies of the immune network are clustered. The use of artificial immune network makes the behavior features with high affinity be preserved, while the behavior features with low affinity be filtered out.

1.4 E-Mail Classification Techniques

1. *Naive Bayes*: Simple and effective, this method is the most common method. Many studies have shown that this method is the most effective way of dealing with spam, with relatively high precision rate and recall rate [11,156]. Some studies indicate that the application of the polynomial mode will acquire higher accuracy rate than that of the Bernoulli rate [164]. Variations have been derived from the traditional naive Bayes. Shrestha [169] has taken advantage of the internal connection features of the same keywords appearing in different places to calculate the co-weighting of the keyword and made great improvement in its property. Li et al. [119] mentions the improved naive Bayes more focused on the users' feedbacks, which has acquired a comparatively low false positive and better performance.

2. *k-Nearest Neighbors*: Sakkis et al. [157] have put into effect the *k*-nearest neighbors—kNN (a classical lazy learning method) in the scope of spam detection. They have studied the influence of domain (*k*), the characteristic dimension, and the practice set on the performance of the testing machine. The experiments have shown that the average performance and properties are better than naive Bayes.

3. *Boosting trees*: Schapire and Singer [162] are, for the first time, to apply this method in the area of text classification, which handles the problems of divisions of multiclass and multilabel through multi-base hypotheses. Carreras and Marquez [33] have applied AdaBoost algorithm in e-mail filtering. Based on two public data sets experiments (PU1 corpus and Ling-Spam corpus), they drew a conclusion that Boosting Trees method was better than naive Bayes theorem, Decision Trees, and kNN algorithms in performance. However, Nicholas [180] thought Boosting Trees and AdaBoost using decision stumps were worse than naive Bayes in terms of accuracy and speed.

4. *Support vector machine*: Support Vector Machine (SVM) is thoroughly discussed in References [66,209,210]. Drucker, et al. [67] have implemented a spam filter based on SVM. Their research shows that SVM filter and Boosting Trees can both meet the lowest error rates, while Boosting Trees spend more time in the training process.

5. *Ripper*: Different from other classification methods, Ripper in [43] concludes the rule of classification from training sample set without the help of feature vectors, which consists of the rules of if-then.

6. *Rocchio*: Classifier of this type [163,179] uses the standardized TF-IDF as vectors of training samples. The advantage of the classifier lies in its fastness in

training and testing, while the disadvantages can be seen from the following two aspects: extra training time is needed when searching for optimum threshold and β in training set, and also these parameters take on a weaker property of generalization.

7. *Clustering*: Sasaki et al. [161] present text clustering based on the feature space model, using spherical k-means to calculate different clusters and then tagging the extracted centroid vector according to its class by counting the distance between the vectors of the new e-mails and centroid vector. This method has shown a good detection performance on Ling-Spam corpus.

8. *Meta-Heuristics*: Yeh et al. [233], on account of the influence the variation of keywords has on the performance of the learning methods of keywords-based robots, present the use of the behavior of spammers to classify e-mails. These behavioral characteristics are described through Meta-Heuristics. Under the given Meta-Heuristics, 113 new features have been extracted. The result shows that this method is superior to the filter type of keywords, and has also shortened the training time.

9. *Artificial neural network*: Clark et al. [41], by using Artificial Neural Network (ANN), have made e-mail classification automatic [154,155,185,189,192]. Linger, a system developed by them, has achieved a higher rate of accuracy, recall, and precision. However, experiment on PU1 corpus has shown a performance reduction. Based on the descriptive properties of words and news, Iran Stuart et al. try to classify e-mails with the help of artificial neural network. The experimental results show that certain extension or modification of the feature set should be made for its improvement on performance.

10. *Artificial immune system*: Secker et al. [167] put forward the concept of AISEC (Artificial Immune System for E-mail Classification), aiming to distinguish e-mails the users are interested in and those they are not. Given that there is no repeating in training, this method can realize advanced e-mail locator on ends and track the change of the users' interests.

    White and Oda [141] have applied this model in spam filtering, taking advantage of the detection principle of *self*/*nonself* and the concept of detector. In the spam-filtering system, a gene library is constructed from various sources, including the lexical vocabularies, words, and expressions in the e-mails collected, contact information in spam, the header information of e-mails, and so on. In the process of system initialization, antibody and its related lymphocyte are produced in a random way. In the process of construction, no similar antibodies are allowed to be produced repeatedly. Each lymphocyte, apart from its attribute of immunity, has another two attributes—message-matched and spam-matched—signifying, respectively, the amount of e-mails matched to lymphocyte and that of spam. In the training process of lymphocyte, modifications on the property values of message-matched and spam-matched are made to the matched lymphocytes. In the process of system operation, the evaluation method of using the weighted average is adopted to sort e-mails. In this way, lymphocytes that have been matched for many times takes a larger proportion in the score.

More advances in research of AIS-based spam filtering will be given in Chapter 2.

1.5 Performance Evaluation and Standard Corpora

1.5.1 *Performance Measurements*

Spam detection is still a hot topic in the information security, many novel anti-spam techniques are increasingly proposed and studied deeply. In order to make it easier to compare and choose an effective way to filter spam, researchers drew up a few measurements to make a comparison of the performance between different ways and systems for filtering spam. This section mainly introduces and analyzes some common ways to evaluate the performance of spam detection and give some public standard corpora.

1. *Spam recall*: Spam recall can figure out the rate of spam correctly spotted and categorized by the arithmetic model. The systematic model with high rate of spam recall can filter spam and reduce the negative influence on people's life by them more effectively. The following formula is to calculate spam recall:

$$R_s = \frac{n_{s \to s}}{n_{s \to s} + n_{s \to l}} \tag{1.4}$$

   where, $n_{s \to s}$ means the number of spam correctly spotted and categorized while $n_{s \to l}$ means the number of spam mistaken as normal mails.

2. *Spam precision*: Spam precision can figure out the precision of measuring spam. It can figure out the rate of spam correctly spotted and categorized. It can also reflect the rate of normal e-mails mistaken as spam. The higher the spam precision is, the less the number of normal e-mails mistaken as spam is. The following formula is for calculating the spam precision:

$$P_s = \frac{n_{s \to s}}{n_{s \to s} + n_{l \to s}} \tag{1.5}$$

   where, $n_{l \to s}$ means the number of normal e-mails that are mistaken as spam.

3. *Legitimate recall and legitimate precision*: Since the spam detection involves two sorts of e-mails (legitimate e-mails and spam), these two measurements are corresponding to the spam recall and spam precision. The formulas can be deduced accordingly.

4. *Accuracy*: Accuracy can reflect the whole performance of a spam filtering system. It can measure out the rate of e-mails categorized correctly by the system, including spam and legitimate e-mails. It is defined as follows:

$$A = \frac{n_{l \to l} + n_{s \to s}}{n_l + n_s} \tag{1.6}$$

where $n_{l \to l}$ means the number of legitimate e-mails correctly categorized while n_l and n_s means the total number of legitimate e-mails and spam, respectively.

5. *Weighted accuracy*: Researchers found that the loss of legitimate e-mails (incorrectly be filtered out by the system) means people will miss important information in life, which may cause more severe consequence than spam being incorrectly categorized. In order to reflect the importance of legitimate e-mails, researchers defined the following formula as the way to calculate the weighted accuracy on the basis of accuracy.

$$A = \frac{\lambda n_{l \to l} + n_{s \to s}}{\lambda n_l + n_s} \tag{1.7}$$

where λ is the parameter reflecting the importance of legitimate e-mails.

The larger its value is, the more important the legitimate e-mail is in the current case. Its value can be 9, 99, or 999. If it is defined as 999, it means the legitimate e-mail is extremely important in such cases. When its value is 1, the weighted accuracy is equal to the accuracy directly.

6. F_β *measure*: Spam recall and precision can only reflect one aspect of the spam filtering system, respectively, while one of the two measurements cannot reflect the whole performance of the system. In order to solve this problem, F_β measure is viewed as a combination of the two measurements and is defined as follows:

$$F_\beta = (1 + \beta^2) \frac{R_s P_s}{\beta^2 P_s + R_s} \tag{1.8}$$

where β represents the weighted accuracy reflecting the importance of precision compared with recall. In most cases, the value of β is 1, and then it is referred to as F_1 measure.

1.5.2 Standard Corpora

In 2000, Androutsopoulos et al. disposed and publicized LingSpam dataset [11]. This dataset is one of the classic datasets, which were publicized earliest:

- *LingSpam:* The dataset contains 2983 e-mails including 2412 legitimate e-mails. The percentage of spam is 16.63%. The e-mails involved in this dataset were all processed in advance. Information in the header of e-mails was all eliminated (except subject). The mark of html was also eliminated. But the deficit of this dataset is that most of the e-mails are on linguistics, which means using this dataset to evaluate spam detection system could bring about an over optimistic estimate.

    In 2004, Androutsopoulos et al. [13] collected, disposed, and publicized classic datasets of PU series, which are now being widely used to evaluate various spam filtering systems. PU series contain four individual datasets as follows:

- *PU1:* It contains 1099 e-mails, of which 481 are spam. All e-mails are normally-written English e-mails. Legitimate e-mails were collected in 36 months by the author firstly referred and spam e-mails were collected by him in later 22 months.
- *PU2:* It contains 721 e-mails, of which 142 are spam. Similar to PU1, e-mails in this dataset are also in English. One of the colleagues of the author firstly referred collected these e-mails in 22 months.
- *PU3:* It contains 4139 e-mails, of which 1826 are spam. Contrast to PU1 and PU2, this dataset covers e-mails both in English and in other languages. Legitimate e-mails in this dataset were collected by the second author while spam were cited from other datasets.
- *PUA:* This one contains 1142 e-mails, 572 of which were spam. Like PU3, this dataset contains some e-mails in other languages and spam were from other datasets. Legitimate e-mails were collected by another colleague.

    Medlock [129] disposed and publicized another large-scale e-mail dataset called GenSpam.

- *GenSpam:* It was composed of three parts. Part one is dataset for training including 8018 legitimate e-mails and 31,235 spam. Part two is dataset for testing including 754 legitimate e-mails and 797 spam e-mails. Part three is dataset for self-adaption including 300 spam and 300 legitimate e-mails, which are used to detect the dynamic and self-adaption features of spam filtering systems.

    Dataset ZH1 is a Chinese e-mail dataset [240]. Chinese words in the e-mails have been separated. After such processing, the words were reflected as integer so as to protect e-mail users' privacy.

- *ZH1:* This dataset contains 1633 e-mails, of which 433 are legitimate e-mails and the percentage of spam is 73.79%. The average length of legitimate e-mails covers 819.06 words. The average length of spam covers 819.06 words. The shortest spam is 819.06 words long while the longest is 32,810 words long.

1.6 Summary

In current anti-spam techniques, intelligent spam detection methods are the most effective and promising approaches. Nevertheless, legal means and simple techniques can also play a role on some spam conforming to the defined characteristics, while it is difficult for the e-mail protocol methods to be put into practice due to the high cost.

Feature extraction approach is the core part of an intelligent spam detection system, which plays a decisive role on the performance of classification. The research on newly proposed and improved feature extraction approaches will greatly promote the development of anti-spam technologies. The intelligent spam detection is wholly a new type of anti-spam technique developed on the basis of the traditional simple anti-spam techniques. Currently, machine learning methods are widely used in the field of intelligent anti-spam and achieved high performance. Research on machine learning methods, especially classification techniques, and their application in spam filtering has a bright prospect in future development.

Chapter 2

Artificial Immune System

Artificial immune system (AIS) is an inter-discipline research area that aims to build computational intelligence models by taking inspiration from Biological immune system (BIS). This chapter first gives some knowledge of BIS and briefly introduces the origin and developments of AIS. Then, several AIS models are described in detail. This chapter then summarizes the main features and applications of AIS. Finally, the AIS-based anti-spam is presented and detailed.

2.1 Introduction

People have a keen interest on the biosphere since ancient times and have gotten inspiration from the structures and functions of biological systems and their regulatory mechanisms continuously. Since mid-twentieth century, researchers have focused on the simulation of the biological systems, especially the structures and functions of human beings. For examples, artificial neural network is to simulate the structure of the nerve system of the human brain, fuzzy control is very similar to the fuzzy thinking and inaccurate reasoning of human beings, and evolutionary computation algorithms are the direct simulations of the evolved processes of natural creatures.

In recent years, BIS has become an emerging bioinformatics research area. The immune system is a complex system consisting of organs, cells, and molecules. The immune system is able to recognize the stimulation of *self* and *nonself*, make a precise response, and retain the memory. It turns out from many researches that the immune system is of a variety of functions such as pattern recognition, learning, memory acquisition, diversity, fault-tolerant, distributed detection, and so on.

These attractive properties of the BIS have drawn extensive attention of engineering researchers who have proposed many novel algorithms and techniques based on those principles of immunology. After introducing the concept of immunity, many researches in engineering have obtained more and more promising results, such as computer network security, intelligent robots, intelligent control, and pattern recognition and fault diagnosis. These researches and applications not only can help us to further understand the immune system itself, but also can help us to reexamine and solve practical engineering problems from the perspective of information processing way in BIS.

Building a computer security system in principle of the immune system opens a new research field of information security. Many structures, functions, and mechanisms of the immune system are very helpful and referential to the research of computer security, such as antibody diversity, dynamic coverage, and distribution. We believe that the excellent features of the immune system are the roots and original springs for us to build perfect computer security systems.

2.2 Biological Immune System

2.2.1 Overview

BIS is a highly complex, distributed, and paralleled natural system with multiple levels, which can identify the *self*, exclude the *nonself*, for maintaining the security and stability in the biological environment. It makes use of the innate immunity and adaptive immunity to generate accurate immune response against the invading antigens outside. BIS is robust to noise, distributed, self-organized, noncentral control, and with enhanced memory [37]. The original substance in an organism is called *self* such as normal cells. The non-original substance in the organism is called *nonself* like the invading antigens.

BIS consists of innate immunity (also known as nonspecific immune) system and adaptive immunity (also known as specific immune) system. The two systems mutually cooperate together to resist the invasion of external antigens. Specifically, innate immune response starts the adaptive immune response, influences the type of adaptive immune responses, and assists adaptive immune to work. Adaptive immune response provides a more intense specific immune response [243].

Innate immune system is an inherent defense system that comes from a long-term evolutionary process. It is the first line of defense against antigens, which provides the innate immune function of the body. Usually, the innate immune system makes use of innate immune cells to recognize the common pattern formed by a variety of *nonself*. Therefore it can identify a variety of antigens, effectively preventing from the invasion of most antigens. If an antigen breaks up the body's innate immune defense barrier, the adaptive immune system of the human body will be invoked and responsible for the immune response to that specific antigen.

Adaptive immune system mainly has the following three functions:

1. Identifying specific antigen
2. Providing the specific immune response to clear the corresponding antigen
3. Providing a mechanism for immune memory

Specific memory cells are able to remember the corresponding antigens. When the same antigen invades the body again, the memory cells will propagate and divide rapidly, providing a more intense immune response to it.

2.2.2 Adaptive Immune Process

Lymphocytes are the mainly effective immune substances in the adaptive immune system, which consists of T lymphocytes and B lymphocytes. The generation process of the lymphocytes is shown in Figure 2.1. After negative selection, bone marrow stem cells grow into the B cells and T cells in the bone marrow and thymus. Other cells involved in the adaptive immune response include phagocytic cells, dendritic cells, and so on.

In the generation process, lymphocytes are affected by a large number of *self*. The lymphocytes that react with *self* will undergo apoptosis, and the remaining lymphocytes will go to lymphoid organs and tissues, cycling in the organism with the lymphatic blood. This process in the BIS is called the negative selection process [175]. Based on the negative selection mechanism, the BIS is able to successfully identify *self* and *nonself*, without the need of any *nonself* information.

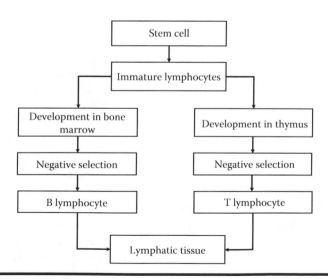

Figure 2.1   The generation and differentiation of lymphocytes.

During the first adaptive immune response, T cells and B cells will proliferate and differentiate into effector T cells and effector B cells, respectively. The effector T cells are able to specifically recognize invading antigens and eliminate the antigens directly through the manner of cell lysis. Such immune process is called cellular immunity. Different from effector T cells, the effector B cells specifically recognize and destroy the antigens by secreting antibodies, which is a kind of immunoglobulin. This method is called humoral immunity. In such a process, a few effector cells will differentiate into memory cells, achieving the immunological memory which is able to remember the antigens for a long time.

When the antigens invade the organism again, the adaptive immune system will produce the secondary immune response. In case of the secondary immune response, the memory cell is capable of proliferation and differentiation quickly, producing a large number of effector cells and providing a more intense immune response.

The proliferation and differentiation process of lymphocytes are actually the processes of clone and mutation of lymphocytes, respectively. Such clone and mutation result in the diversity of immune cells in the BIS. It is this kind of diversity that makes the BIS have the ability to identify unknown antigens and new variants of known antigens.

2.2.3 Characteristics of BIS

AIS is a bionic system inspired from immunology principles of the BIS. The key to design the AIS is how to take full advantage of the immunology principles and how the effectiveness and capability of the BIS in computer systems reappear. The BIS has a number of inspirational characteristics that the AIS can borrow from.

1. *Distributivity*: Lymphocytes in the BIS are able to detect abnormity independently, with the control of a center, which means that they constitute a highly distributed system. When to design the AIS, this feature is very helpful to the *self* protection and robustness of AIS. The architecture based on agents has been proposed to simulate the distribution of the immune system.
2. *Multilayered*: The BIS has a multilayer structure. A single layer of the BIS cannot protect the organism from all invasions, but the cooperation of multiple layers is able to achieve the security protection of the system. Although this feature is not unique to the BIS, it is a very important feature of the BIS. The studies and implementations of the multilayered feature in the AIS for computer systems can greatly enhance security of computer systems.
3. *Diversity*: In nature, although the bodies protected by the BIS are the same on the whole, each body has its own differences. The diversity of different bodies is also very helpful to the protection against invasions. Diversity is from two aspects: one is the body's own diversity, and the other is the diversity of the BIS. The combination of the two aspects increases the "diversity" greatly and

is very good to protect our body. In the field of computer system security, the implementation of the "diversity" can also be achieved in two aspects, that is, the diversity of computer operating systems and the diversity of the AIS.

4. *Disposability*: No immune cells in the BIS are indispensable. Every immune cell has a life cycle. In the study of the AIS, we can borrow the mechanism to achieve the life cycle of immune antibodies.

5. *Autonomy*: The BIS does not require a central control node. They can automatically recognize and destroy invading antigens, and unitize the illness and death of immune cells to update themselves, achieving the immunologic function on their own.

6. *Adaptability*: The BIS is able to learn new found invading pathogens, and form the memory. The speed of response to the same pathogen invasion will be accelerated. Learning mechanisms of the BIS is very important to the AIS. The AIS should not only remember the abnormal immune information found in the past, but also dynamically learn the immune rules to handle the emerging unknown anomalies.

7. *No secure layer*: In the BIS, any cell can be invaded by the pathogens, including lymphocytes. But other lymphocytes can kill the invading pathogens. The mutual help between the lymphocytes forms the basis of security of the BIS.

8. *Dynamically changing coverage*: The BIS can maintain a good balance between the space and time of the detector set. The BIS cannot form a large detector set to contain all the invasion information. The detector set flowed in the body at any time is just a small portion of the entire detector set. The flowed detector set will update itself over time and the life cycle. Such a mechanism has great benefits for enhancing the portability and coverage of the BIS.

9. *Identity via behavior*: For identification, the encryption algorithm is used in the field of encryption, whereas the representations of antibody and antigen are used in the BIS. In the field of computer systems, any representation is based on "0" and "1" at the bottom. Finding a reasonable representation will result in good recognition effect.

10. *Anomaly detection*: The BIS is able to recognize the pathogen that is never seen. This phenomenon is called as anomaly detection. This feature is conducive to the AIS for achieving the function to detect unknown anomaly or find new viruses in the field of computer security.

11. *Incomplete detection*: The antibodies and antigens do not match completely. This feature can enhance diversity and generalization of detectors. Just a few antibodies are able to detect a large number of antigens.

12. *Numbers game*: The numbers game mainly refers to the time of the invasion and the protective response. Immune response must be faster than the speed of invasion, otherwise the immune protection will be overwhelmed by the invasion. Researches of AIS indicate that more attention should be paid to the lightweight of the system.

2.3 Artificial Immune System

2.3.1 Overview

AIS is a computational intelligence system inspired by the working mechanism and principle of BIS. Based on the concept and idea of "getting wisdom from nature", and by simulating the working mechanism of BIS, AIS successfully achieved many advantages of BIS, including noise patience to learn without a teacher, distributed, self-organized, noncentral control, strengthening memory, etc. [135]. Now AIS has developed into a hot-spot research field of computational intelligence [107], and attracted many interested researchers.

There are a variety of immune algorithms and models in AIS. Among them, most algorithms try to utilize the mechanisms of learning and memory of BIS for problem solving. Most algorithms and models achieved great success. In artificial immune algorithm, the antigen is corresponding to the objective function for solving problems and constraints; the antibody is corresponding to candidate solution, antigen and antibody affinity matching degree is corresponding to candidate solution with objective function. The general steps of AIS Algorithm 2.1 is shown as follows. In Algorithm 2.1, when suspended, it was the best match with the antigen–antibody, which had optimized the solution that solved the problem successfully.

Based on the negative selection mechanism of BIS, Forrest et al. first proposed a negative selection algorithm [70], as shown in Algorithm 2.2, for anomaly detection in computer systems. This algorithm is one of the most important AIS algorithms and is of very good robustness in identifying *self* and *variant*, without reference

---

Algorithm 2.1 General steps of AIS

Step 1 input antigen;
Step 2 initialize antibody populations;
Step 3 calculate affinity for each antibody;
Step 4 check the life cycle of each antibody and update the antibody;
Step 5 if the abort condition, then go to **Step 6**, otherwise steer for **Step 3**;
Step 6 output antibodies.

Algorithm 2.2 Negative Selection Algorithm

Step 1 define *self* as a category of detector set;
Step 2 generate a detector randomly, this detector undergoes "autologous" match, if a match occurs, then this detector is removed, otherwise it is added to the *variant* detector concentration;
Step 3 abort condition judgment, if the *variant* does not contain a sufficient concentration detector, steer for **Step 2**, otherwise abort.

---

to information of *variant*, which can be used to detect unknown antigens. It is especially suitable for unknown computer security monitoring, fault diagnosis under changing environments, computer malware detection, anomaly detection, intrusion detection, and so on.

According to the clonal selection theory proposed by the Australian immunologist Burnet et al. [30], Castro and Zuben proposed clonal selection algorithm inspired by the clonal selection mechanism of AIS [59,61]. In the B cell cloning process, according to the affinity, clonal selection algorithm in the vicinity of the candidate is to produce a variation of individual clones as a population of individuals for expanding the search. In such a way, clonal selection algorithm can help prevent from the premature of an evolutionary algorithm to avoid falling into local minima [242], then lead to improve the optimization speed of the algorithm [106].

Application of biological diversity mechanism in the immune system helps to improve global search ability of optimization algorithms, and accelerate their convergence speeds. Negative expression mechanism of BIS, self-organization, and unsupervised learning may provide us useful mechanisms to cognize unknown environments by the use of the known information. The mechanism of immune memory that can save the previous knowledge learned is very important and vital for many intelligent systems. Besides, other artificial immune models and algorithms such as artificial immune network model, dendritic cells algorithm, etc. are not introduced here due to limited space. Amid the rapid development of artificial immune algorithm, many people continue to put forward a variety of novel artificial immune models and algorithms for a plenty of real-world problems.

Now AIS has been successfully applied to many practical fields, including computer security, optimization, fault diagnosis, and pattern recognition, to name a few. In particular, computer malware detection based on immune principle has been developed rapidly and achieved many fruitful results and achievements, attracting more and more researchers. Nevertheless, these AISs and malware detection methods are not perfect. Most of them have some deficiencies and shortcomings that stimulate researchers to explore more efficient models and algorithms in future.

2.3.2 AIS Models and Algorithms

BIS is a dynamic and adaptive system with the learning, memory, and cognitive abilities to effectively identify and remove antigens [201]. In the research and analysis of BIS, immunologists propose many biological immune theories and models, typically including "autologous and allogeneic" theory, clonal selection theory, immune network model, and danger theory [128]. These immune theories of the immune system not only give reasonable explanations, but also provide theoretical basis for the development of AIS [53,202].

2.3.2.1 Negative Selection Algorithm

Inspired by the generation process of T cells in immune systems, Forrest et al. [70] proposed negative selection algorithm, which has now becomes one of the most famous AIS algorithms [35,191,221]. BIS has the ability to distinguish between *self* cells and *nonself* cells, which makes it able to recognize invading antigens. T cells play a key role in this process. The generation of T cells includes two stages: the initial generation stage and the negative selection stage. Firstly, T-cell receptors are generated by a random combination of genes. In order to avoid the erroneous recognition of *self* T cells are filtered in the thymus (i.e., negative selection process). The T cells that can recognize the *self* cells will be removed, while others which are approved by the T cells are able to participate in the immune response. Forrest et al. applied the same principle to the distinction of *self* and *nonself* in computer systems. They generate the detector set by negative selection to recognize the *nonself* which invades the computers.

The process of negative selection algorithm is shown in Algorithm 2.3. Negative selection algorithm includes the detector set generation stage and the *nonself* detection stage. In the detector set generation process, the *self* gene library is constructed from the *self* files. Then the detector set is randomly generated. The detectors that match the *self* gene library are removed from the detector set according to the negative selection principle. The main role of the detector sets is that it can fully cover the *nonself* data space. Therefore the number of detectors tend to be more substantial. In the *nonself* detection stage, the algorithm conducts the *r*-contiguous bits match between the sample and the detectors in the detector set one by one. Once a match occurs, the sample will be labeled as *nonself.*

Algorithm 2.3 Negative Selection Algorithm

Input: The self set $SELF = self_i$.
Output: The detector set $D = d_i$.

  1: $D = \phi$.
  2: **while** termination condition does not meet **do**
  3:      Randomly generate a detector set N.
  4:      **for all** detector d in the detector set N **do**
  5:          **for all** self $self_i$ in the self set $SELF$ **do**
  6:              **if** $Affinity(d, self_i) < \theta$ **then**
  7:                  remove d from the detector set N.
  8:                  continue.
  9:              **end if**
10:          **end for**
11:      **end for**
12:      $D = D \cup N$.
13: **end while**

The key to negative selection algorithm is the design of the detector representation and matching functions. Regarding these two aspects, researchers have carried out a lot of negative selection algorithm researches [105].

Dasgupta and González [51] represented the detector as a rectangular function of the real number space, which is able to measure the degree of "abnormal".

González et al. [79] analyzed the limitations of the binary string representation and its matching process. They discussed the experimental performance of binary-type detector and analyzed distribution of such type of detector set in the data space. They pointed out that binary type of detector was not able to characterize the data spatial structure well of certain issues.

Balachandran et al. [17] conducted the investigation on multiple shapes of detectors in the real value space: super rectangle, super sphericity, super spheroidicity, and so on. Besides, they gave a uniform negative selection model.

Balthrop et al. [18] proposed the *r*-block matching function. The matching process measures the match status of the detectors and the text character block. The matching method can reduce the vulnerabilities of detection and improve the detection range of the detector set.

Ji and Dasgupta [104] adopted the Euclidean distance as the detector matching function in the real value space, and dynamically adjusted the matching threshold value according to the length of detectors.

In the traditional negative selection algorithm, the detector set for *nonself* is generated randomly. This random way without wizard will consume a lot of resources. Furthermore, the traditional negative selection algorithm is more concerned about *nonself* characteristic of the samples, while what the BIS really cares about is the danger of antigen. The concern of anomaly detection in computer system is the risk of the sample. Therefore how to improve the negative selection algorithm to concern about the risk of the sample becomes a valuable work.

2.3.2.2 Clonal Selection Algorithm

In BIS, each B cell produces a kind of antibody, in order to identify the corresponding antigen. When the antibody and antigen match (i.e., binding) and receive a stimulus signal emitted by the helper T cells, the corresponding B cells of antibodies are activated and cloned and differentiated into plasma cells and memory B cells. When the memory B cells encounter the same antigen again, they will generate a lot of antibodies with high affinities. Burnet [29] proposed the biological clonal selection theory to explain the process of cloning and the relationship between proliferation and differentiation of the immune cells and the affinities.

Inspired by this theory, De Castro and Von Zuben [61] proposed the clonal selection algorithm. The core idea of the algorithm is selecting and cloning the cells with high affinities, clearing the cells with low affinities, and cloning and mutating the cells based on affinities of antigens and antibodies.

Algorithm 2.4 Clonal Selection Algorithm

Input: The pattern set S.
Input: n, the number of antibodies to be cloned.
Input: d, the number of new antibodies at each iteration.
Output: The memory detector set M.
  1: Randomly generate the candidate antibody set P_r.
  2: Randomly generate the memory detector set M.
  3: **while** termination condition does not meet **do**
  4:      $P = P_r \cup M$.
  5:      Select n antibodies with best affinities from P, denote the set as P_n.
  6:      $C = \phi$
  7:      **for all** antibody $a \in P_n$ **do**
  8:          Clone a to get new antibodies, denote the set as A, the size of the set A is proportional to the affinity of a.
  9:          $C = C \cup A$
10:      **end for** $C* = \phi$
11:      **for all** antibody $a \in C$ **do**
12:          Mutate the antibody a to $a*$, the degree of mutation is proportional to the affinity of a.
13:          $C* = C * \cup a*$
14:      **end for**
15:      Select the best antibodies from $C*$, replace M with the best set.
16:      Randomly generate the candidate antibody set N_d with size d.
17:      Replace the d antibodies with lowest affinities in P_r and M with antibodies in N_d.
18: **end while**

Algorithm 2.4 gives the pseudo-code of the clonal selection algorithm (CSA). Firstly, initial solution set is regarded as the set of immune cells, and n solutions with the highest affinities are selected from the set. Then the selected n solutions are cloned. The amount of offspring is proportional to the affinity, and the degree of mutation is inversely proportional to the affinity. According to the affinity, immune cells with low affinity in the collection will be replaced with a certain probability. If optimal solution is not found, the algorithm goes to the next iteration. It can be seen that the algorithm gradually approaches the optimal affinity set in the iterative process, like the reinforcement learning. Furthermore, the random replacement in the algorithm is able to effectively maintain the diversity of the immune cell set.

De Castro and Von Zuben [61] further analyzed and discussed this algorithm, and applied it to learning and optimization problems. They used the binary encoding for solutions.

On the basis of De Castro and Von Zuben's work, researchers have proposed a number of clonal selection algorithm variants. Clonal selection algorithm gradually became an important branch of AIS.

Cutello and Nicosia [50] gave a new strategy to maintain diversity. For each B cell, they defined the probabilistic half-life period to control the cycle of the B cell and updated the immune cell set according to the life cycle.

Garrett [78] added the parameters of the clonal selection algorithm to the representation of solutions, and used the real value to encode the solution. The parameters of the algorithm can be automatically adjusted in an iterative process. This method avoids the process of parameter selection, which is very useful to problems with uncertainty parameters.

Watkins et al. [223] researched on the distributed nature of clonal selection algorithm and gave the parallel implementation of this algorithm. This method divided memory B cells into multiple independent groups, and each group evolves independently. At last the solutions from all of the groups are integrated to obtain the final result.

Cruz-Cortés et al. [49] discussed different variants of clonal selection algorithm. The binary encoding strategy and the real value encoding strategy were compared. They also analyzed the effect of Cauchy mutation and Gaussian mutation to the performance of clonal selection algorithm.

Brownlee [28] made a comprehensive analysis of the development of clonal selection algorithm. They pointed out the common character of clonal selection algorithm variants in aspect of operators and the framework, and compared clonal selection algorithms with evolutionary computation algorithms.

2.3.2.3 Immune Network Model

Immune network theory [103] explains the relationship between the immune system B cells: no matter the presence or absence of the antigen, B cells in the immune system have excitation and inhibition affect with each other. The mutual excitation and inhibition of B cell make the B cell network to be stable. The excitation of a B cell is not only affected by the antigen, but also affected by the excitation and inhibition from other B cells in the immune network.

Inspired by the ideology of the immune network theory, Hunt and Cooke [100] proposed an artificial immune network method, and applied it to the DNA sequence recognition. In this method, B cells are correlated according to the degree of affinity and inhibition. The population of B cells includes two subgroups: the initial population and the cloned population. In the training phase, the training set is divided into two parts, one for generating the initial B cell network, and the other part is used as antigens to stimulate B cell network. When the affinity between an antigen and a B cell exceeds a predetermined threshold, B cell is excited and will be cloned and mutated. The generated B cells then join the network, and excited state of the network to dynamically adjust it.

This work founds the basic of the immune network theory. Regarding the mechanisms of the immune network and the representation method of B cells, researchers have proposed a variety of artificial immune network approaches [73].

Timmis and Neal [203] proposed the idea of artificial recognition balls. Each artificial recognition ball represents a group of similar B cells. There exist excitation and inhibition among the artificial recognition balls to maintain the stability of the immune network. This method assumes that the network resources are limited; the overall number of B cells represented by the artificial recognition balls is limited.

Neal [138] proposed the self-stable artificial recognition balls, which are controlled distributively. Each artificial recognition ball automatically controls its own resources.

Nasaroui et al. [137] applied the fuzzy theory to the artificial immune network. The artificial recognition balls are represented as fuzzy sets in the data space. The method also proposed to merge artificial recognition balls according to affinity, which is similar to the crossover operator in evolutionary computation.

De Castro and Von Zuben [60] combined the clonal selection algorithm and the immune network theory. In the adjustment process of the network, then conducted clonal selection and suppression to the immune cells based on the affinity.

2.3.2.4 Danger Theory Model

Matzinger [127] analyzed the limitations of *self* and *nonself* theory, and proposed the immune danger theory on this basis. According to the traditional immune theory, the function of BIS is to distinguish between *self* and *nonself*. However, some harmless variant, such as food, embryos, and transplanted organ will not trigger an immune response. Therefore, Matzinger pointed out that immune system's function is to detect danger, rather than detect *nonself*. Danger signals are generally released by injured cells before death and can synergistically stimulate the antigen-presenting cells.

From the perspective of AIS, Aickelin and Cayzer [2] analyzed the danger theory and discuss how to build the corresponding artificial immune models. They proposed the concept of the danger zone. The core of the danger theory is the cooperative stimulation of danger signals, and scope for danger signals is the local area of the injured cells (i.e., danger zone). The B cells activation requires two conditions: one is the matching of the antibody with the corresponding antigen, the other one is locating in a danger zone and being stimulated by the danger signal.

The key to build a danger model is to define a reasonable danger signal and danger zone based on the original matching principle. In practical problems, danger signals can be dangerous independent mechanism, and can be regarded as the information representation of a problem. For the definition of danger zones, the similarity in the space or the time can be used, and the correlation between the data can also be used. The danger theory has the potential to be used in anomaly detection and data mining.

On the basis of Aickelin and Cayzer's work, researchers have proposed a number of artificial immune models based on the danger theory [36,146,236].

Secker et al. [166] explored how to apply the danger theory to web mining. The definition of danger signals is based on the user's behavior and interests. The danger zone is defined according to the distance in time and space of the documents. This work mainly discussed ideas and model's framework, without giving a specific implement algorithm.

Aickelin et al. [3] analyzed the relationship between the danger theory based AIS and the intrusion detection system. They discussed how to define the danger signals and danger zones based on the intrusion behavior, in order to build a more robust intrusion detection system.

Prieto et al. [146] applied the danger theory to the control strategy of robot soccer goalkeeper. When football is located in our region, a first immune signal is generated. When an opposing player comes into the penalty area with the ball (danger zone), the danger signal will be generated.

Chao et al. [36] detected the anomaly in the software system based on the danger theory. In the running process of the software, the abnormal changes of the system resources will result in a danger signal, indicating the anomaly of the software.

2.3.2.5 Immune Concentration

Immune concentration is an immune inspired algorithm for feature extraction. Let's take the spam detection as an example to introduce the concept of immune concentration.

The essence of the feature extraction method lies in the construction of concentration feature vectors. In References [155,190], Tan et al. presented Global Concentration (GC) based feature extraction methods for spam filtering. In References [246,248], Local Concentration (LC) based feature extraction methods were proposed. In these methods, statistical term selection methods [232] are utilized to remove uninformative terms. Then a tendency function is well designed to generate two detector sets [246,248]. The tendency of a term t_i is defined in Equation 2.1. $T(t_i)$ measures the difference between the term's occurrence frequency in two types of messages. Terms are added to corresponding detector sets according to their tendency. Detector concentration, which corresponds to antibody concentration in BIS, is then extracted from messages by using the detector sets. In addition, a sliding window is utilized to slide over a message to extract position-correlated information from messages. By using a sliding window, a message is divided into local parts. At each movement of the window, a spam detector concentration S_i and a legitimate detector concentration L_i are calculated with respect to the two detector sets and the terms in the window according to Equations 2.2 and 2.3.

$$T(t_i) = P(t_i|c_l) - P(t_i|c_s) \qquad (2.1)$$

where

$P(t_i|c_l)$ denotes the probability of t_i's occurrence, given messages are legitimate e-mails

$P(t_i|c_s)$ denotes the probability of t_i's occurrence estimated in spam

$$S_i = \frac{\sum_{j=1}^{w_n} M(t_j, D_s)}{N_t} \qquad (2.2)$$

$$L_i = \frac{\sum_{j=1}^{w_n} M(t_j, D_l)}{N_t} \qquad (2.3)$$

where

N_t is the number of distinct terms in the window

D_s denotes the spam detector set

D_l denotes the legitimate e-mail detector set

$M(\cdot)$ denotes the match function, which measures the number of terms in the window matched by detectors

Each sliding window defines a specific local area in a message. To explore the effects of a sliding window, we design two strategies using a sliding window with fixed-length (FL) and using a sliding window with variable length (VL). When a fixed-length sliding window is utilized, messages may have different number of local areas (corresponding to different number of feature dimensionality), as messages vary in length. To handle this problem, we may either expand a short message by reproducing the existing features, or reduce the dimensionality of long messages by discarding uninformative features. In VL strategy, the length of a sliding window is designed to be proportional to the length of a message, and there is no need for specific process of feature dimensionality. Preliminary experiments showed that both the two strategies are effective in extracting discriminative features. In the circumstance that the size of a window is set to infinite, a message is taken as a whole for getting concentration features, GC feature vectors are extracted. When the window size is smaller than the message length, the window divides a message into individual local parts, and LC features are extracted from each window.

Very recently, there are a number of concentration-based methods that are derived from the global and local concentration methods and applied to several practical problems [77,132,133,219,220].

2.3.2.6 *Other Models and Algorithms*

Dasgupta et al. [52] made a comprehensive analysis of a variety of biological immune models, and pointed out that BIS is highly complex network composed of biological tissue, immune cells, chemical molecules, etc. On this basis, they proposed a multilayer multi-resolution immune learning model, which integrated a variety of immunization strategies, including dynamical detector generation, clonal selection, and the interactions of immune cells. The method is able to make full use of the function of various immune cells; helper T cells, suppressor T cells, B cells, and antigen-presenting cells will synergistically interact information to detect anomalies.

Wang et al. [217] presented a complex immune system to simulate the representation and process of antigens. This method also used the interactions among a variety of immune cells. It comprised five immune processes, and mainly concerned the processing and representation of the antigens, and the interactions between the antigen-presenting cells, T cells, and B cells. Experiments show that the system has a good memory and noise immunity.

Zhang and Hou [244] combined the niche strategy and clonal selection algorithm, and proposed a hybrid immunological method. This method combined the negative selection, clonal selection, mutation, and niche strategies, which is able to effectively reduce the number of detectors.

Li et al. [121] proposed an efficient artificial immune network, which combined with particle swarm optimization algorithm. In the particle swarm optimization, particles' behavior can be affected by the optimal particle in the population. By interacting with the optimal particle, the swarm is able to speed up the convergence of the particle swarm. With regard to the immune network, they introduced the interaction between immune cells and the optimal immune cell, making the immune network converging to a stable state with a faster speed.

De Castro and Von Zuben [62] proposed the Bayesian AIS that replace the basic clone and mutation operator with a probabilistic model for solving complex optimization problems.

2.3.3 *Characteristics of AIS*

The BIS has been evolving for hundreds of millions of years and plays a very important role in the protection of the body from bacterial invasion. Although the immune system may encounter problems sometimes, generally speaking, we can see its unique protective effect. The working principles of the BIS will have some inspiration and reference meaning on the research field of security protection technologies of computer systems, providing a brand new thinking of computer security, if the computer systems are seen as "human bodies" and the external intrusions as "harmful viruses."

Immunity refers to the ability of the body to identify *self* or *nonself* and exclude *nonself*. The BIS is the body's natural system with functions of resistance to the disease itself and prevention of invasion from harmful bacteria. This system itself has many characteristics, some of which obtain certain significance on the research of computer system security.

1. *Distributed detection*: The immune system works in a way of distributed detection, in which the "detector" to detect the bacteria invasion is very small but with high detection efficiency, and centralized control center and collaboration are not required. Computer security systems are not equipped with the function of distributed detection, and the use of the control center has actually reduced the factor of safety protection of the system.

2. *Detection of abnormality*: The immune system is able to identify the invading bacteria that the system has never seen and take corresponding measures. The specific targets of the current computer security protection system are generally decided by the protective strategies or the protection system itself, without automatic intrusion detection of the latest way of invasion [85,124,218].

3. *Learning and memory*: The immune system is able to automatically learn the structure of invading bacteria, and memorize these information in order to reply to this type of bacteria faster and timely subsequently. Current computer security systems do not have the ability of self-learning.

4. *Diversity*: Different biological bodies have different immune systems. A certain weakness of one immune system is not the weakness of another. A virus might be able to break through one protective immune system, but the possibility of breaking through other immune systems is very small. Thus, the immune systems have strong ability to protect the overall population. While for computer systems, the security systems are always the same. Once a loophole is found, any computer system using this kind of security system will suffer the threat of invasion through this loophole.

5. *Incomplete detection*: The immune system does not require making *nonself* test on every invading cell. It has great flexibility and may sacrifice a portion of the body functions or resources in order to ensure the normal functions of the body in general. Computer security systems generally do not have the ability of overall analysis of the system and its functions are generally specific and fixed.

2.3.4 Application Fields of AIS

1. *Robot*: D. W. Lee proposes a controlling method in distributed robots based on the principle of homeostasis in the immune system. In this method, each robot is regarded as a B cell and each environment condition as an antigen, while the behavior strategies adopted by the robots are taken as antibodies and the controlling parameters of the robots as T cells. Under different environment conditions, each robot will first select a set of behavioral strategies that

are adapted to the environment conditions of itself. Then this set of behavioral strategies are individually communicated with other robots one by one, and some behavioral strategies will be stimulated while some others are suppressed. The behavioral strategies that are stimulated more than others will finally be adopted by the robot [184]. Based on the distributed controlling mechanism of the immune system, A. Lshiguro implements the gait controlling and speed measuring of a six-legged walking robot. The action strategies based on the principle of interaction between B cells in the immune system are used to control the movement of self-regulation robots. The main idea of this strategy is: several basic and different operators of the self-regulation robot are pre-designed, and each operator is regarded as an Agent that can make action decisions based on its surrounding environment and send controlling commands to the system, and the system will dynamically determine the robot's actions according to the collaboration and competition status between the Agents.

2. *Controlling engineering*: AIS can be readily identified as a feedback controller based on the principles of fast response and rapid determination of foreign intrusions. It has been applied to the car's rear collision prevention system by comprehensive processing signals transmitted from sensors and controlling each actuator executing corresponding operations quickly and accurately. K. Takahashi designs an immune feedback controller of proportion integration differentiation (PID) with activation item of controlling the response speed and suppression item of controlling the stabilizing effect. The validity of the controller is verified by simulating a discrete, single-input and single-output system. In addition, AIS is also used in sequence controlling, dynamic and complex controlling, and other aspects.

3. *Fault diagnosis*: Distributed diagnosis system that combines immune network and learning vector quantization (LVQ) can be used to accurately detect the sensors where failure occurs in controlled object. This system has two modes: training mode and diagnosis mode. In the training mode, data of sensors working normally are trained and achieved through LVQ; in the diagnosis mode, the immune network determines the sensors with faults based on the knowledge acquired by LVQ. Experiments show that the system can automatically identify the failed sensors in the group of working sensors; while in the past, this was implemented by detecting the output of each sensor independently. The self-learning ability of the immune system is also used in the monitoring system of computer hardware, in which the system marks out the area when fault occurs in and takes appropriate recovery actions once the computer hardware system goes wrong.

4. *Optimized design*: For the nonlinear optimization problem with multiple local minima, the general optimization methods are difficult to find the global optimal solution, while genetic mechanism based on diversity of the immune system can be used for optimal search. It can avoid premature convergence

for improving the genetic algorithm and dealing with multi-criteria problems. It is being currently used for function testing, the traveling salesman problem, VLSI layout, structure design, parameter correction of permanent magnet synchronous motor, etc.

5. *Data analysis*: AIS has the ability of data analysis and classification by combining the advantages of classifiers, neural networks, and machine inference. Therefore, it has been used in the fields of data mining and information processing. J. Timmis discusses how to implement an unsupervised and self-learning AIS specifically.

6. *Virus detection*: According to the ability of distinguishing *self* and *nonself* of the immune system, Forrest proposes principles and laws of BIS that AIS can take inspiration from and has done a lot of research work. By taking inspiration from the mechanism of BIS resisting and destroying unknown biological virus, T. Okamolo proposes a distributed Agent-based antivirus system. It consists of two parts: the immune system and the recovery system. The function of the immune system is identifying the *nonself* information (computer virus) by grasping the *self* information; the recovery system copies files from the noninfected computer to the computer which has been infected through the network to cover the files on it. Based on the same principles, AIS is also used for hacking prevention, network security maintenance, and system maintenance.

2.4 Applications of AIS in Anti-Spam

2.4.1 Heuristic Methods

In AIS, immune cells constantly update over time, which provides a good ideological inspiration for building dynamic detection systems. Secker et al. [167] proposed an immune-based dynamic e-mail classification system, in which they extract information from the subjects and senders' e-mail addresses that the users are not interested in to generate B cells (feature library), and classify e-mails, as e-mail users are interested in and those users are not interested in according to the affinity between B cells and antigens (new e-mails). Two categories of B cells are designed in the system: primary B cells and memory B cells, and the life cycles of memory B cells are longer. When the feedback confirmation from user is received, primary B cells are upgraded to memory B cells. In the update process, the B cells whose life cycles are terminated are replaced with new B cells generated by the clonal selection algorithm. In the clonal selection algorithm, number and mutation degree of clones are controlled based on the affinity. This method can achieve an accuracy of 90% in the experiment.

The rules of generating antibodies and matching function between antibodies and antigens are key factors in the detection system, directly affecting the overall performance of the system. Oda and White [139] give an AIS for spam detection, in which antibodies are expressed as regular expressions in order to match a large number of antigens. Reference [140] deeply analyzes and discusses this method. It generates the antibody library by referring the immune matching principle and gives the update strategy of the antibody library. In the training phase, the antibody library is first generated by randomly selecting genes from the gene library (word or meta-heuristic information), and then the antibodies are given corresponding weights according to their matching with two types of e-mails. When classifying a new e-mail, antibodies matching the e-mail are first selected and the category of the e-mail is ultimately obtained according to the weighted matching value calculated based on the weights of the matching antibodies. In the detection process, the weights of antibodies are updated in real time based on the matching of the antibodies with e-mails, and the antibodies whose weights are too small will be replaced by new randomly generated antibodies. Experimental results show that the performance of this method is slightly lower than that of naive Bayes. The important significance of this approach is providing a new mechanism. In Reference [190], corresponding gene libraries for two categories of e-mails are constructed, respectively, and they compute the concentrations to enhance the ability of noise tolerance. Reference [147] gives a dual-detector immunological method for spam detection, where two detector sets are constructed respectively by extracting information from two types of e-mails. In the detection process, two types of detectors are simultaneously used to detect new e-mails. This method can effectively reduce the rate of false positive, while resulting in a decline of spam recall.

Wang et al. [215] apply the immune principles into collaborative detection of spam in P2P networks. In P2P networks, when one of the nodes recognizes the antigen, antibodies are generated according to the antigen and information of antibodies are transferred to the adjacent nodes, avoiding repeated learning of other nodes. Sarafijanovic and Le Boudec [160] propose an immune-based collaborative spam detection method. This method expresses antibodies by calculating hash values of the similarity of random sampling characters in e-mails, preventing character confusion attacks from spammers. In the spam identification process, the actions of deleting e-mails from users are defined as danger signals, in order to ensure the reliability of information sharing. In the collaborative process, only reliable category information and hash values that are confirmed by the danger signals are used for interaction between multiple users to ensure the validity of the collaborative information.

2.4.2 Negative Selection

Immune negative selection algorithm is a simulation of autologous tolerance process and can reduce the false positive rate of detection systems. Sirisanyalak and Sornil [171] apply the immune negative selection algorithm to the generation process of the antibody library, and update the antibody library based on user needs. Users can specify the time when to update the antibody library according to the actual needs to meet their individual requirements. Another characteristic of this method is that it takes the match between the antibody and the antigen as feature vector and uses the logistic regression method for further classification instead of directly classifying the e-mails according to the match between the antibody and the e-mail in the classification phase. Reference [125] adopts the immune negative selection algorithm to detect spam in condition that there is no spam information. They define the problem as: how to detect spam e-mails in the case that only information of normal e-mails can be obtained. In the process of antibody generation, antibodies are randomly generated and selected according to the negative selection algorithm and information of normal e-mails. This method is suitable for detection of new spam e-mails.

2.4.3 Immune Network

In immune networks, immune cells interact each others. Cells with high affinity get cloned and propagated, and to be updated according to the stimulation and suppression in the network to ensure that the performance of the network is tending to the optimal. Bezerra et al. [21] apply the supervised method of real-value antibody network to spam detection. The main characteristics of this method are: the antibody network is a supervised learning network with strong ability of learning; the antibody network is built legitimately by adjusting the size of the network according to clonal selection principle in the building process; and the connection weights are real values with strong expression ability. Yue et al. [235] propose an incremental clustering artificial immune network algorithm. The algorithm first gets the original set of memory antibodies by using the artificial immune network algorithm, and generates clusters on the antibody set. When a new batch of e-mails (antigens) arrives, the affinities between memory antibodies and antigens are computed. On the basis of this, antibodies of high affinities are cloned and mutated, while the number of low-affinity antibodies is restrained, so that the immune network can dynamically adjust to the changes of antigens. To reduce the computational complexity, the algorithm uses a time-window technique to control the time of update.

2.4.4 Dynamic Algorithms

Guzella et al. [88] propose dynamic AIS method to detect spam. This method combines the immune negative selection algorithm and clonal selection algorithm, and defines the corresponding macrophages, B cells, T cells, and the way of dynamic interaction between B cells and T cells. In the algorithm, macrophages, B cells, and helper T cells are generated by extracting information from *nonself* data (spam), while controlling T cells are generated by extracting information from *self* data (normal e-mails). B cells and helper T cells are selected by a negative selection algorithm during the process of generation. In the detection process, these immune cells classify e-mails collaboratively, and the set of immune cells is dynamically adjusted based on user feedback. Reference [1] applies the immune cross-regulation model to dynamic spam detection. In the immune cross-regulation model, the effector T cells, regulatory T cells, and antigen-presenting cells interact dynamically and are capable of detecting harmful antigens. Effector T cells and regulatory T cells work together to distinguish harmful antigens and harmless antigens. In this spam detection algorithm, terms in subject and content of e-mails are randomly sampled and expressed by antigen-presenting cells. Effector T cells and regulatory T cells are virtually expressed as category tendency associated with features in the algorithm. Eventually, the e-mail classification is completed by computing the category score according to the interaction between the two types of T cells.

2.4.5 Hybrid Models

On the basis of AIS, researchers carry out hybrid immune algorithms by combining advantages of different methods to improve the overall performance of detection systems. Ruan and Tan [154] propose a dynamic intelligent learning method combining the incremental support vector machine and AIS. This method trains the support vector machine on the training set and takes the obtained support vectors as immune antibodies. When the number of e-mails that an antibody correctly identifies reaches a predetermined threshold, this antibody will be added into the memory antibody set. The time-window technology is used to control the support vector machines that are currently active during the dynamic update process. When the time for updating comes, new support vector machines are generated based on the existing antibodies and antigens that exceed the classification boundaries, and the newly obtained support vectors are added to the antibody set, while the support vector machine which is the first to enter the time window is removed. Reference [155] combines the immune concentration method with artificial neural network, and the immune antibody concentration vector is taken as the input of artificial neural networks to detect antigens (spam). Reference [123] proposes a method that combines AIS with Naive Bayes, where antibody cells are produced by using AIS and affinities between antibodies and antigens are calculated according to Naive Bayes. The use of Naive Bayes enhances the classification performance of AIS. Reference [216] combines immune method with rough set to detect spam e-mails, where the number of genes could be effectively reduced by the rough set method.

Tan [181] makes a combination of clonal selection algorithm and particle swarm optimization (i.e., so-called clonal PSO) to optimize the parameters of spam detection algorithms, tending to select the optimal parameter setting. Experimental results show that this method can effectively improve the performance of detection algorithms by optimizing the parameters. In Reference [249], the genetic algorithm is used to optimize AIS based on spam detection method. On one hand, this method adopts the genetic algorithm to dynamically adjust the weights of antibodies in the AIS. On the other hand, the genetic algorithm is also used to control the updating process of antibodies. Introducing the genetic algorithm enhances the recognition ability of AIS to new e-mails. Reference [158] applies the particle swarm optimization algorithm for optimizing a simple AIS. In this system, the particle swarm optimization algorithm and immune mutation are combined together to improve the discrimination capacity of e-mail categories of the system.

Very recently, Zhang and Tan [241] propose an immune cooperation mechanism-based learning framework for virus detection and anti-spam with a good performance.

2.5 Summary

By taking inspiration from BIS, variety of immune theories and models have been proposed. This chapter introduced the BIS and AIS from a complete and comprehensive perspective, giving an intuitive understanding of this research area. Classical immune theories and models were presented in detail. Descriptions of features and applications further verified the reliability and rationality of AIS.

Chapter 3

Term Space Partition-Based Feature Construction Approach

This chapter presents a novel feature construction approach based on term space partition (TSP), which aims to establish a mechanism to make terms play more sufficient and rational roles in e-mail categorization [132]. First, motivation of proposing the TSP approach is described. The main principle of the TSP approach is then introduced. Detailed implementation of the TSP approach for spam filtering is given next, including preprocessing, term space partition, and feature construction as three core steps. Finally, conducted experiments are shown to indicate the effectiveness of the TSP approach.

3.1 Motivation

Feature selection plays quite important roles in spam filtering and other text categorization problems, as the removal of less informative terms can reduce not only computational complexity but also affect possible noisy terms [132,133]. In decades, several feature selection metrics have been proposed and applied in text categorization as well as other pattern recognition issues. There are mainly two kinds of feature selection metrics: class independent ones and class dependent ones. They also are referred to as unsupervised and supervised feature selection metrics. We take document frequency (DF) and information gain (IG) as representatives of unsupervised and supervised feature selection metrics, respectively, to investigate

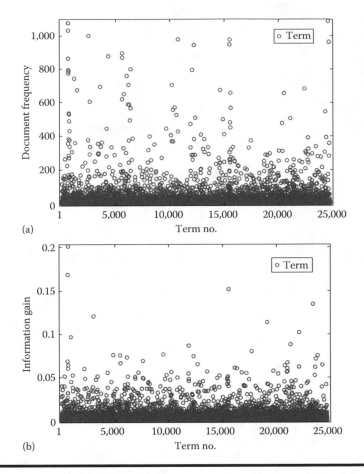

(a)

(b)

**Figure 3.1   Distribution of terms in PU1 with respect to feature selection metrics.
(a) Document frequency of terms and (b) information gain of terms.**

the distribution of terms with respect to these feature selection metrics in e-mail categorization. Figure 3.1a and b show the distribution of terms in a commonly used benchmark corpus, which is named PU1 and contains nearly 25,000 distinct terms, with respect to DF and IG, respectively, where the terms are numbered continuously.

As we can see, no matter which kind of feature selection metrics is employed, similar distribution reveals that rare terms can get much higher and discriminative scores while the great majority of terms are given relatively low and similar scores, though term distribution with respect to IG in high-score space is sparser than that of DF due to the consideration of term-class associations. Terms are selected according to the scores they get. The distribution of terms suggests that only a few terms with obvious superiority can be selected confidently, while the others are with weak confidence as they are not so superior and discriminative with each other on the evaluation.

Terms reserved by feature selection metrics are further utilized to construct feature vectors of e-mails. Therefore, the extent of feature selection is determined by the corresponding feature construction (CFC) approach employed. For the traditional bag of words (BoW) approach, several hundred terms are selected. Each selected term corresponds to an individual dimension of the feature vector and plays a sufficient role in e-mail categorization. In our consideration, BoW has the following restraints: (1) terms reserved far exceed with obvious superiority in the term space, and it is not reasonable that low score terms are considered equally important with that given much higher scores; (2) only a small part of terms in the term space are utilized, which indicates waste of information; and (3) several hundred dimensional feature vectors still lead to a heavy computational burden. While for the heuristic approaches, that is CFC and local concentration (LC) by taking inspiration from biological immune system (BIS), more terms (empirically more than 50% of the terms in the original term space [155,190,248]) are reserved for further constructing feature vectors, and feature vector's dimension is reduced by computing concentration features. However, there exists a similar but more prominent deficiency in these two approaches as in BoW that terms with obvious superiority are treated equally with terms given much lower scores, which weakens the contributions on categorization from the superior terms.

3.2 Principles of the TSP Approach

The proposed TSP approach aims to establish a mechanism to make the terms play more sufficient and rational roles in e-mail categorization by dividing the original term space into subspaces and designing corresponding feature construction strategy on each subspace, so as to improve the performance and efficiency of spam filtering.

Feature selection metrics give terms reasonable and effective goodness evaluation. According to the distribution characteristics of terms with respect to feature selection metrics, a vertical partition of the term space is performed to separate the *Dominant Terms* from *General Terms*. By dominant terms, we mean the terms given high and discriminative scores by feature selection metrics and considered to lead the categorization results, and this part of terms has the following features: small amount, sparse distribution, discriminative, and informative. While large amount of general terms congregate in a narrow range of the term space with similar low scores. Though general terms are less informative than dominant terms and adulterated with redundant and noisy terms, most of them can also contribute to e-mail categorization, which cannot be ignored easily. Undoubtedly, dominant terms and general terms should play different roles in e-mail categorization.

To construct discriminative features, we introduce *Class Tendency* to perform a transverse partition of the term space to separate the *Spam Terms* from *Ham Terms*. By class tendency, we mean the tendency of a term occurring in e-mails of a certain class, defined as

$$tendency\ (t_i) = P(t_i|c_h) - P(t_i|c_s) \tag{3.1}$$

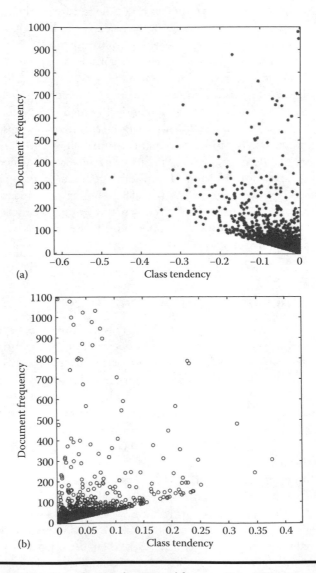

(a)

(b)

Figure 3.2   Distribution of terms in PU1 with respect to DF. (a) Spam terms and (b) ham terms.

where

    $P(t_i|c_h)$ is the probability of t_i's occurrence, given the e-mail is ham

    $P(t_i|c_s)$ is the probability of t_i's occurrence, given the e-mail is spam

Spam terms occur more frequently in spam than in ham with negative tendency, and ham terms occur more frequently in ham than in spam with positive tendency.

In this case, each term in the original term space can be represented by a two-dimensional vector, that is, $\vec{t} = <tendency, goodness>$. Distribution of terms in PU1 with respect to DF and IG in the newly constructed term space is shown in Figures 3.2 and 3.3. As we can see, the whole term space is divided into a spam term space and a ham term space. The spam term space and ham term space contain both dominant terms and general terms. Therefore, the original term space is decomposed into four independent and nonoverlapping subspaces: spam-dominant, ham-dominant, spam-general, and ham-general.

For the partition between dominant terms and general terms, we finally employed a thresholding method through analysis and experiments. *Spam Term Ratio* and *Ham Term Ratio* are defined as features on dominant terms, while *Spam Term Density* and *Ham Term Density* are computed on general terms, which will be introduced next.

3.3 Implementation of the TSP Approach

We decompose the TSP approach into the following steps:

3.3.1 Preprocessing

The purpose of preprocessing is transforming e-mails into terms by examining the existence of blank spaces and delimiters, also referred to as tokenization. It is a quiet simple but indispensable step. The followings are essential steps of the TSP approach.

3.3.2 Term Space Partition

Algorithm 3.1 gives a detailed description of the term space partition step, which mainly contains term selection and term space partition. Term selection is involved to reduce the computational complexity and affect possible noisy terms. Parameter p determines the extent of term selection.

The vertical partition is performed to separate dominant terms and general terms by defining a threshold θ_{dg} with respect to the corresponding feature selection metrics employed, as shown in Equation 3.2.

$$\theta_{dg} = \frac{1}{r}(\tau_{max} - \tau_{min}) \tag{3.2}$$

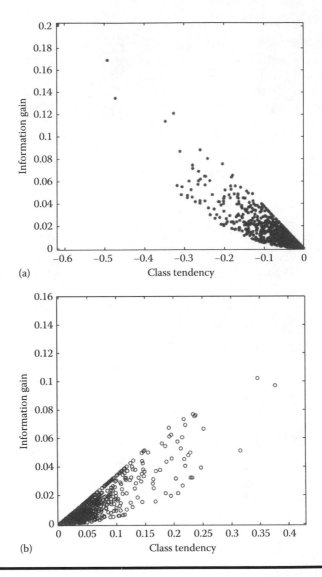

Figure 3.3 Distribution of terms in PU1 with respect to IG. (a) Spam terms and (b) ham terms.

where

τ_{max} and τ_{min} depict the highest and lowest evaluation of terms in the training set, respectively

variable r controls the restriction level of dominant terms

Term t_i with $\tau(t_i) \geq \theta_{dg}$ is considered as dominant term, and general term otherwise

---

Algorithm 3.1 Term space partition

1: initialize preselected term set TS_p, spam-dominant term set TS_{sd}, ham-dominant term set TS_{hd}, spam-general term set TS_{sg} and ham-general term set TS_{hg} as empty sets
2:
3: **for** each term t_i occurs in the training set **do**
4:     calculate goodness evaluation $\tau(t_i)$ according to the feature selection metrics employed
5: **end for**
6: sort the terms in descending order of evaluation
7: add the front $p\%$ terms to TS_p
8:
9: calculate partition threshold θ_{dg} according to Equation 3.2
10: **for** each term t_i in TS_p **do**
11:     calculate *tendency*(t_i) according to Equation 3.1
12:     **if** *tendency*$(t_i) < 0$ **then**
13:         **if** $\tau(t_i) \geq \theta_{dg}$ **then**
14:             add t_i to TS_{sd}
15:         **else**
16:             add t_i to TS_{sg}
17:         **end if**
18:     **else**
19:         **if** *tendency*$(t_i) > 0$ **then**
20:             **if** $\tau(t_i) \geq \theta_{dg}$ **then**
21:                 add t_i to TS_{hd}
22:             **else**
23:                 add t_i to TS_{hg}
24:             **end if**
25:         **end if**
26:     **end if**
27: **end for**

When performing the transverse partition to separate spam terms and ham terms, terms with *tendency*$(t_i) = 0$ are considered useless and discarded directly.

3.3.3 Feature Construction

To construct discriminative and effective feature vectors of e-mails, we define *Term Ratio* and *Term Density* on dominant terms and general terms, respectively, as features to make the terms play sufficient and rational roles in e-mail categorization. Algorithm 3.2 shows the process of feature construction.

Algorithm 3.2 Feature construction

1: calculate spam term ratio TR_s according to Equation 3.3
2: calculate ham term ratio TR_h according to Equation 3.4
3: calculate spam term density TD_s according to Equation 3.5
4: calculate ham term density TD_h according to Equation 3.6
5: combine TR_s, TR_h, TD_s and TD_h together to form the feature vector

---

For the very small amount of dominant terms, which are considered to lead the categorization results, each individual term should be given more weights to play sufficient roles in e-mail categorization. Spam term ratio and ham term ratio are calculated on spam-dominant terms and ham-dominant terms, respectively. Spam term ratio is defined as

$$TR_s = \frac{n_{sd}}{N_{sd}} \tag{3.3}$$

where

n_{sd} is the number of distinct terms in the current e-mail which are also contained in spam-dominant term space TS_{sd}
N_{sd} is the total number of distinct terms in TS_{sd}

Similarly, ham term ratio is defined as

$$TR_h = \frac{n_{hd}}{N_{hd}} \tag{3.4}$$

where

n_{hd} is the number of distinct terms in the current e-mail, which are also contained in ham-dominant term space TS_{hd}
N_{hd} is the total number of distinct terms in TS_{hd}

While for the large amount of general terms, which are less informative and may be adulterated with redundant and noisy terms, the affect of individual term should be weakened. Spam term density and ham term density are calculated on spam-general terms, and ham-general terms, respectively. Spam term density is defined as

$$TD_s = \frac{n_{sg}}{N_e} \tag{3.5}$$

where

n_{sg} is the number of distinct terms in the current e-mail, which are also contained in spam-general term space TS_{sg}
N_e is the total number of distinct terms in the current e-mail

And ham term density is defined as

$$TD_h = \frac{n_{hg}}{N_e} \tag{3.6}$$

where n_{hg} is the number of distinct terms in the current e-mail, which are also contained in ham-general term space TS_{hg}.

In this step, term ratio and term density are two essential but completely different concepts. Term ratio indicates the percentage of dominant terms that occur in the current e-mail, emphasizing the absolute ratio of dominant terms. In this way, the contributions to categorization from dominant terms are strengthened and not influenced by other terms. While term density represents the percentage of terms in the current e-mail that are general terms, focusing on the relative proportion of terms in the current e-mail that are general terms. The affect on categorization from general terms is weakened and so is the affect from possible noisy terms.

Finally, the achieved features are combined together to form the feature vector, that is $\vec{v} = [TR_s, TR_h, TD_s, TD_h]$.

3.4 Experiments

All the experiments were conducted on a PC with E4500 CPU and 2G RAM. SVM was employed as classifier and LIBSVM [34] was applied for implementation of SVM. Ten-fold cross validation was utilized on PU corpora and six-fold cross validation on Enron-Spam according to the number of parts each of the corpora has been already divided into. Accuracy and F_1 measure are the main evaluation criteria, as they can reflect the overall performance of spam filtering.

3.4.1 Investigation of Parameters

Experiments have been conducted on PU1 to investigate the parameters of the TSP approach. Ten-fold cross validation was utilized. There are two important parameters. Parameter p in the term space partition step determines the percentage of terms reserved for feature construction. As mentioned earlier, removal of less informative terms can reduce not only computational complexity but also affect from possible noisy terms, so as to improve the efficiency and performance of spam filtering. The parameter r, which is much more essential and controls the restriction level of dominant terms in the term space partition step, depicts the core idea of this TSP approach. With small r, the restriction level of dominant terms is high and thus the number of dominant terms as defined is small, and vice versa.

Since the distribution of dominant terms with respect to supervised feature selection metrics is sparser than that of unsupervised ones, we first investigate the parameters in TSP with respect to unsupervised feature selection metrics and DF is selected as the representative. Figure 3.4 shows the performance of TSP with respect

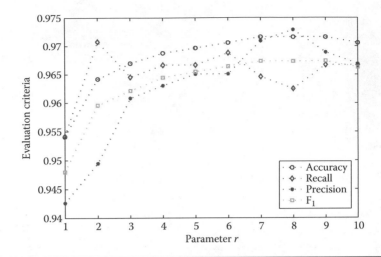

Figure 3.4 **Performance of TSP with respect to DF under varied *r*.**

to DF under varied *r*. As expected, the performance of TSP shows improvements with *r* getting larger in the first half. Thus, *r* = 7 is considered a suitable selection of parameter *r*, where the TSP approach performs best and relatively high precision and recall are achieved.

The performance of TSP with respect to DF under varied *p* is shown in Figure 3.5. As we can see, the TSP approach always performs quite well though *p* varies, and better performance can be achieved with larger *p* values. For efficiency consideration,

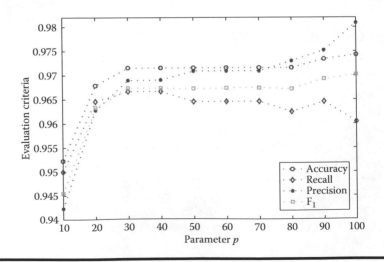

Figure 3.5 **Performance of TSP with respect to DF under varied *p*.**

$p = 30$ is selected, which means the front 30% terms with respect to DF are reserved for feature construction. On the other hand, better performance on larger p values indicates that the term density strategy is effective to make general terms play roles in e-mail categorization.

Similar experiments were conducted to tune the parameters of TSP when supervised feature selection metrics are employed, and IG is selected as the representative of this kind of metrics. From the experimental results, $r = 3$ and $p = 30$ are selected.

3.4.2 Performance with Different Feature Selection Metrics

In the proposed TSP approach, the vertical partition of the term space is performed according to term evaluation given by feature selection metrics. Therefore, it is quite necessary to verify whether the TSP approach can cooperate well with both unsupervised and supervised feature selection metrics.

We selected DF and IG as representatives of unsupervised and supervised feature selection metrics, respectively, to conduct comparison experiments, because these two metrics are widely applied in spam filtering and other text categorization issues. Performance of TSP with respect to DF and IG on five benchmark corpora PU1, PU2, PU3, PUA, and Enron-Spam is shown in Table 3.1. Abbreviations in the tables of this chapter are as follows: Cor., Corpus; FSM, Feature Selection Method; App., Approach; Pre., Precision; Rec., Recall; Acc., Accuracy; FD, Feature Dimensionality. As the experimental results reveal, the TSP approach performs quite well with both

Table 3.1 Performance of TSP with respect to Different Feature Selection Metrics

Cor.	FSM	Pre. (%)	Rec. (%)	Acc. (%)	F_1 (%)
PU1	DF	96.90	96.67	**97.16**	**96.74**
	IG	96.07	96.46	96.70	96.21
PU2	DF	94.09	83.57	**95.63**	**88.12**
	IG	96.32	80.00	95.35	87.09
PU3	DF	95.69	95.88	96.20	95.73
	IG	96.37	97.09	**97.05**	**96.69**
PUA	DF	95.91	96.49	**96.05**	**96.11**
	IG	95.62	94.74	95.00	95.06
Enron	DF	94.29	98.21	**97.02**	**96.14**
	IG	94.18	98.23	96.90	96.12

Note: Bold digits means better results.

DF and IG, which represent unsupervised and supervised feature selection metrics correspondingly. It is worth noting that DF outperforms IG with TSP as feature construction approach in most cases of the experiments, indicating that the transverse partition of term space is effective to make use of the information of term-class associations.

3.4.3 Comparison with Current Approaches

Experiments were conducted on PU1, PU2, PU3, PUA, and Enron-Spam to compare the performance of the proposed TSP approach with that of current approaches. The selected current approaches are BoW, CFC, and LC. Table 3.2 shows the performance of each feature construction approach in spam filtering when incorporated with SVM, and the corresponding dimensionality of feature vectors constructed. As mentioned earlier, we take accuracy and F_1 measure as comparison criteria without focusing on precision and recall, which are incorporated into the calculation of F_1 measure and can be reflected by F_1 measure.

BoW is a traditional and one of the most widely used feature construction approach in spam filtering. As we can see, the proposed TSP approach not only makes significant reduction on the feature vector dimension so as to improve efficiency but also achieves much better performance in terms of both accuracy and F_1 measure when compared with BoW, indicating that the TSP approach is effective for e-mail categorization.

CFC and LC are heuristic and state-of-the-art approaches in spam filtering by taking inspiration from BIS. The CFC approach transforms e-mails into two-dimensional feature vectors by calculating *self* and *nonself* concentrations, while the LC approach extracts position-correlated information from messages additionally to CFC by constructing concentration features on local areas. LC-FL and LC-VL utilize different strategies of defining local areas respectively. The CFC and LC approaches achieve not only good performance but also high efficiency. The experimental results show that the TSP approach far outperforms CFC and LC in terms of both accuracy and F_1 measure, which verified that the proposed term space partition strategy and newly defined features—term ratio and term density—are successful to make terms play more sufficient and rational roles in e-mail categorization. Meanwhile, the TSP approach reduces the feature vector dimension with fixed four-dimensional feature vectors, compared with both LC-FL and LC-VL. It is worth noting that the TSP approach achieves much higher and stabler precision in spam filtering, which is warmly welcomed in spam filtering as e-mail users would rather accept more spam than discard useful e-mails.

We conducted experiments on PU1 to compare the efficiency of TSP with that of the selected current feature construction approaches. Ten-fold cross validation was utilized. Table 3.3 shows the average time spent on each approach on processing one incoming e-mail. As we can see, all of the CFC, LC, and TSP approaches perform

Table 3.2 Performance Comparison of TSP with Current Approaches

Cor.	App.	Pre. (%)	Rec. (%)	Acc. (%)	F_1 (%)	FD
PU1	BoW	93.96	95.63	95.32	94.79	600
	CFC	94.97	95.00	95.60	94.99	2
	LC-FL	95.12	96.88	96.42	95.99	20
	LC-VL	95.48	96.04	96.24	95.72	6
	TSP	96.90	96.67	**97.16**	**96.74**	4
PU2	BoW	88.71	79.29	93.66	83.74	600
	CFC	95.12	76.43	94.37	84.76	2
	LC-FL	90.86	82.86	94.79	86.67	20
	LC-VL	92.06	86.43	**95.63**	**88.65**	6
	TSP	94.09	83.57	**95.63**	88.12	4
PU3	BoW	96.48	94.67	96.08	95.57	600
	CFC	96.24	94.95	96.05	95.59	2
	LC-FL	95.99	95.33	96.13	95.66	20
	LC-VL	95.64	95.77	96.15	95.67	6
	TSP	96.37	97.09	**97.05**	**96.69**	4
PUA	BoW	92.83	93.33	92.89	93.08	600
	CFC	96.03	93.86	94.82	94.93	2
	LC-FL	96.01	94.74	95.26	95.37	20
	LC-VL	95.60	94.56	94.91	94.94	6
	TSP	95.91	96.49	**96.05**	**96.11**	4
Enron	BoW	90.88	98.87	95.13	94.62	600
	CFC	91.48	97.81	95.62	94.39	2
	LC-FL	94.07	98.00	96.79	95.94	20
	LC-VL	92.44	97.81	96.02	94.94	6
	TSP	94.29	98.21	**97.02**	**96.14**	4

Note: Bold digits means better results.

Table 3.3   Efficiency Comparison of TSP with Current Approaches

App.	BoW	CFC	LC-FL	LC-VL	TSP
Seconds/e-mail	$9.57e^{-3}$	$3.75e^{-4}$	$5.52e^{-4}$	$4.50e^{-4}$	$3.91e^{-4}$

far more efficiently than BoW, due to significant reduction on feature vector dimension. Since the LC approach needs to calculate concentrations on each local area and finally construct feature vectors with more dimensions, the TSP approach can process incoming e-mails faster than both LC-FL and LC-VL. Although the feature vectors constructed by TSP have additional two dimensions compared with CFC, TSP can achieve similar efficiency as CFC, as the term space partition strategy is dividing the original term space into four non-overlapping subspaces and less time is spent on computing term ratio and term density compared with the computation of concentrations in CFC. On the other hand, less terms are reserved in TSP than CFC and LC for feature construction to achieve better performance as the dominant terms can play sufficient roles in TSP.

3.5 Summary

In this chapter, the TSP-based feature construction approach for e-mail categorization, which divides the original term space into subspaces and constructing features on each subspace independently, is introduced. In this approach, the vertical and transverse partitions are performed with respect to feature selection metrics and class tendency, respectively. Discriminative features are constructed by computing term ratio and term density on corresponding subspaces. The TSP approach is proved effective in establishing a mechanism to make terms in the original term space play more sufficient and rational roles in e-mail categorization by comprehensive experiments. Furthermore, it achieves high efficiency by transforming e-mails into four-dimensional feature vectors.

Chapter 4

Immune Concentration-Based Feature Construction Approach

This chapter presents the immune concentration-based feature construction (CFC) approach, which was proposed by taking inspiration from biological immune system (BIS) and utilizes a two-element concentration vector as the feature vector for spam detection [155,190]. After an analysis of diversity of detector representation in artificial immune system (AIS), the motivation of CFC approach is described. Then, the overview of CFC approach is given. Implementation of CFC approach, including gene library generation and concentration vector construction, is described in detail. This chapter then analyzes the relation of CFC approach with other methods as well as the complexity of CFC approach. Finally, experimental validation and discussions are given.

4.1 Introduction

Inspired by the functions and principles of BIS, AIS was proposed in the 1990s as a novel computational intelligence model [54] and has received attentions of researchers. In recent years, numerous AIS models have been designed for spam filtering [54,88,139,155,194]. One main purpose of both BIS and AIS is to discriminate *self* from *nonself*. In the anti-spam field, detectors (antibodies) are

59

designed and created to discriminate spam from legitimate e-mails, and the ways of creation and manipulation of detectors are quite essential in these AIS models.

BIS is a system that distinguishes *self* from *nonself* such as foreign substances and pathogenic organisms by producting immune response. Specialized white blood cells, for example, B and T *lymphocytes*, are used for immune recognition. On the surface of each lymphocyte there is a *receptor*. The lymphocyte can be activated by the binding of the receptor to patterns presented on *antigens*. It takes longer for BIS to mount a response for the first time when some pathogen is encountered, for example, the process of *Primary Response*, but when the same pathogen or its likeness appears again, BIS can respond very quickly because of immune memory, for example, the process of *Secondary Response*. During each immune response, a large amount of antibodies are generated to purge out antigens. The concentration of white blood cells in blood rises sharply at the early stage of immune response and this phenomena is used as the evidence of intrusion of pathogens in clinical diagnosis.

Figure 4.1 depicts the immune response processes.

4.2 Diversity of Detector Representation in AIS

AISs are adaptive systems, inspired by theoretical immunology and observed immune functions, principles, and models, which are applied to problem solving [57]. These AISs are applied in a wide variety of domains, including machine learning, pattern recognition, optimization, data mining, computer security, etc. [55,57].

When using AIS in detection, the main difficult problem is mostly decreasing the anomaly detection hole. A detection hole is caused by the limited coverage of

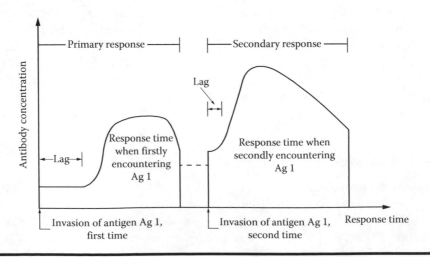

Figure 4.1   Immune response processes of biological immune system.

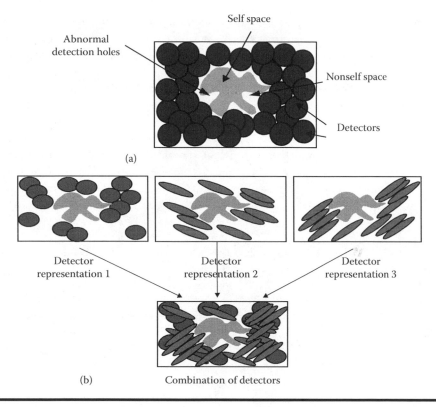

(a)

(b)   Combination of detectors

Figure 4.2 Anomaly detection hole and diversity of detector representation. (a) Anomaly detection hole and (b) diversity of detector representation.

detectors as shown in Figure 4.2a. BIS solves this problem very well by use of the diversity of MHC (Major Histocompatibility Complex) cell representations, which decides the diversity of antibody touching surface of T cells. This property is very useful in increasing the power of detecting mutated antigens, and decreasing the anomaly detection hole. According to this principle, the diversity of detector representation can be used to decrease the detection hole in real-world applications such as malicious executables detection [86]. Figure 4.2b depicts the effectiveness of diversified representation.

4.3 Motivation of Concentration-Based Feature Construction Approach

Feature selection plays a very important role in pattern recognition in particular in spam filtering. Well-defined features greatly improve the performance and are not sensitive to the changing of the contents of e-mails and user's interests. For most of proposed anti-spam approaches, words vector is formed through term frequency analysis and served as the feature vector for various classification algorithms. Though several methods such as stop list, words stemming, mutual information, information gain are used for selection among candidate words and dimension reduction, the dimensionality of final feature vector is still in the order of thousands. Heuristic approaches reduce the dimension to some extent, however the matching process between all the prediscovered patterns and those patterns appeared in an e-mail to be classified is time consuming, especially when the library of patterns is very large. Meanwhile, mining a proper pattern is also very difficult. In BIS, the intrusion of pathogens can be simply concluded by the raised concentration of antibodies, which is a desirable property of which we are going to make use in the spam detection system in this chapter.

4.4 Overview of Concentration-Based Feature Construction Approach

Immune construction-based feature construction approach can be mainly divided into three parts. (1) Generate *self* gene library and *nonself* gene library from training samples; (2) Construct the concentration vector of each training sample through earlier two gene libraries, then these concentration vectors are used as the input of a successive classification algorithm for training; and (3) The trained classifier is used to predict the label of testing samples characterized by concentration vectors. Here we focus on the feature construction and do not emphasize the classification algorithms, which would be support vector machine (SVM), artificial neural networks (ANN), Adaboost, just to name a few. The overview of the proposed algorithm is outlined in Algorithm 4.1. Each step of Algorithm 4.1 is described in detail in the following sections.

4.5 Gene Library Generation

Two gene libraries—*self gene library* and *nonself gene library* are generated from training samples in the immune concentration-based feature construction approach. The gene fragment in gene library is simply a word. *Self gene library* is composed of words with utmost representative of nonspam e-mails. By contrast, *nonself gene library* contains those words with utmost representative of spam e-mails. Intuitively, a word that appears most in nonspam e-mails while seldom in spam e-mails is a good representative of nonspam e-mails. Consequently, the difference of its frequency in nonspam e-mails minus that in spam e-mails can be used to reflect a word's *proclivity*. After calculating the difference of each word, words are sorted in terms of their differences. Consider the queue of words sorted in descendent order, for instance, then two portions of words derived from the front and the rear of the queue with certain proportion can be used to construct *self gene library* and *nonself gene library*,

---

Algorithm 4.1   Spam detection

Generate *self gene library* and *nonself gene library* from training samples.

for each *sample$_i$* in training set **do**
    Construct the *concentration vector* of *sample$_i$* through two gene libraries.
end for

Use these *concentration vectors* of training samples to train a successive classification algorithm to obtain a *classifier*.

while Algorithm is running **do**
    if *e-mail* is received **then**
        Characterize the *message* by *concentration vector*.
        Use trained *classifier* to predict the label of the e-mail.
    end if
end while

---

respectively. Preprocessing is used to select candidate words. According to [250], the features that appear in most of the documents are not relevant to separate these documents because all the classes have instances that contain those features. For simplification, words that appear more than 95% in all messages of the corpus are discarded and stop word list is also used to remove those trivial words. The generation of gene libraries is described in Algorithm 4.2. Parameters $P_N\%$ and $P_S\%$ are determinants that uniquely determine *self gene library* and *nonself gene library*, respectively.

4.6 Concentration Vector Construction

The *concentration* of an e-mail is defined as the proportion of the number of words of the e-mail which appear in *gene library* to the number of different words in the e-mail, which can be formulated as

$$c = \frac{N}{W} \tag{4.1}$$

where
    c denotes the concentration
    N is the number of words appearing in both e-mail and *gene library*
    W is the number of words in the e-mail

Calculation of the *concentration* is described in Algorithm 4.3. The *gene library* in Algorithm 4.3 can be either the *self gene library* or the *nonself gene library*.

Algorithm 4.2   Generation of gene libraries

Use stop word list to exclude those trivial words in training set.

Drop the word whose frequency is more than 95% in training set.

for each remaining word **do**

    Calculate its frequency appearing in nonspam (denoted by f_n) and spam (denoted by f_s), respectively.

end for

for each remaining word **do**

    Calculate its "proclivity" via following formula:

    $f_d = f_n - f_s.$

end for

Sort the words in terms of f_d, in descendent order.

Extract P_N% of words in front of the queue to form *self gene library* and P_S% of words in rear of the queue to form *nonself gene library*, respectively.

Algorithm 4.3   Algorithm for feature construction

For an e-mail to be classified, calculate the number of *different* words in this e-mail (denoted by *words-Num*).

counter $= 0$.

for each different word in this e-mail **do**

    if it appears in gene library **then**

        counter++;

    end if

end for

concentration $=$ *counter* / *words-Num*.

Therefore for an e-mail to be classified, a *self concentration* that describes its similarity to nonspam and a *nonself concentration*, which describes its similarity to spam can be constructed, respectively. When parameters P_N and P_S take different values, different *self gene libraries* and *nonself gene libraries* are obtained. Consequently, different *concentrations* can be constructed. Theses *concentrations* are used to form a feature vector that is served as the input of a successive classification algorithm.

4.7 Relation to Other Methods

In this section, we analyze the relation of the immune concentration-based feature construction approach to other methods such as term frequency analysis approaches and heuristic approaches. In Algorithm 4.2, the *self gene library* and *nonself gene library* are composed of words in front of the queue and in rear of the queue, respectively. Now let us consider the following extreme circumstance, assuming the number of words in the sorted queue is N, and now we are going to construct N libraries each of which only contains one word with none overlapping interval with size of 1%, that is, the N different words are used to construct N different gene libraries, respectively. Then for an e-mail to be classified, each library scans the e-mail to check whether the contained word appears in the e-mail or not, if so, it gives a bit 1, otherwise a bit 0 is given. Subsequently, a binary vector consisted of earlier n bits is used as the feature vector of the e-mail. In such circumstance, the immune concentration-based feature construction approach is equivalent to the binary representation of term frequency analysis approach.

Compared to simple approaches and frequency analysis approaches that use words in a relative direct way, heuristic approaches and the immune concentration-based feature construction approach mine semantic information to construct features. For heuristic approaches, phrases are mainly used to generate patterns in forms of regular expressions. Though heuristic approach is less sensitive to the variation of a single word, a changed phrase while expressing the same meaning can often avoid the match of the regular expression. The immune concentration-based feature construction approach utilizes the words but do not closely rely on the words as frequency analysis approaches do. The words at one end of the queue work together to give out a feature. Variation of individual word, especially the words in the middle of the queue, will not influence the constructed concentration. Besides, the immune concentration-based feature construction approach is also insensitive to the variation of phrases and has much stronger robustness and stability.

The significance of different samples differs a lot, as in SVM, the most important samples are the ones determining the optimal hyperplane, that is, the so-called support vectors. Support vectors of same class work together to position the separating hyperplane, and the corresponding coefficient of support vector reflects the relative importance of the support vector. Analogically, different features have different weights, some of which have strong capability in discriminating samples, while others can only introduce noises. In Algorithm 4.2, the importance of a feature (word) is measured by f_d, and the words in front of the queue and in rear of the queue are grouped, respectively. Each group of words give out a concentration that can be regarded as a mapped feature by using a subset of original features (words). The word in each group plays a role similar to that of the support vector and accordingly the corresponding f_d can be regarded as its relative importance.

4.8 Complexity Analysis

In Algorithm 4.2, the time complexity of sorting m words is

$$O(m \log m) \tag{4.2}$$

where m is the number of candidate words after preprocessing and this process only carries out once during training stage. During running stage, according to Algorithm 4.3, the time complexity of constructing *self concentration* and *nonself* concentration is

$$O(n_s * n_m + n_n * n_m) \tag{4.3}$$

where
 n_s and n_n are the number of words in *self gene library* and *nonself* gene library, respectively
 n_m is the number of words in the e-mail to be classified

As n_m is usually at the scale of constant, Equation 4.3 can be further expressed as

$$O(n_s + n_n) \tag{4.4}$$

When $n_s + n_n < m$, the time complexity for constructing a two-element feature vector for an e-mail is at most $O(m)$.

4.9 Experimental Validation

Experiments were conducted on standard spam corpus introduced earlier to verify performance of the concentration-based feature construction approaches. WEKA toolkit [89] was utilized in implementation of classification methods, as well as the library LIBSVM [34], which is an implementation of SVM.

Two corpora used to test the concentration-based feature construction approach are the PU1 corpus [14] and Ling corpus [11]. All the messages in both corpora have header fields, attachment, and HTML tags removed, leaving only subject line and mail body text. In PU1, each token is mapped to a unique integer to ensure the privacy of the content while keeping its original form in Ling. Each corpus is divided into 10 partitions with approximately equal amount of messages and spam rate. There are four versions of the corpus: with or without stemming and with or without stop-word removal. Words like "of," "and," "the" in stop list are trivial, while certain forms of a word (such as the active tense) may be meaningful in semantics [67]. Consequently, the version with stop-word removal is used in experiments.

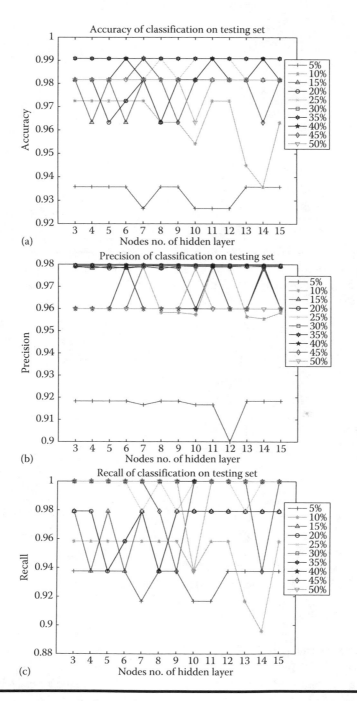

Figure 4.3 **(a) Accuracy, (b) precision, and (c) recall.** **(*Continued*)**

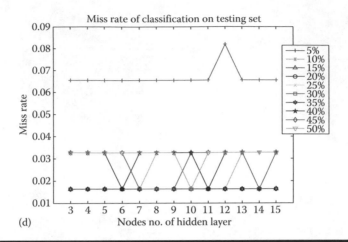

Figure 4.3 (*Continued*)   (d) Miss rate with different *self* concentrations on corpus PU1, leaving partition 1 as testing set.

4.9.1 Experiments on Different Concentrations

In this part, different *self concentrations* and *nonself concentrations*, which correspond to *self gene libraries* and *nonself gene libraries* with different P_N and P_S are tested, aiming to find the *concentrations* with best performance. The tested P_N and P_S range from 5% to 50% at a step size 5%. Ten-fold cross validation is used to measure the performance. That is, in each iteration, 90% data are used for training while the rest 10% are used for its test.

A three layer BP network is used as the implementation of ANN algorithm. The number of nodes of input layer equals to the size of *concentration vector*. In this scenario, the *concentration vector* is unary. The number of nodes of hidden layer ranging from 3 to 15 is tested. There is only one node in output layer, output 1 indicates nonspam e-mail and output 0 is for spam e-mail. The transfer functions of hidden layer and output layer are "tansig" and "purelin", respectively. The training function is "trainlm." Performance function used is MSE. The network is trained for a maximum of 50 epochs to an error goal of 0.01. Figures 4.3 and 4.4 show when leaving partition 1, the accuracy, precision, recall, and miss rate on corpus PU1 with different *self concentrations* and *nonself concentrations*, respectively. Figures 4.5 and 4.6 show when leaving partition 1, the accuracy, precision, recall, and miss rate on corpus Ling with different *self concentrations* and *nonself concentrations*, respectively. The performance measured by 10-fold cross validation shows that *self concentration* with $P_N = 30\%$ and *nonself concentration* with $P_S = 30\%$ perform best on corpus PU1, respectively. On corpus Ling, best performance is *self concentration* with $P_N = 50\%$ and *nonself concentration* with $P_S = 5\%$, respectively.

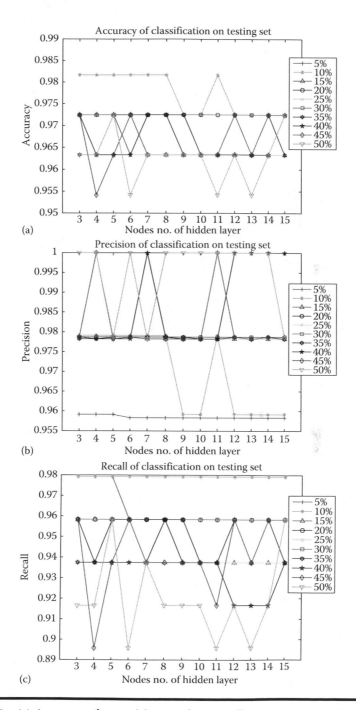

Figure 4.4   **(a) Accuracy, (b) precision, and (c) recall.**   (*Continued*)

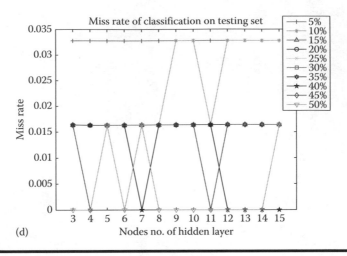

(d)

Figure 4.4 (*Continued*) **(d) Miss rate with different *nonself* concentrations on corpus PU1, leaving partition 1 as testing set.**

4.9.2 Experiments with Two-Element Concentration Vector

In this part, a *self concentration* and a *nonself concentration* are used together to form a two-element vector to reduce the detection hole caused by the unary *concentration vector*. *Self concentration* with $P_N = 30\%$ and *nonself concentration* with $P_S = 30\%$ are used to form a two-element *concentration vector* to characterize each e-mail on corpus PU1. On corpus Ling, two-element *concentration vector* is composed of *self concentration* with $P_N = 50\%$ and *nonself concentrations* with $P_S = 5\%$. Figure 4.7 shows the data distribution of nonspam and spam on corpus PU1 and Ling after feature construction with two-element *concentration vector*. Linear discriminant, SVM (with linear kernel and RBF kernel), and BP neural network are used as classification algorithm to test the effectiveness and robustness of *concentration vector*. According to Reference [67], the performance of the SVM is remarkably independent of the choice of C as long as C is large (over 50). The parameter C of SVM is set to be 100 for both SVM with linear kernel and SVM with RBF kernel in the experiments. In the initial tentative experiments, a range of parameter γ for RBF kernel are tested, and the performance is not sensitive to the variation of parameter γ. The γ is set to be 10 for SVM with RBF kernel in the experiments. For BP neural network, the difference of performance with different number of nodes of hidden layer is inapparent. Figure 4.8 shows when leaving partition 3, the accuracy, precision, recall, and miss rate on corpus PU1 with BP neural network with number of hidden layer ranging from 3 to 15. The number of nodes of hidden layer is set to be 3 in the experiments. The performances of linear discriminant,

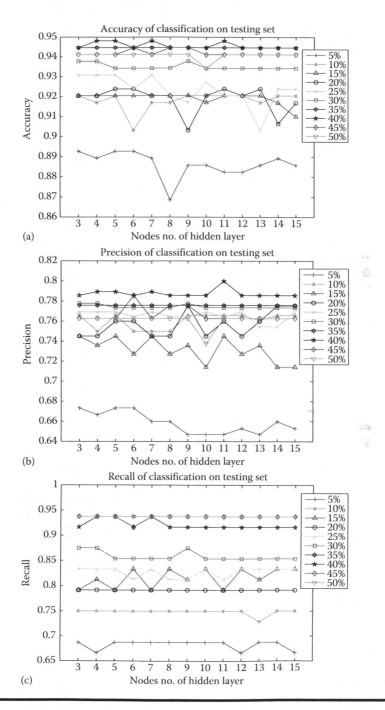

Figure 4.5 (a) Accuracy, (b) precision, and (c) recall.　　　*(Continued)*

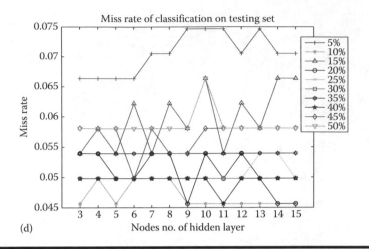

Figure 4.5 (*Continued*) **(d) Miss rate with different *self* concentrations on corpus Ling, leaving partition 1 as testing set.**

SVM (with linear kernel and RBF kernel), and BP neural network with two-element concentration vector as input on corpus PU1 and Ling are listed in Tables 4.1 and 4.2, respectively.

Tables 4.3 and 4.4 show the performances of Naïve Bayesian, Linger-V, and SVM-IG on corpus PU1 and Ling reported in References [11,14,41,112]. Linger-V is a NN-based system for automatic e-mail classification. For Naïve Bayesian, the version of the corpus adopted in the experiments is the original version, for Linger-V and SVM-IG, it is the stemming version. All these results are obtained by using 10-fold validation. In References [11,14,41,112], the authors only report the accuracy, precision, and recall, the miss rate given here is derived through the aforementioned three indexes. For Naïve Bayesian, 50 words with the highest mutual information scores are selected. LINGER-V and SVM-IG uses variance (V) and information gain (IG) as feature selection criteria, respectively, and the best scoring 256 features are chosen. Figures 4.9 and 4.10 show the comparison of performance on corpus PU1 and Ling among the presented approach and the approaches discussed here, respectively.

4.9.3 Experiments with Middle Concentration

In Algorithm 4.2, the gene library is generated by the words in the front or rear of the queue. In this part, the words in the middle of the queue are used to construct a relatively "neutral" library compared to previous *self gene library* and *nonself gene*

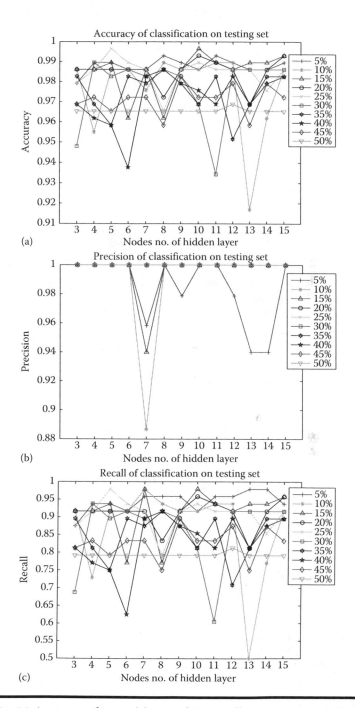

Figure 4.6   **(a) Accuracy, (b) precision, and (c) recall.**   *(Continued)*

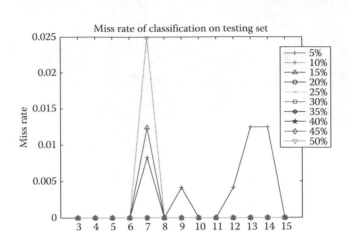

Figure 4.6 (*Continued*) **(d) Miss rate with different *nonself* concentrations on corpus Ling, leaving partition 1 as testing set.**

library. In PU1, the words between the interval, of [30%, 40%], [40%, 50%], and [30%, 50%] from the front and the rear of the queue are used to construct "neutral" libraries (Tables 4.3 and 4.4). Consequently, correspondent concentration can be derived. Table 4.5 shows when using *self concentration* with $P_N = 30\%$ and *nonself concentration* with $P_S = 30\%$ together with two concentrations derived by neutral library as a four-dimensional feature vector, the performance of Linear Discriminant on corpus PU1. The interval in the parentheses denotes the range of the words used to construct the neutral library. Figure 4.11 shows the data distribution of nonspam and spam on corpus PU1 with earlier three neutral libraries, respectively. The result indicates that the ability of "neutral" library in discriminating different classes is weaker than that of *self* and *nonself* libraries.

4.10 Discussion

In this section, we analyze the experimental results in detail and give some explanations. In Section 4.9.1, different P_N and P_S ranging from 5% to 50% at a step size 5% are tested. The values of P_N and P_S from which best *self concentration* and *nonself concentration* are achieved are quite different for corpus Ling compared to corpus PU1. On corpus Ling, there is an unbalance between the number of negative examples and that of positive examples, the spam rate of Ling is only 16.63%. On corpus PU1, the spam rate and nonspam rate are proportional, the percentage of spam is 43.77%. Consequently, after sorting the words in terms of Algorithm 4.2,

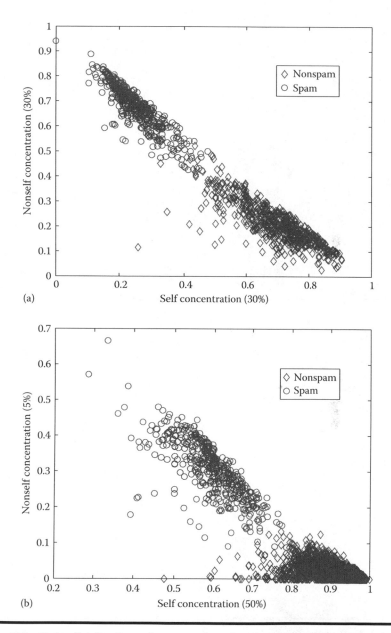

Figure 4.7   Data distribution of nonspam and spam on corpus PU1 and Ling. (a) Data distribution of nonspam and spam on corpus PU1 and (b) data distribution of nonspam and spam on corpus Ling.

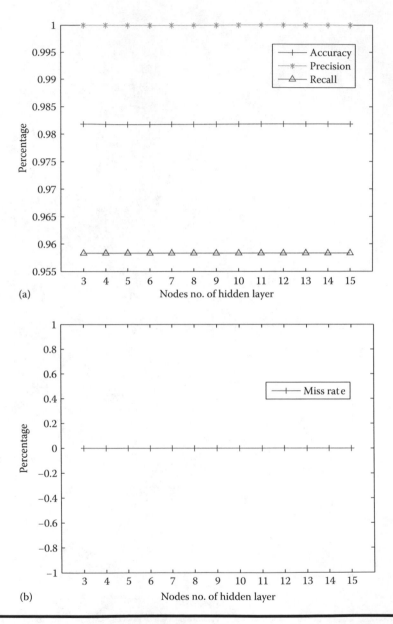

Figure 4.8 Performances on corpus PU1 using BP neural network with a number of hidden layers ranging from 3 to 15, leaving partition 3 as testing set. (a) Accuracy, precision, and recall and (b) miss rate.

Table 4.1   Performances of Linear Discriminant (LD), SVM, and BP Neural Network with Two-Element Concentration Vector on Corpus PU1, Using 10-Fold Cross Validation

Met.	Ac. (%)	Pr. (%)	Re. (%)	MR (%)	NF
LD	96.36	97.02	94.38	2.27	2
SVM (linear kernel)	97.09	97.02	97.38	2.11	2
SVM (RBF kernel)	97	97.5	95.63	1.95	2
BP neural network	97.37	97.09	96.97	2.36	2

Met., method; Ac., accuracy; Pr., precision; Re., recall; MR, miss rate; NF, number of feature.

Table 4.2   Performances of Linear Discriminant (LD), SVM, and BP Neural Network with Two-Element Concentration Vector on Corpus Ling, Using 10-Fold Cross Validation

Met.	Ac. (%)	Pr. (%)	Re. (%)	MR (%)	NF
LD	98.55	99.77	91.49	0.041	2
SVM (linear kernel)	99	97.72	96.26	0.45	2
SVM (RBF kernel)	99.2	98.34	96.88	0.33	2
BP neural network	99.13	98.93	95.84	0.21	2

Met., method; Ac., accuracy; Pr., precision; Re., recall; MR, miss rate; NF, number of feature.

Table 4.3   Performances of Naïve Bayesian (NB), Linger-V, and SVM-IG on Corpus PU1, Using 10-Fold Cross Validation

Met.	Ac. (%)	Pr. (%)	Re. (%)	MR (%)	NF
NB	91.076	95.11	83.98	3.4	50
Linger-V	93.45	96.46	88.36	2.588	256
SVM-IG	93.18	95.7	88.4	3.1	256

Met., method; Ac., accuracy; Pr., precision; Re., recall; MR, miss rate; NF, number of feature.

Table 4.4   Performances of Naïve Bayesian (NB), Linger-V, and SVM-IG on Corpus Ling, Using 10-Fold Cross Validation

Met.	Ac. (%)	Pr. (%)	Re. (%)	MR (%)	NF
NB	96.408	96.85	81.10	0.539	50
Linger-V	98.2	95.62	93.56	0.875	256
SVM-IG	96.85	99	81.9	0.17	256

Met., method; Ac., accuracy; Pr., precision; Re., recall; MR, miss rate; NF, number of feature.

the words at the rear of the sorted queue show more strong *proclivity* to spam for corpus Ling compared to PU1. Analogically, the words at the front of the queue give less class information for corpus Ling compared to corpus PU1. For corpus Ling itself, the words at the rear have more class information compared to those at the front. While for corpus PU1, the representation ability for correspondent class of the words at two ends is almost the same. The best P_N and P_S are both 30% for corpus PU1, which shows a good symmetry. For corpus Ling, the best P_N and P_S are 50% and 5%, respectively.

In Section 4.9.2, the best *self concentration* and *nonself concentration* are used to form a two-element *concentration vector* to characterize each e-mail in corpus. The data distribution as shown in Figure 4.7 demonstrates the effectiveness of the proposed feature construction approach intuitively. The data points of two classes are almost separable except very few overlaps in the adjacent area of two classes. Experimental results on corpus PU1 and Ling listed in Tables 4.1 and 4.2 show good performance by using the unary *concentration vector*, even using linear discriminant as the classifier. Compared to current methods reported in Tables 4.3 and 4.4, the immune concentration-based feature construction approach excels in terms of accuracy, precision, and miss rate. Besides, as there are only two features, the speed of classification is very fast.

In Section 4.9.3, some "neutral" concentrations are also tested. The experimental results in Table 4.5 show that the prospective improvement is not achieved. The reason is that words in the middle of the queue are not representative as words at two ends, therefore the constructed concentrations contribute little for classification.

4.11 Summary

In this chapter, the immune concentration-based feature construction (CFC) approach for spam detection is introduced. Both *self gene library* and *nonself gene library* that contain words with utmost representative of nonspam mail and spam

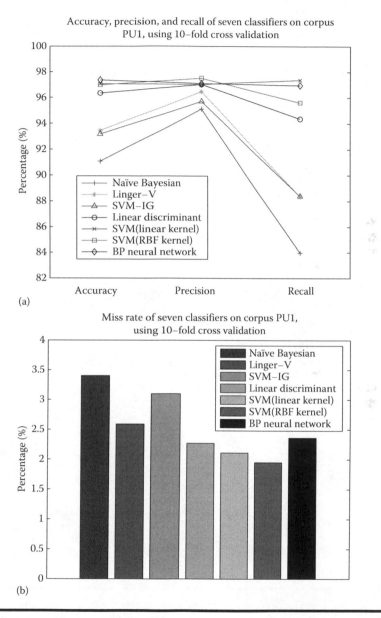

Figure 4.9 Comparison of performances on corpus PU1 among Naïve Bayesian, Linger-V, SVM-IG, and the presented approach. (a) Accuracy, precision, and recall and (b) miss rate.

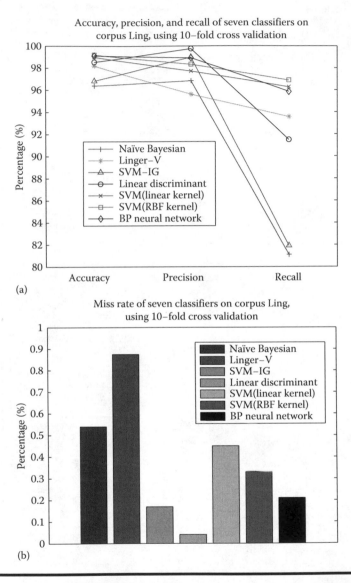

Figure 4.10 Comparison of performances on corpus Ling among Naïve Bayesian, Linger-V, SVM-IG, and the presented approach. (a) Accuracy, precision, and recall and (b) miss rate.

Table 4.5 Performances of Linear Discriminant (LD) with Different Middle Concentrations on Corpus PU1, Using 10-Fold Cross Validation

Met.	Ac. (%)	Pr. (%)	Re. (%)	MR (%)	NF
LD (30%–40%)	96.35	98.9	92.71	0.81	4
LD (40%–50%)	96.45	98.46	93.33	1.14	4
LD (30%–50%)	95.9	98.45	92.09	1.3	4

mail, respectively, are generated. The representative of a word for nonspam or spam is measured by the difference of its frequency in nonspam e-mails minus that in spam e-mails. *Self concentration* together with *nonself concentration* for an e-mail to be classified are constructed in terms of *self gene library* and *nonself gene library*, respectively. A two-element concentration vector composed of earlier two concentration values is used as the feature vector to characterize the e-mail. Several classifiers including linear discriminant, artificial neural networks (ANN), support vector machine (SVM) are employed to verify the effectiveness as well as robustness of the CFC approach. Comprehensive experiments are conducted on two public benchmark corpus PU1 and Ling. Experimental results show that CFC approach gives impressive performance and will be effective tools in practical applications for spam detection in future.

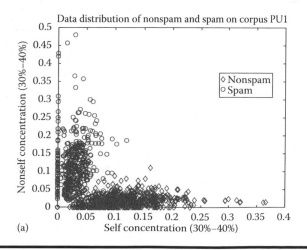

(a)

Figure 4.11 Data distributions of nonspam and spam on corpus PU1 with different neutral libraries: (a) 30%–40%. **(*Continued*)**

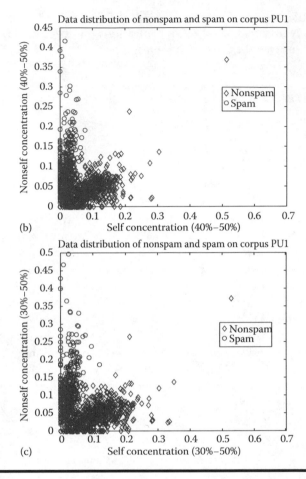

Figure 4.11 (*Continued*) Data distributions of nonspam and spam on corpus PU1 with different neutral libraries: (b) 40%–50% and (c) 30%–50%.

Chapter 5

Local Concentration-Based Feature Extraction Approach

This chapter presents the local concentration (LC)-based feature extraction approach for anti-spam, which is considered to be able to effectively extract position-correlated information from messages by transforming each area of a message to a corresponding LC feature [246,248]. After a brief introduction of the background, the structure of the LC model is given. Then described in detail is the implementation of the LC approach for anti-spam, including term selection, generation of detector sets, and construction of local concentration-based feature vectors. Two strategies for defining local areas and analysis of the LC model are also presented. Finally, the experimental validation is given.

5.1 Introduction

BIS is an adaptive distributed system with the capability of discriminating *self* cells from *nonself* cells. It protects our body from attacks of pathogens. Antibodies, produced by lymphocytes to detect pathogens, play core roles in the BIS. On the surfaces of them, there are specific receptors which can bind corresponding specific pathogens. Thus, antibodies can detect and destroy pathogens by binding them. All the time, antibodies circulate in our body and kill pathogens near them without any central controlling node. In the BIS, two types of immune response may happen: a primary response and a secondary response. The primary response happens when a pathogen appears for the first time. In this case, the antibodies with affinity to the pathogen are produced slowly. After that, a corresponding long-lived B memory cell (a type of lymphocyte) is created. Then when the same pathogen appears again, a secondary response is triggered, and a large amount of antibodies with high affinity to that pathogen are proliferated.

In this chapter, we introduce local concentration-based feature construction approach, which takes inspirations from BIS and CFC [155] presented in Chapter 4 and gives a way of generating LC features of messages. To mimic the functions of BIS, one key step is to define corresponding antibodies in an application. In the LC model for spam filtering, antibodies (spam genes and legitimate e-mail genes) are extracted from messages through term selection methods and tendency decisions. In addition, the difference between a primary response and a secondary response shows that the local concentrations of antibodies play important roles in immune behavior. Accordingly, two strategies are designed for calculating local concentrations for messages. As local concentrations of antibodies help detect antigens in BIS, it is reasonable to believe that the proposed LC approach will provide discriminative features for spam filtering.

5.2 Structure of Local Concentration Model

To incorporate the LC feature extraction approach into the whole process of spam filtering, a generic structure of the LC model is designed, as shown in Figure 5.1. The tokenization is a simple step, where messages are tokenized into words (terms)

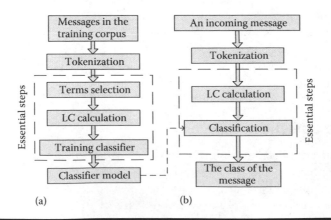

Figure 5.1 (a) Training and (b) classification phases of the LC model.

by examining the existence of blank spaces and delimiters, while term selection, LC calculation, and classification are quite essential to the model:

■ *Term selection*: In the tokenization step of the training phase, messages in the training corpus are transformed into a huge number of terms, which would cause high computational complexity. To reduce computational complexity, term selection methods should be utilized to remove less informative terms. Three term selection methods —IG, TFV, and DF were, respectively, applied to the LC model. The experiments were conducted to compare their performances, aiming to show that the proposed model is compatible with various term selection methods. In addition, the experiments could reflect the effectiveness of the three methods. For a detailed introduction of term selection methods, please refer to Section 1.3.1.

■ *Local concentration calculation*: In BIS, antibodies distribute and circulate in bodies. Meanwhile, they detect and destroy specific pathogens nearby. In a small area of a body, if the concentration of the antibodies with high affinity to a specific pathogen increases above some threshold, the pathogen would be destroyed. Thus, the local concentrations of antibodies determine whether the corresponding pathogens could be culled from the body. Inspired from this phenomenon, the LC-based feature extraction approach is proposed. A detailed description and analysis of it can be found in the following sections.

■ *Classification*: In the training phase, messages in the training corpus are at first transformed into feature vectors through the steps of tokenization, term selection, and LC calculation. Then the feature vectors are taken as the inputs of a certain classifier, after which a specific classifier model is acquired. Finally, the classifier model is applied to messages for classification. At this stage, the main focus is on the proposal of the LC-based feature extraction approach, so only SVM is adopted in the step of classification. The effects of different classifiers on the performance of the model could be investigated exactly in the same.

5.3 Term Selection and Detector Sets Generation

Algorithm 5.1 shows the process of term selection and generation of detector sets. The terms, generated by the step of tokenization, are at first selected by utilizing one certain term selection method, which can be any one of the approaches introduced in Section 1.3.1. In term selection, importance of the terms is measured by the criterion defined in the term selection method. Then unimportant (uninformative) terms are removed, and important terms are added to the preselected set, which should be initialized as an empty set at the beginning. The purposes of term selection are to reduce the computational complexity of the LC calculation step and reduce

---

Algorithm 5.1 Term selection and DS generation

Initialize preselected set and DS as empty sets;

for each term in the terms set (generated by tokenization) **do**
  Calculate importance of the term according to a certain term selection methods;
end for

Sort the terms in descending order of the importance;
Add the front $m\%$ terms to the preselected set;

for each term t_i in the preselected set **do**
  Calculate *Tendency*(t_i) of the term t_i according to Equation (5.1);

  if $\| P(t_i|c_l) - P(t_i|c_s) \| > \theta, \theta \geqslant 0$ **then**
    if $P(t_i|c_l) - P(t_i|c_s) < 0$ **then**
      Add the term to DS_s;
    else
      Add the term to DS_l;
    end if
  else
    Discard the term;
  end if

end for

---

possible noises brought by uninformative terms. The noises may occur when the uninformative terms are taken as discriminative features.

Taking the preselected set as a source, the detector set (DS) are built based on tendencies of terms. The tendency of a term t_i is defined as follows.

$$Tendency(t_i) = P(t_i|c_l) - P(t_i|c_s) \tag{5.1}$$

where
  $P(t_i|c_l)$ is the probability of t_i's occurrence, given messages are legitimate e-mails
  $P(t_i|c_s)$ is defined similarly, that is the probability of t_i's occurrence estimated in spam

Tendency(t_i) measures the difference between the term's occurrence frequency in legitimate e-mails and that in spam. According to Algorithm 5.1, the terms, which occur more frequently in spam than in legitimate e-mails, are added to spam detector set (DS_s), in which the terms represent spam genes. On the contrary, the terms, tending to occur in legitimate e-mails, are added to legitimate e-mail detector set

(DS_l), in which the terms represent legitimate genes. The two DS (DS_s and DS_l) are then utilized to construct the LC-based feature vector of a message.

5.4 Construction of Local Concentration–Based Feature Vectors

To construct an LC-based feature vector for each message, a sliding window of w_n-term length is utilized to slide over the message with a step of w_n-term, which means that there is neither gap nor overlap between any two adjacent windows. At each movement of the window, a spam genes concentration SC_i and a legitimate genes concentration LC_i are calculated according to the two DS and the terms in the window as follows.

$$SC_i = \frac{N_s}{N_t} \tag{5.2}$$

$$LC_i = \frac{N_l}{N_t} \tag{5.3}$$

where
 N_t is the number of distinct terms in the window
 N_s is the number of the distinct terms in the window, which has been matched
  by detectors in DS_s
 N_l is the number of the distinct terms in the window which has been matched
  by detectors in DS_l

Algorithm 5.2 shows the construction process of a feature vector. For the purpose of better understanding, we give an example as follows.

Algorithm 5.2 Construction of an LC-based feature vector

Move a sliding window of w_n-term length over a given message with a step of w_n-term;

for each position i of the sliding window **do**
  Calculate the spam genes concentration SC_i of the window according to Equation 6.4;
  Calculate the legitimate genes concentration LC_i of the window according to Equation 5.3;
end for

Construct the feature vector likes:
 $\langle (SC_1, LC_1), (SC_2, LC_2), \ldots, (SC_n, LC_n) \rangle$.

Suppose one message is *"If you have any questions, please feel free to contact us ...,"* $DS_s = \{free, any\}$, $DS_l = \{If, you, questions, feel, to, contact\}$, and the parameter $w_n = 5$. Then according to Algorithm 5.2, the first window would be *"If you have any questions,"* $SC_1 = 0.2$, and $LC_2 = 0.6$. Similarly, the second window would be *"please feel free to contact,"* $SC_2 = 0.2$, and $LC_2 = 0.6$. The rest of SC_i and LC_i can be calculated in the same way by continuing to slide the window and do similar calculation. Finally, a feature vector $\langle (0.2, 0.6), (0.2, 0.6), \ldots \rangle$ can be acquired.

5.5 Strategies for Defining Local Areas

In this section, we present two strategies for defining local areas in messages—using a sliding window with fixed length (FL) and using a sliding window with variable length (VL).

5.5.1 Using a Sliding Window with Fixed Length

When a fixed-length sliding window is utilized, messages may have different number of local areas (corresponding to different number of feature dimensionality), as messages vary in length. To handle this problem, we design two specific processes for dealing with the feature dimensionality of messages.

1. *Implementation for short messages*: Suppose a short message has a dimensionality of 6, and its dimensionality should be expanded to 10. Two methods could be utilized with linear time computational complexity. One is to insert zeros in the end of the feature vector. For example, a feature vector
   $\langle (SC_1, LC_1), (SC_2, LC_2), (SC_3, LC_3) \rangle$
   can be expanded as
   $\langle (SC_1, LC_1), (SC_2, LC_2), (SC_3, LC_3), (0,0), (0,0) \rangle$.
   The other is to reproduce the front features. For example, the feature vector would be expanded as
   $\langle (SC_1, LC_1), (SC_2, LC_2), (SC_3, LC_3), (SC_1, LC_1),$
   $(SC_2, LC_2) \rangle$.

   In our preliminary experiments, the latter one performed slightly better. As we see, the reason is that the front features contain more information than simple zeros. Therefore, the second method is utilized in the LC model.

2. *Implementation for long messages*: For long messages, we reduce their dimensionality by discarding terms at the end of the messages (truncation). The reason for choosing this method is that we will not do much reduction of features, but just do small adjustment so that all messages can have the same feature dimensionality. One advantage of it is that no further computational complexity would be added to the model. Preliminary experiments showed that the truncation performed well with no loss of accuracy for the

remaining features could provide quite enough information for discrimination. It is shown in Reference [165] that truncation of long messages can both reduce the computational complexity and improve the overall performance of algorithms.

In the model, we utilize both the two specific processes—implementation for short messages and implementation for long messages. We at first conduct parameter tuning experiments to determine a fixed value for the feature dimensionality. Then, if the dimensionality of a feature vector is greater than the value, the first kind of process will be utilized. Otherwise, the second one will be utilized. The parameter tuning experiments can ensure that the two specific processes do not affect the overall performance, and the LC model performs best with respect to the parameter of feature dimensionality.

5.5.2 Using a Sliding Window with Variable Length

In this strategy, the length of a sliding window is designed to be proportional to the length of a message. Suppose we want to construct a $2N$ dimensional feature vector for each message. Then for an M-term length message, the length of the sliding window would be set to M/N-term for the message. In this way, all the messages can be transformed into $2N$ dimensional feature vectors without loss of information.

5.6 Analysis of Local Concentration Model

For the purpose of better understanding, we now analyze the LC model from a statistical point of view. According to Algorithm 5.1, each term t_j in the DS_l satisfies:

$$P(t_j|c_l) > P(t_j|c_s) \tag{5.4}$$

Thus, the terms in legitimate e-mails are more likely to fall into the DS_l, compared to those in spam, that is:

$$P(t_j \in DS_l|c_l) > P(t_j \in DS_l|c_s) \tag{5.5}$$

According to Algorithm 5.2, the LC_i of a sliding window depends on the number of terms (N_l) falling into the DS_l. From a statistical point of view, the probable number of terms (N_l) falling into the DS_l can be regarded as a good approximation of binomial distribution, that is

$$P(N_l = r) \sim B_r(n, p) \tag{5.6}$$

$$B_r(n, p) = C_n^r p^r (1 - p)^{n-r}, r = 0, 1, 2, \ldots, n \tag{5.7}$$

where
$p = P(t_j \in DS_l)$
n is the length of the sliding window

Then we can obtain the expectation value of N_l for legitimate e-mails as follows.

$$E(N_l|c_l) = \sum_{r=0}^{n} rC_n^r p_l^r (1 - p_l)^{n-r}$$

$$= np_l$$

$$= nP(t_j \in DS_l|c_l) \tag{5.8}$$

Similarly, we can obtain the expectation value of N_l for spam as follows.

$$E(N_l|c_s) = \sum_{r=0}^{n} rC_n^r p_s^r (1 - p_s)^{n-r}$$

$$= np_s$$

$$= nP(t_j \in DS_l|c_s) \tag{5.9}$$

From Equations 5.5, 5.8, and 5.9, we can obtain

$$E(N_l|c_l) > E(N_l|c_s) \tag{5.10}$$

which indicates that a sliding window in a legitimate e-mail tends to contain more legitimate genes than a sliding window in spam from a statistical point of view. Similarly, we can obtain $E(N_s|c_l) < E(N_s|c_s)$. Thus, an LC_i of a legitimate e-mail tends to be larger than that of spam, and an SC_i of a legitimate e-mail tends to be smaller than that of spam. In conclusion, the LC model can extract discriminative features for classification between spam and legitimate e-mails.

5.7 Experimental Validation

Experiments were conducted on five benchmark corpora PU1, PU2, PU3, PUA [13], and Enron-Spam [131], using cross validation. The corpora have been pre-processed with removal of attachments, HTML tags, and header fields except for the subject. In the four PU corpora, the duplicates were removed from the corpora for duplicates may lead to over-optimistic conclusions in experiments. In PU1 and PU2, only the duplicate spam, which arrived on the same day, are deleted. While in PU3 and PUA, all duplicates (both spam and legitimate e-mails) are removed, even if they arrived on different days. In the Enron-Spam corpus, the legitimate messages sent by the owners of the mailbox and duplicate messages have been removed to avoid over-optimistic conclusions. Different from the former PU1 corpus (the one released in 2000) and Ling corpus, the corpora are not processed with removal of stop words, and no lemmatization method is adopted. The details of the corpora are given as follows.

In addition, experiments for tuning the parameters of the LC model have been conducted on PU1 corpus by utilizing 10-fold cross validation, and IG was used as the term selection method of the models.

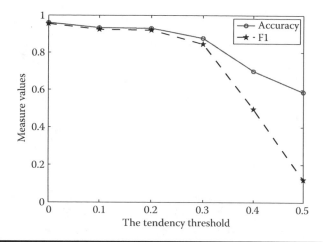

Figure 5.2   Performance of the model with varied tendency threshold.

5.7.1 Selection of a Proper Tendency Threshold

Experiments were conducted with varied tendency threshold θ to investigate the effects of θ on the performance of the LC model. As shown in Figure 5.2, the LC model performs well with small θ. However, with the increase of θ, the performance of the LC model degrades in terms of both accuracy and F_1 measure. As we can see, the term selection methods have already filtered the uninformative terms, thus the threshold is not quite necessary. In addition, a large θ would result in loss of information. It is recommended that θ should be set to zero or a small value.

5.7.2 Selection of Proper Feature Dimensionality

For the LC model using a fixed-length sliding window (LC-FL), short messages and long messages need to be processed specifically so that all the messages can have the same feature dimensionality. Before that, the feature dimensionality needs to be determined. Therefore, we conducted experiments to determine the optimal number of utmost front sliding windows for discrimination. Figure 5.3 depicts the results, from which we can see that the model performed best when 10 utmost front sliding windows of each message were utilized for discrimination. In this case, all the messages would be transformed into 20-dimensional feature vectors through the specific process introduced in Section 5.5.1.

For the LC model using a variable-length sliding window (LC-VL), all the messages are directly transformed into feature vectors with the same dimensionality. However, there is still the necessity for determining the feature dimensionality, which corresponds to the number of local areas in a message. We conducted some preliminary experiments on PU1 and found that the LC-VL model performed optimally when the feature dimensionality was set to 6 or 10.

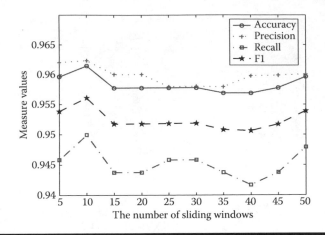

Figure 5.3   Performance of the LC-FL model with different window numbers.

5.7.3 Selection of a Proper Sliding Window Size

For the LC-FL model, the sliding window size is quite essential as it defines the size of local area in a message. Only if the size of local area is properly defined can we calculate discriminative LC vectors for messages. Figure 5.4 shows the performance of the LC-FL model under different values of sliding window size. When the size was set to 150 terms per window, the model performed best in terms of both accuracy and F_1 measure. It also can be seen that the model performed acceptably when the parameter was set to other values.

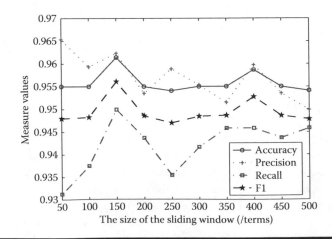

Figure 5.4   Performance of the LC-FL model with different sliding window sizes.

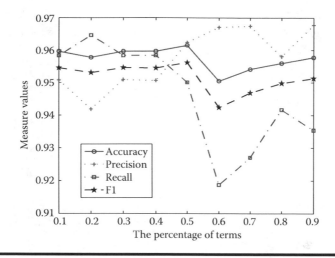

Figure 5.5   Performance of the model with different percentage of terms.

5.7.4 Selection of Optimal Terms Percentage

The phase of term selection plays an important role in the LC model. The removal of less informative terms can reduce computational complexity and improve the overall performance of the model. We conducted experiments to determine the percentage of terms reserved after the phase of term selection. Therefore, the removal of uninformative terms can be maximized while avoiding removing informative ones.

Figure 5.5 gives the results of the LC-FL model. When 50% terms were reserved after term selection, the model performed best in terms of both accuracy and F_1 measure. In the following experiments, we set the parameter to 50% for both the LC-FL model and the LC-VL model. We should pay attention to that the model performed quite well when only 10% terms were reserved. This configuration can be applied to the cost-sensitive situations.

5.7.5 Experiments of the Model with Three Term Selection Methods

To construct discriminative feature vectors for messages, both the term selection method and the feature extraction approach play quite essential roles. To some extent, a feature extraction approach depends on a proper term selection method. Therefore, it is necessary to verify whether the proposed LC approach can be incorporated with prevalent term selection methods.

Comparison experiments of the model were conducted with three term selection methods IG, TFV, and DF. All these experiments were conducted on corpora PU1, PU2, PU3, and PUA using 10-fold cross validation, and on corpus Enron-Spam

Table 5.1 Experiments of the LC-FL Model with Three Different Terms Selection Methods on Corpora PU1, PU2, PU3, and PUA, Utilizing Cross Validation

Cor.	FSM	Pre. (%)	Rec. (%)	Acc. (%)	F_1 (%)	FD
PU1	IG	96.04	95.42	96.24	95.73	20
	TFV	95.12	96.88	**96.42**	**95.99**	20
	DF	94.38	96.67	95.96	95.51	20
PU2	IG	95.74	75.71	94.37	84.55	20
	TFV	93.37	74.29	93.80	82.74	20
	DF	90.86	82.86	**94.79**	**86.67**	20
PU3	IG	95.99	95.33	**96.13**	**95.66**	20
	TFV	95.80	95.05	95.91	95.43	20
	DF	95.15	95.99	96.00	95.57	20
PUA	IG	96.01	94.74	**95.26**	**95.37**	20
	TFV	95.83	94.39	94.91	95.10	20
	DF	95.25	94.56	94.74	94.90	20
Enron	IG	94.07	98.00	96.79	**95.94**	20
	TFV	93.73	98.10	**96.80**	95.79	20
	DF	93.67	98.10	96.68	95.77	20

Note: Bold digits means better results.

Cor., corpus; App., approach; FSM, feature selection method; Pre., precision; Rec., recall; Acc., accuracy; FD, feature dimensionality.

using six-fold cross validation. The performance of the LC-FL strategy and the LC-VL strategy are listed in Tables 5.1 and 5.2, respectively.

The two strategies performed quite well incorporated with any of these term selection methods. On one hand, the experiments showed that the proposed LC strategies could be incorporated with different term selection methods. On the other hand, the experiments had also reflected the effectiveness of the three term selection methods.

5.7.6 Comparison between the LC Model and Current Approaches

In this section, we compared the two LC strategies with some prevalent approaches through the experiments on four PU corpora using 10-fold cross validation and

Table 5.2 Experiments of the LC-VL Model with Three Different Terms Selection Methods on Corpora PU1, PU2, PU3, and PUA, Utilizing Cross Validation

Cor.	FSM	Pre. (%)	Rec. (%)	Acc. (%)	F_1 (%)	FD
PU1	IG	94.85	95.63	95.78	95.21	6
	TFV	95.48	96.04	**96.24**	**95.72**	6
	DF	95.07	96.25	96.15	95.63	6
PU2	IG	95.74	77.86	94.79	85.16	6
	TFV	94.43	79.29	94.79	85.47	6
	DF	92.06	86.43	**95.63**	**88.65**	6
PU3	IG	96.68	94.34	96.03	95.45	6
	TFV	96.46	94.29	95.91	95.32	6
	DF	95.64	95.77	**96.15**	**95.67**	6
PUA	IG	95.60	94.56	**94.91**	**94.94**	6
	TFV	95.22	94.39	94.65	94.67	6
	DF	95.95	93.33	94.56	94.52	6
Enron	IG	92.44	97.81	**96.02**	**94.94**	6
	TFV	92.07	97.88	95.90	94.77	6
	DF	92.11	97.93	95.95	94.82	6

Note: Bold digits means better results.

Cor., corpus; App., approach; FSM, feature selection method; Pre., precision; Rec., recall; Acc., accuracy; FD, feature dimensionality.

on corpus Enron-Spam using six-fold cross validation. The approaches utilized in comparison are Naive Bayes-BoW, SVM-BoW [13], SVM-Global Concentration (SVM-GC), SVM-LC-FL, and SVM-LC-VL.

In Naive Bayes-BoW and SVM-BoW, Naive Bayes and SVM are utilized as their classifiers, respectively, BoW is utilized as the feature extraction approach, and IG is used as the term selection method [13]. In both SVM-LC-FL and SVM-LC-VL, SVM is utilized as their classifier. SVM-GC is a specific configuration of SVM-LC, in which the sliding window size is set to infinite. In such case, each message is recognized as a whole window, and a two-dimensional feature (including a spam genes concentration and a legitimate genes concentration) is constructed for each message. In this way, it is degraded as the CFC approach [155]. The results of these experiments are shown in Table 5.3.

Table 5.3 Comparison between the LC Model and Current Approaches

Cor.	App.	Pre. (%)	Rec. (%)	Acc. (%)	F_1 (%)	FD
PU1	NB-BoW	89.58	99.38	94.59	94.23	600
	SVM-BoW	93.96	95.63	95.32	94.79	600
	SVM-GC	94.97	95.00	95.60	94.99	2
	SVM-LC-FL	95.12	96.88	**96.42**	**95.99**	20
	SVM-LC-VL	95.48	96.04	96.24	95.72	6
PU2	NB-BoW	80.77	90.00	93.66	85.14	600
	SVM-BoW	88.71	79.29	93.66	83.74	600
	SVM-GC	95.12	76.43	94.37	84.76	2
	SVM-LC-FL	90.86	82.86	94.79	86.67	20
	SVM-LC-VL	92.06	86.43	**95.63**	**88.65**	6
PU3	NB-BoW	93.59	94.84	94.79	94.21	600
	SVM-BoW	96.48	94.67	96.08	95.57	600
	SVM-GC	96.24	94.95	96.05	95.59	2
	SVM-LC-FL	95.99	95.33	96.13	95.66	20
	SVM-LC-VL	95.64	95.77	**96.15**	**95.67**	6
PUA	NB-BoW	95.11	94.04	94.47	94.57	600
	SVM-BoW	92.83	93.33	92.89	93.08	600
	SVM-GC	96.03	93.86	94.82	94.93	2
	SVM-LC-FL	96.01	94.74	**95.26**	**95.37**	20
	SVM-LC-VL	95.60	94.56	94.91	94.94	6
Enron	NB-BoW	79.34	99.17	88.41	87.32	600
	SVM-BoW	90.88	98.87	95.13	94.62	600
	SVM-GC	91.48	97.81	95.62	94.39	2
	SVM-LC-FL	94.07	98.00	**96.79**	**95.94**	20
	SVM-LC-VL	92.44	97.81	96.02	94.94	6

Note: Bold digits means better results.

Cor., corpus; App., approach; FSM, feature selection method; Pre., precision; Rec., recall; Acc., accuracy; FD, feature dimensionality.

The comparison with Naive Bayes-BoW and SVM-BoW is mainly to compare the two LC strategies with the prevalent BoW approach. The results show that both the two LC strategies outperformed the BoW approach in accuracy and F_1 measure. As mentioned in Chapter 1, we take accuracy and F_1 measure as comparison criteria without focusing on precision and recall. Because they are incorporated into the calculation of F_1 measure and can be reflected by the value of F_1 measure.

The comparison between the two LC strategies and SVM-GC is to verify whether the two LC strategies can extract useful position-correlated information from messages. Both the two LC strategies correspond different parts of a message to different dimensions of the feature vector, while SVM-GC extracts position independent feature vectors from messages. As shown in Table 5.3, both the two LC strategies outperformed SVM-GC in accuracy and F_1 measure, which verified that the proposed LC approach (including the LC-FL strategy and the LC-VL strategy) could effectively extract position-correlated information from messages.

Compared to BoW, the proposed LC strategies can greatly reduce feature vector dimensionality and have advantages in processing speed. As shown in Table 5.4, the two LC strategies outperformed BoW approach significantly in terms of feature dimensionality and processing speed. However, BoW obtained poor performance when feature dimensionality was greatly reduced [13], while LC strategies performed quite promisingly with a feature dimensionality of 20.

5.7.7 Discussion

In Section 5.7.6, it is shown that both the LC-FL strategy and the LC-VL strategy outperform the GC approach on all the corpora. The success of the LC strategies is considered to lie in two aspects. First, the LC strategies can extract position-correlated information from a message by transforming each area of a

Table 5.4 The Processing Speed of the Approaches

App.	Seconds/E-Mail	FD
NB-BoW	0.2	120
SVM-BoW	0.5	120
NB-BoW	3	600
SVM-BoW	5	600
SVM-GC	0.06	2
SVM-LC-FL	0.07	20
SVM-LC-VL	0.06	6

message to a corresponding feature dimension. Second, the LC strategies can extract more information from messages, compared to the GC approach. As the window size can be acquired when the parameter of the LC strategies are determined, the GC can be approximately expressed by the weighted sum of LC, and the weights are correlated with the window size. However, the LC cannot be deduced from GC. Thus, the LC contains more information than the GC does.

The essence of the LC strategies is the definition of local areas for a message. As the local areas may vary with message length, we conducted experimental analysis to see whether drift of message length would affect the performance of the LC strategies. The average message length of corpora PU1, PU2, PU3, PUA, and Enron-Spam are 776 terms, 669 terms, 624 terms, 697 terms, and 311 terms, respectively. It can

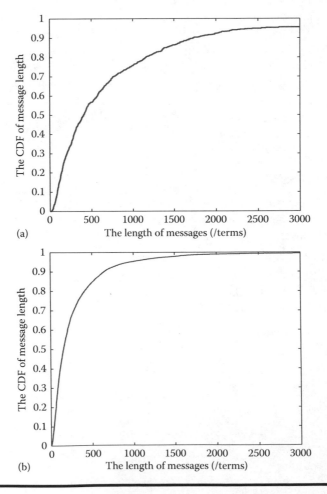

Figure 5.6 The CDF curves of message length in (a) PU1 corpus and (b) Enron-Spam corpus.

be seen that the average message length of Enron-Spam is quite shorter than the other four PU corpora. To further demonstrate the difference between Enron-Spam corpus and the PU corpora, the Cumulative Distribution Function (CDF) of the message length in PU1 corpus and Enron-Spam corpus is depicted in Figure 5.6.

Even though the message length distribution in Enron-Spam corpus is quite different from that of PU corpora, it is shown in Section 5.7.6 that the LC strategies perform well on both Enron-Spam corpus and PU corpora. Thus, a preliminary conclusion can be drawn that the LC strategies are robust against variable message length, and the coexistence of short messages and long messages does not decrease the performance of the LC strategies. As long as the average message length is larger than the size of a window, the LC strategies can extract local concentration from messages. When almost all the messages become shorter than a window, the performance of the LC strategies would decay and become equivalent to that of the GC approach. However, the window size could be tuned accordingly when the message length changes too much. In that way, the LC strategies can still extract local concentration from messages with variable length. In future, we intend to focus on developing adaptive LC approaches, so that the definition of local area can be automatically adapted to the change of message length.

5.8 Summary

The LC approach for extracting local-concentration features for messages is introduced in this chapter. There are two implementation strategies of the approach: the LC-FL strategy and the LC-VL strategy. Extensive experiments show that the proposed LC strategies have quite promising performance and advantage in the following aspects.

- Utilizing sliding windows, both the two LC strategies can effectively extract the position-correlated information for messages.
- The LC strategies cooperate well with three term selection methods, which endows the LC strategies with flexible applicability in real world.
- Compared to the prevalent BoW approach and the GC approach, the two LC strategies perform better in terms of both accuracy and F_1 measure.
- The LC strategies can greatly reduce feature dimensionality and have much faster speed, compared to the BoW approach.
- The LC strategies are robust against messages with variable message length.

Chapter 6

Multi-Resolution Concentration-Based Feature Construction Approach

This chapter presents the multi-resolution concentration (MRC)-based feature construction approach for spam filtering, which depicts a dynamic process of gradual refinement in locating the pathogens by calculating concentrations of detectors on local areas and is considered to be able to extract the position-correlated and process-correlated information from e-mails [33]. After a brief introduction of the background, a generic structure of the MRC model, which mainly contains detector sets construction and MRC calculation, is given and the implementation of the MRC approach for spam filtering is described in detail. Then the weighted MRC (WMRC) approach is presented by considering the different activity levels of detectors in calculation of concentrations. Finally, the experimental validation is given.

6.1 Introduction

Biological immune system (BIS) is an adaptive distributed system with the capability of discriminating *self* and *nonself* and further protecting the biological system from invasion of pathogens. In the BIS, antibodies, produced by lymphocytes, can detect and destroy pathogens by binding them. Two types of immune response may happen in the BIS. The primary response happens when a pathogen appears for the first time and antibodies with affinity to the pathogen are produced slowly. A secondary response is triggered when the same pathogen appears again and a large amount of antibodies with high affinity to the pathogen are proliferated as a corresponding long-lived B memory cell is created during the primary response. Therefore, concentrations of antibodies with affinity to pathogens increase no matter a primary or secondary response happens. Concentrations of antibodies in local areas can reflect the corresponding pathogens precisely.

In this chapter, we introduce the multi-resolution concentration-based feature construction approach, which mimics the dynamic process of gradual refinement in locating the pathogens by calculating the local concentrations of antibodies. E-mails are transformed into multi-resolution concentration feature vectors with respect to "antibodies" by this approach.

6.2 Structure of Multi-Resolution Concentration Model

The structure of MRC model, which depicts the dynamic process of gradual refinement in locating the pathogens by calculating local concentrations of antibodies on smaller and smaller resolutions, is shown in Figure 6.1. The purpose of preprocessing step in the model is transforming e-mail into terms (words) by examining the existence of blank spaces and delimiters. Detector sets construction and MRC calculation are essential steps of the MRC model.

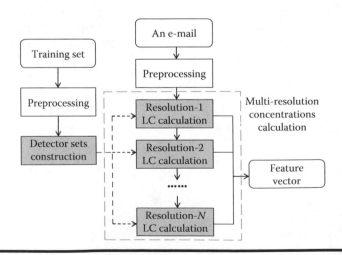

Figure 6.1   Structure of the MRC model.

6.2.1 Detector Sets Construction

Detector (antibody) sets, utilized for calculating concentrations, are constructed on the training set. A detector represents an individual term. After preprocessing of the training set, huge number of terms are gotten. In order to reduce the computational complexity of the model and the affect from possible noisy terms, a certain term selection strategy is utilized. For the informative terms reserved, tendency to spam or ham is employed to finish the construction of *self* detector set and *nonself* detector set.

6.2.2 Calculation of Multi-Resolution Concentrations

The calculation step of multi-resolution concentrations depicts a natural and direct strategy of gradual refinement in locating the pathogens by calculating the local concentrations of detectors. It presents a dynamic process with the resolutions getting smaller and smaller till the concentrations become stable. After finishing the refinement process, all the concentration features calculated are combined together to form the feature vector.

6.3 Multi-Resolution Concentration-Based Feature Construction Approach

Algorithm 6.1 gives a detailed description of the detector sets construction process, which mainly contains term selection and tendency calculation. The purpose of term selection is to reduce the computational complexity and affect from possible noisy terms. The parameter p determines the extent of term selection.

Information gain (IG) [232], the most frequently employed term goodness criterion in machine learning area, which measures the number of bits of information obtained for text classification by knowing the presence or absence of a term in a text, is selected as the term selection strategy. When applied to spam filtering, information gain of term t_i can be defined as

$$\tau(t_i) = \sum_{c \in (s,h)} \sum_{t \in (t_i, \bar{t}_i)} P(t, c) \log \frac{P(t, c)}{P(t)P(c)} \tag{6.1}$$

where
   c denotes the class of an e-mail
   s stands for spam
   h stands for ham
   t_i and $\bar{t}_i$ denote the presence and absence of term t_i, respectively

---

Algorithm 6.1 Construction of detector sets

1: initialize preselected term set TS_p, "ham" detector set DS_h, and "spam" detector set DS_s as empty sets

2:

3: **for** each term t_i occurs in the training set **do**

4:    calculate evaluation $\tau(t_i)$ according to a certain term selection strategy

5: **end for**

6: sort the terms in descending order of evaluation

7: add the front $p\%$ terms to TS_p

8:

9: **for** each term t_i in TS_p **do**

10:    **if** *tendency*$(t_i) > 0$ **then**

11:       add t_i to DS_h

12:    **else**

13:       **if** *tendency*$(t_i) < 0$ **then**

14:          add t_i to DS_s

15:       **end if**

16:    **end if**

17: **end for**

The tendency of term t_i is defined as

$$tendency(t_i) = P(t_i|c_h) - P(t_i|c_s) \tag{6.2}$$

where

$P(t_i|c_h)$ is the probability of t_i's occurrence, given the e-mail is ham

$P(t_i|c_s)$ is the probability of t_i's occurrence, given the e-mail is spam

The different *tendency*(t_i) shows which class of e-mails term t_i tends to occur in. Term t_i with *tendency*$(t_i) < 0$, which means t_i occurs more frequently in spam than in ham, is added into the spam detector set, and vice versa.

The feature vector is constructed by calculating local concentrations of detectors on smaller and smaller resolutions. Algorithm 6.2 shows the process of MRC calculation. For efficiency consideration, the resolution set is initialized to determine the whole process of gradual refinement in locating the pathogens, which is quite essential to the MRC approach. It is initialized as $RS = \{1, 2, 2^2, \ldots, 2^{n-1}\}$ by adopting the bisection method. Each member in the resolution set denotes a certain resolution, which means how many local areas the given e-mail should be partitioned into. The parameter n determines when the process of gradual refinement should stop.

$$RS = \{1, 2, 2^2, \ldots, 2^{n-1}\} \tag{6.3}$$

Algorithm 6.2 Multi-resolution concentrations calculation

1: initialize resolution set RS

2:

3: **for** each resolution r_i in RS **do**

4:     partition the given e-mail into local areas according to resolution r_i

5:     **for** each local area la_j with respect to resolution r_i **do**

6:         calculate spam detectors concentration SC_{ij}

7:         calculate ham detectors concentration HC_{ij}

8:     **end for**

9: **end for**

10:

11: combine the achieved concentrations together to form the feature vector

---

Concentrations of spam detectors and ham detectors are calculated on each local area achieved under a certain resolution. Spam detectors concentration is defined as

$$SC = \frac{N_s}{N_t} \qquad (6.4)$$

where

N_s is the number of distinct terms in the local area, which has been matched by detectors in DS_s

N_t is the number of distinct terms in the local area

Ham detectors concentration is defined similarly, which is

$$HC = \frac{N_h}{N_t} \qquad (6.5)$$

where

N_h is the number of distinct terms in the local area which has been matched by detectors in DS_h

Finally, the MRC-based feature vector of the given e-mail can be acquired by combining all the achieved concentration feature during the refinement process.

6.4 Weighted Multi-Resolution Concentration-Based Feature Construction Approach

Antibodies play core roles in the BIS. On the surface of the antibodies, there are specific receptors that can bind corresponding specific pathogens. All the time, a wide variety of antibodies are circulating in the BIS to detect and destroy different kinds of antigens. Since the invading frequency of different antigens varies, the corresponding specific antibodies have different activity levels, which means some kinds of antibodies are activated more frequently than others. Taking inspiration from this, we propose a WMRC approach by considering the different activity levels of detectors during the refinement process in locating the pathogens.

In the WMRC approach, each detector in the constructed detector sets is given a weight, which depicts the activity level of the detector. The weight is defined as

$$w_i = \frac{\tau(t_i)}{\max\limits_{t_j \in DS_s \cup DS_h} \tau(t_j)} \tag{6.6}$$

where

$\tau(t_i)$ is the evaluation of t_i achieved in the detector sets construction process
$w_i \in [0, 1]$

The weights of detectors are reflected in the MRC calculation process. The weighted concentration of spam detectors is defined as

$$SC_w = \frac{\sum_{t_i \in TS_s} w_i}{N_t} \tag{6.7}$$

where

TS_s is the term set with distinct terms in the local area, which have been matched by detectors in DS_s
w_i is the weight of the corresponding detector in DS_s

Similarly, the weighted concentration of ham detectors is defined as

$$HC_w = \frac{\sum_{t_i \in TS_h} w_i}{N_t} \tag{6.8}$$

where

TS_h is the term set with distinct terms in the local area, which have been matched by detectors in DS_h

6.5 Experimental Validation

Experiments were conducted on PU1, PU2, PU3, PUA [13], and Enron-Spam [131], which are all benchmark corpora widely used for effectiveness evaluation in spam filtering. PU1 contains 1099 e-mails, 481 of which are spam. PU2 contains 721 e-mails, and 142 of them are spam. 4139 e-mails are included in PU3 and 1826 of them are spam. 1142 e-mails are included in PUA and 572 of them are spam. Enron-Spam contains $33,716$ e-mails, $17,171$ of which are spam. E-mails in the five corpora all have been preprocessed by removing header fields, attachment and HTML tags, leaving subject and body text only. For privacy protection, e-mails in PU corpora have been encrypted by replacing meaningful terms with specific numbers.

6.5.1 Investigation of Parameters

Experiments have been conducted on PU3 corpus with SVM as the classification method to investigate the parameters of the MRC approach. Ten-fold cross validation was utilized. There are two important parameters as mentioned earlier. Parameter p determines the percentage of terms reserved after term selection in the detector sets construction process. The removal of less informative terms can reduce not only the computational complexity but also the affect from possible noisy terms, so as to improve the efficiency and performance, while parameter n, which is much more essential, determines the whole process of MRC calculation, especially when the refinement process should stop.

Figure 6.2 describes the performance of the MRC approach under different values of n. As we can see, along with the gradual refinement process, the performance shows improvements till $n = 4$. However, with further increase of n, the performance of the MRC approach degrades in terms of both accuracy and F_1 measure, which reveals the decreased generation capability due to overfitting on training set. Thus, $n = 4$ properly defines the termination of the gradual refinement process.

The performance of the MRC approach with varied p is shown in Figure 6.3. As we can see, the MRC approach always performs quite well though p varies, but better performance can be achieved with smaller ps, which is consistent with our expectation. The MRC approach performs best with $p = 20$. In this case, the front 20% terms are reserved after the term selection phase.

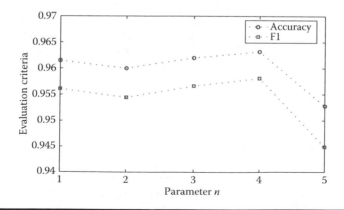

Figure 6.2 Performance of the MRC approach with varied *n*.

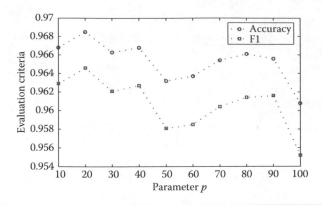

Figure 6.3   Performance of the MRC approach with varied p.

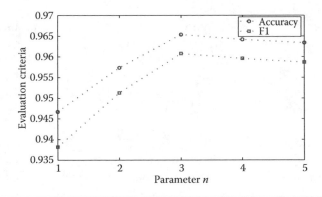

Figure 6.4   Performance of the WMRC approach with varied n.

Similarly, we conducted experiments on PU3 corpus with SVM as the classification method to tune the parameters of the WMRC approach. As shown by the experimental results, $n = 3$ and $p = 20$ lead to the best performance, see Figures 6.4 and 6.5.

6.5.2 Comparison with the Prevalent Approaches

Experiments were conducted on PU1, PU2, PU3, PUA, and Enron-Spam to compare the performance of the proposed MRC and WMRC approaches with the prevalent approaches. The selected prevalent approaches are BoW, CFC, and LC. Table 6.1 shows the spam filtering performance of each feature construction approach when incorporated with SVM, and the corresponding dimensions of feature vectors constructed. As mentioned earlier, we take accuracy and F_1 measure as

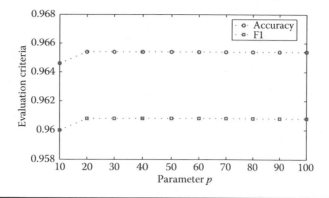

Figure 6.5   Performance of the WMRC approach with varied *p*.

comparison criteria without focusing on precision and recall, which are incorporated into the calculation of F_1 measure and can be reflected by F_1 measure.

As we can see, compared with BoW, the proposed MRC and WMRC approaches not only make significant reduction on the feature vector dimension, but also achieve much better performance, which is average 1.58% higher than BoW in terms of accuracy and 2.15% higher in terms of F_1 measure. This demonstrates the MRC and WMRC approaches are effective.

The CFC approach calculates *self* and *nonself* concentrations on the entire e-mail, which is defined as resolution-1 in the proposed MRC and WMRC approaches, to transform an e-mail into a two-dimensional vector. While the LC approach partitions the e-mail on a single resolution to extract position-correlated information by calculating *self* and *nonself* concentrations on each local area. The experimental results show that the MRC and WMRC approaches outperform both CFC and LC in accuracy and F_1 measure, which verified that the proposed MRC model could effectively extract not only position-correlated information but also process-correlated information through the dynamically gradual refinement process in locating pathogens.

The comparison between MRC and WMRC is to verify whether considering the activity levels of detectors in calculation of concentrations is effective. The results indicate that the WMRC approach performs better than MRC on most cases. Moreover, the introduction of weights enables the WMRC approach reduce the number of resolutions that the e-mail should be partitioned on by accelerating the process of gradual refinement and further reduce the dimension of feature vectors constructed.

We conducted experiments on PU1 with SVM as the classification method to compare the efficiency of the feature construction approaches mentioned earlier. The 10-fold cross validation was utilized. The average speed of processing one e-mail is calculated, as shown in Table 6.2. As we can see, all of the CFC, LC,

Table 6.1 Performance Comparison of the MRC and WMRC Approaches with the Prevalent Approaches

Cor.	App.	Pre. (%)	Rec. (%)	Acc. (%)	F_1 (%)	FD
PU1	BoW	93.96	95.63	95.32	94.79	600
	CFC	94.97	95.00	95.60	94.99	2
	LC	94.85	95.63	95.78	95.21	6
	MRC	95.49	95.62	96.06	95.51	30
	WMRC	96.34	96.46	**96.79**	**96.33**	14
PU2	BoW	88.71	79.29	93.66	83.74	600
	CFC	95.12	76.43	94.37	84.76	2
	LC	95.74	77.86	94.79	85.16	6
	MRC	94.16	82.14	95.07	86.98	30
	WMRC	94.44	85.71	**96.06**	**89.37**	14
PU3	BoW	96.48	94.67	96.08	95.57	600
	CFC	96.24	94.95	96.05	95.59	2
	LC	96.68	94.34	96.03	95.45	6
	MRC	96.47	96.54	**96.85**	**96.46**	30
	WMRC	96.58	95.66	96.54	96.08	14
PUA	BoW	92.83	93.33	92.89	93.08	600
	CFC	96.03	93.86	94.82	94.93	2
	LC	95.60	94.56	94.91	94.94	6
	MRC	95.00	95.09	94.91	**94.95**	30
	WMRC	96.95	93.16	**95.00**	94.94	14
Enron	BoW	90.88	98.87	95.13	94.62	600
	CFC	91.48	97.81	95.62	94.39	2
	LC	92.44	97.81	96.02	94.94	6
	MRC	92.74	98.42	96.29	**95.42**	30
	WMRC	92.76	98.08	**96.30**	95.26	14

Note: Bold values mean the best values among the comparing methods.

Cor., corpus; App., approach; Cla., classifier; Pre., precision; Rec., recall; Acc., accuracy; FD, feature dimensionality.

Table 6.2 Efficiency Comparison of the MRC and WMRC Approaches with the Prevalent Approaches

Approach	BoW	CFC	LC	MRC	WMRC
Seconds/e-mail	$9.57e^{-3}$	$3.75e^{-4}$	$4.50e^{-4}$	$6.46e^{-4}$	$5.22e^{-4}$

MRC, and WMRC approaches perform far more efficient than BoW, due to significant reduction on feature vector dimension. Although the MRC and WMRC approaches depict the dynamic process of gradual refinement in locating pathogens and increase the feature vector dimension, the processing efficiency decreases not so much. Because less terms are reserved after term selection in MRC and WMRC, and the resolution set is initialized to determine the whole process of MRC calculation.

6.5.3 Performance with Other Classification Methods

To filter spam effectively, both the feature construction approach and the classification method are essential. Since the performance of a feature construction approach must be reflected by cooperating with certain classification methods, it is necessary to verify whether the proposed MRC and WMRC approaches can be incorporated with different classification methods.

We conducted experiments on PU1, PU2, PU3, PUA, and Enron-Spam to investigate the performance of the proposed approaches with different classification methods. The selected classification methods are naive Bayes, C4.5 decision tree, AdaBoost with ID3 as the base classifier (AdaBoost1), and AdaBoost with C4.5 as the classifier (AdaBoost2), which are all commonly used classification methods in machine learning area. The performances of the MRC and the WMRC approaches with different classifiers are listed in Tables 6.3 and 6.4, respectively. As we can see, both the MRC and WMRC approaches can perform well with varieties of classifiers, which endow them with flexible capability in the real world.

6.6 Summary

This chapter introduced the MRC-based feature construction approach, in which feature construction is considered as a process of gradual refinement in locating the pathogens by dynamically calculating local concentrations of detectors on smaller and smaller resolutions. By introducing activity level of detector, the WMRC-based feature construction approach was presented. Sufficient experiments illustrated that the MRC and WMRC approaches outperform prevalent feature construction approaches in spam filtering and achieve high efficiency.

Table 6.3   Performance of the MRC Approach Incorporated with Different Classification Methods

Cor.	Cla.	Pre. (%)	Rec. (%)	Acc. (%)	F_1 (%)
PU1	Naive Bayes	94.92	92.25	96.06	95.54
	C4.5	94.15	93.33	94.50	93.70
	AdaBoost1	94.52	95.21	95.41	94.81
	AdaBoost2	95.50	95.21	95.87	95.29
PU2	Naive Bayes	85.22	87.86	93.80	85.62
	C4.5	89.08	80.00	93.80	83.70
	AdaBoost1	91.97	82.86	94.93	86.57
	AdaBoost2	93.06	79.29	94.37	84.95
PU3	Naive Bayes	95.73	94.07	95.47	94.85
	C4.5	93.89	96.04	95.40	94.88
	AdaBoost1	93.37	96.59	95.38	94.89
	AdaBoost2	95.56	96.26	96.30	95.86
PUA	Naive Bayes	94.57	94.74	94.39	94.50
	C4.5	91.90	94.04	92.63	92.82
	AdaBoost1	92.11	94.21	92.89	93.04
	AdaBoost2	94.96	93.86	94.30	94.30
Enron	Naive Bayes	90.98	98.68	95.89	94.55
	C4.5	92.43	98.07	95.87	95.07
	AdaBoost1	90.28	98.81	95.48	94.19
	AdaBoost2	93.64	98.50	96.71	95.94

Cor., corpus; App., approach; Cla., classifier; Pre., precision; Rec., recall; Acc., accuracy; FD, feature dimensionality.

Table 6.4   Performance of the WMRC Approach Incorporated with Different Classification Methods

Cor.	Cla.	Pre. (%)	Rec. (%)	Acc. (%)	F_1 (%)
PU1	Naive Bayes	95.96	97.71	97.16	96.80
	C4.5	94.27	95.83	95.60	95.02
	AdaBoost1	96.16	95.62	96.33	95.77
	AdaBoost2	95.88	96.46	96.61	96.13
PU2	Naive Bayes	82.10	93.57	94.08	86.74
	C4.5	88.22	85.00	94.65	86.17
	AdaBoost1	86.20	88.57	94.51	86.69
	AdaBoost2	88.39	87.14	94.93	87.40
PU3	Naive Bayes	95.37	96.26	96.22	95.76
	C4.5	95.21	94.73	95.50	94.92
	AdaBoost1	93.24	95.55	94.87	94.32
	AdaBoost2	95.59	95.99	96.22	95.75
PUA	Naive Bayes	93.92	94.91	94.04	94.25
	C4.5	92.92	94.04	93.07	93.31
	AdaBoost1	91.18	95.79	92.98	93.30
	AdaBoost2	94.30	94.74	94.30	94.40
Enron	Naive Bayes	91.37	98.48	95.95	94.67
	C4.5	92.59	98.04	96.14	95.13
	AdaBoost1	90.08	98.78	95.37	94.06
	AdaBoost2	93.79	98.46	96.78	95.99

Cor., corpus; App., approach; Cla., classifier; Pre., precision; Rec., recall; Acc., accuracy; FD, feature dimensionality.

Chapter 7

Adaptive Concentration Selection Model

This chapter presents an adaptive concentration selection model which selects concentration construction methods adaptively according to the match between testing samples and different kinds of concentration features [77]. After a brief introduction of the background, the overview of the adaptive concentration selection model is given. Then implementation of the model is described in detail. Finally, the experimental validation is presented.

7.1 Overview of Adaptive Concentration Selection Model

In global concentration method, an e-mail is transformed into a two-dimensional feature vector, which reflects the global information of the e-mail. Similarly, we could use local concentration method to reflect e-mails' local information. However, global concentration may be, too simple to cover some "necessary" information-based and lose some important information of the e-mail, while local concentration may cover some "unnecessary" information and get some redundant information. As a result, the adaptive concentration selection model is constructed to transform e-mails into global or local feature vectors adaptively, according to distinctive information of different e-mails.

The adaptive concentration selection model can be mainly divided into four steps: (1) Set up *self* and *nonself* gene library from training e-mails;

(2) Generate global and local concentration vectors of each e-mail using the gene library; (3) Judge which concentration method each e-mail should apply; and (4) Train and classify on the corpora. k-Nearest Neighbor (kNN) is used to calculate the evaluation, which is the reference standard of concentration selection method in the initial work.

7.2 Setup of Gene Libraries

Intuitively, if a word appears mostly in spam e-mails, it belongs to the *nonself* gene library largely. Accordingly, a word which can provide more information for spam than nonspam e-mails usually will be put into the *nonself* gene library, and vice versa. This inspires us to calculate information gain (IG) of each of the words, and sort them in a decent order. Considering the amount of words is too big to build a gene library and most documents contain the same common words, 95% of the words that appear in all the e-mails are discarded, just as [190] does.

7.3 Construction of Feature Vectors Based on Immune Concentration

Getting the gene libraries, we can construct the feature vectors (Algorithms 7.1 through 7.3). According to the generation of detector set, it is obvious that the DS_s can match spam, and the DS_l can match the legitimate e-mails with large probability. As a result, the match between two detector sets and e-mails can reflect the class information of e-mails, and the two detector sets have complementary advantages with each other, which provides a guarantee for the effectiveness of detection.

$$SC_i = \frac{\sum_{j=1}^{\omega_n} M(t_j, DS_s)}{N_t} \tag{7.1}$$

where
  N_t is the number of distinct terms in the window
  $M(t_j, DS_s)$ is the matching function, which is used to measure the matching degree of term t_j and detector DS_s

$$LC_i = \frac{\sum_{j=1}^{\omega_n} M(t_j, DS_l)}{N_t} \tag{7.2}$$

where
  $M(t_j, DS_l)$ is the matching function, which is used to measure the matching degree of term t_j and detector DS_l.

Algorithm 7.1   Generation of gene libraries

1: Initialize gene libraries, detector DS_s and DS_l to the empty
2: Initialize tendency threshold θ to predefined value
3: Tokenization about the emails
4: **for** each word t_k separated **do**
5:      According to the term selection method, calculate the importance of t_k and the amount of information $I(t_k)$
6: **end for**
7: Sort the terms based on the $I(t)$
8: Expand the gene library with the top $m\%$ terms
9: **for** each term t_i in the gene library **do**
10:      **if** $\|P(t_i|c_l) - P(t_i|c_s)\| > \theta, \theta \geq 0$ **then**
11:          **if** $P(t_i|c_l) - P(t_i|c_s) < 0$ **then**
12:              add term t_i to the spam detector set DS_s
13:          **else**
14:              add term t_i to the legitimate detector set DS_l
15:          **end if**
16:      **else**
17:          abandon this term, because it contains little information about those emails
18:      **end if**
19: **end for**

Algorithm 7.2   Construction of feature vectors based on global concentration

---

1: **for** each term t_j in the e-mail **do**
2:      calculate the matching $M(t_j, DS_s)$ between term t_j with spam detector set;
3:      calculate the matching $M(t_j, DS_l)$ between term t_j with legitimate detector set
4: **end for**
5: According to Equation 7.1, calculate the concentration of spam detector set SC;
6: According to Equation 7.2, calculate the concentration of legitimate detector the set LC;
7: Combine the above, concentration values to construct the global concentration feature vectors $< SC, LC >$

$$SC_i = \frac{\sum_{j=1}^{\omega_n} M(t_j, DS_s)}{N_t} = \frac{\sum_{j=1}^{\omega_n} \sum_{d_k \in DS_s} M(t_j, d_k)}{N_t} \tag{7.3}$$

$$LC_i = \frac{\sum_{j=1}^{\omega_n} M(t_j, DS_l)}{N_t} = \frac{\sum_{j=1}^{\omega_n} \sum_{d_k \in DS_l} M(t_j, d_k)}{N_t} \tag{7.4}$$

Algorithm 7.3 Construction of feature vectors based on local concentration

---

1: According to the length of each email and preset number of windows to calculate the value of ω_n

2: Move the ω_n-term sliding window to separate the email, with each moving length being ω_n

3: **for** each moving window **do**

4:     **for** each term in the moving window **do**

5:         calculate the matching $M(t_j, DS_s)$ between term t_j with spam detector set;

6:         calculate the matching $M(t_j, DS_l)$ between term t_j with legitimate detector set;

7:     **end for**

8:     According to Equation 7.3, calculate the concentration of spam detector set SC_i;

9:     According to Equation 8.2, calculate the concentration of legitimate detection set LC_i

10: **end for**

11: Combine local concentration values in each sliding window to construct the local concentration feature vector $\langle (SC_1, LC_1), (SC_2, LC_2), \ldots, (SCn, LCn) \rangle$

7.4 Implementation of Adaptive Concentration Selection Model

Global concentration reflects entire features of e-mails and the local concentration reflects local characteristics. However, the CFC lacks some detailed information and the LC separates the e-mails quite meticulously. As a result, the adaptive concentration selection model is proposed to combine their advantages and make up for their disadvantages. The key point of our model is the evaluation that is used to determine concentration methods. KNN is used to calculate the evaluation. As we all know, the main idea of KNN is to count the numbers of neighbors belonging to different kinds of classes. However, if the numbers of different classes are close, it is hard to judge which class the undetermined point belongs to. So in the proposed model, we make use of this characteristic of KNN and adapt it to determine concentration methods as shown in Figure 7.1 [77].

Firstly, after preprocessing, data is converted to CFC feature vectors and use KNN classifier to evaluate them. During the evaluation, if the number of a particular class, which belongs to the neighbors of an undetermined point, is larger than certain proportion, we can classify the point to this class. But if the number is less than the proportion, we consider this point as a fuzzy one. Secondly, for those fuzzy points, we convert them to LC feature vectors which can reflect their details and evaluate

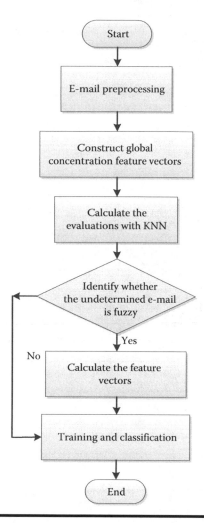

Figure 7.1 Implementation of the adaptive concentration selection model.

them with KNN classifier again. Thirdly, we manipulate all classification results based on them with precision, recalls, accuracy, and F_1 measure.

7.5 Experimental Validation

7.5.1 Experimental Setup

Experiments were conducted on PU series e-mail corpora, which contain PU1, PU2, PU3, and PUA which were collected and published by Androutsopoulos [13] in 2004. The PU series e-mail corpora were widely utilized in spam detection related experiments. To ensure the objectivity, all the experiments are organized with 10-fold cross validation. At the stage of classification, the KNN method is chosen to verify the spam and legitimate e-mails. Besides, recall, precision, accuracy, and F_1 measure are used to assess the results. Among them, the F_1 measure is taken as the most important evaluating indicator, for its reflection of the recalls and precision. All experiments were conducted on a PC with Intel P7450 CPU and 2G RAM.

7.5.2 Parameter Selection

■ *Proportion of term selection*: In the term selection stage, we choose top $m\%$ of the terms according to their information quantity, which decides the size of the gene library. When we screen the terms, on one hand, we need to cut off those noise terms, on the other hand, the important terms should be held back. In a practical application, this parameter can be adjusted based on the need of time and space complexity.

According to Reference [248], when the parameter m is set to 50%, the performance of experiments is optimality. Therefore, the value of m is set to 50% in our experiments.

■ *Tendency threshold*: Tendency function is mainly used to measure the difference between the terms and the two kinds of e-mails and add corresponding terms to the related detector. In Reference [248], with the increasing of the tendency threshold θ, the whole performance of the algorithm degrades. As a result, the value of θ is set to 0.

■ *Dimensionality of feature vectors*: In the global concentration method, each e-mail is reconstructed with the *self* and *nonself* concentrations, which means the dimension is two. And in the local concentration method, this model adopts variable length sliding window strategy, which means that if we assume N is the number of sliding window, each e-mail is transformed into an $2N$-dimensional feature vector. Parameter N is set to 3 according to Reference [190]. As a result, the dimension of local concentration method is six.

■ *Parameter k in KNN*: We have done some experiments to determine the value of parameter k. And the results are shown as follows. As mentioned earlier, the PU2 is a corpus containing only English e-mails and the PUA contains not only English e-mails but also other languages (Figure 7.2). So the experiments on these two corpora reflect general characteristics. Besides, we find that different experiments based on different values of parameter k perform similarly. As we all know, if the value of k is set too large, the computation complexity will increase. Consequently, we choose a moderate value, which sets the value of k to five.

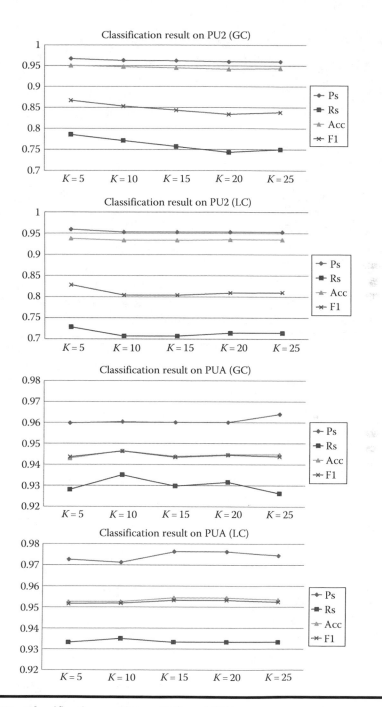

Figure 7.2   Classification results on PU2 and PUA.

7.5.3 Experiments of Proposed Model

Comparison experiments of the model were conducted with selection method IG and mainly compares the performance among CFC, LC, and the proposed model. These experiments are mainly conducted on corpora PU1, PU2, PU3, and PUA using 10-fold cross validation. The average performance experiments are reported in Tables 7.1 through 7.4.

Compared to CFC and LC, the proposed adaptive concentration selection model achieves a better performance on the four corpora. Although in the experiment with PU1, the precision and recall indexes are less than CFC or LC, the overall evaluation index, F_1 measure, is better than CFC and LC. And we can still conclude that our model performs better on this corpus.

As a result, we can come to a conclusion that the proposed model combines the advantages of CFC and LC, and it can enhance the experimental effects so as to classify e-mails more precisely.

Table 7.1   Performance of Three Feature Construction Methods on PU1

App.	Pre. (%)	Rec. (%)	Acc. (%)	F_1 (%)
GC	95.59	94.37	95.60	94.97
LC	96.54	92.92	95.41	94.69
AC	96.18	94.17	**95.78**	**95.16**

Note: Bold values are the best values among comparing methods.

App., approach; Pre., precision; Rec., recall; Acc., accuracy.

Table 7.2   Performance of Three Feature Construction Methods on PU2

App.	Pre. (%)	Rec. (%)	Acc. (%)	F_1 (%)
GC	96.74	78.57	**95.07**	**86.71**
LC	95.95	72.86	93.80	82.83
AC	96.74	78.57	**95.07**	**86.71**

Note: Bold values are the best values among comparing methods.

App., approach; Pre., precision; Rec., recall; Acc., accuracy.

Table 7.3   Performance of Three Feature Construction Methods on PU3

App.	Pre. (%)	Rec. (%)	Acc. (%)	F_1 (%)
GC	96.14	93.57	95.40	94.84
LC	96.95	92.86	95.47	94.86
AC	96.78	94.07	**95.91**	**95.41**

Note: Bold values are the best values among comparing methods.

App., approach; Pre., precision; Rec., recall; Acc., accuracy.

Table 7.4   Performance of Three Feature Construction Methods on PUA

App.	Pre. (%)	Rec. (%)	Acc. (%)	F_1 (%)
GC	95.98	92.81	94.30	94.37
LC	97.27	93.33	**95.26**	95.17
AC	97.44	94.21	94.65	**95.79**

Note: Bold values are the best values among comparing methods.

App., approach; Pre., precision; Rec., recall; Acc., accuracy.

7.5.4 Discussion

The adaptive concentration selection model is proposed for adaptively making use of concentration methods' feature construction characteristics. The improvement of the model can be explained with the defects of CFC and LC. Although CFC approach extracts global information of e-mails into two-dimensional feature vectors, it may miss some information because of its rough data processing. On the contrary, LC processes data in detail, which may be too excessive to retain some noise terms. By contrast, our proposed model first uses CFC feature vectors to evaluate data, and divide all data into two parts: certain classes and fuzzy ones. For those fuzzy ones, the proposed model further makes use of the detailed information based on LC feature vectors and finally we obtain better performance according to the experimental results. Generally speaking, the model combines both advantages of CFC and LC, and avoids large computational complexity of only using LC method.

7.6 Summary

This chapter presents a spam filtering system that combines CFC and LC feature construction methods that further makes the system adaptive to different e-mails. In the stage of feature extraction, IG is used to estimate terms' importance and concentration methods are employed to transform e-mails into reconstructed feature vectors. In the classification, according to different characteristics of e-mails, the system adaptively chooses feature construction methods with the benefit of the promising performance.

Chapter 8

Variable Length Concentration-Based Feature Construction Method

---

In this chapter, we introduce the variable length concentrations (VLC)-based feature extraction method, which aims to break through the limit of feature vector's length. Specifically, this method uses a fixed-length sliding window to divide each e-mail into several sections. The number of sections depends on the length of each e-mail. Consequently, the length of feature vectors varies from each other. This method can acquire adaptive feature vectors according to different lengths of e-mails.

8.1 Introduction

As detailed in previous researches, global or local concentration methods [155,190, 246,248] converts each e-mail into a fixed-length feature vector. As a result, the feature vectors may have redundant information when an e-mail is short, and they may have based information missing when an e-mail is long. In this chapter, we introduce the variable length concentration (VLC)-based feature construction method for anti-spam system, which acquires feature vectors adaptively according to different lengths of e-mails. Similar to previously proposed LC approach, the implement of VLC approach is also designed using a sliding window. But the difference between

LC approach and VLC approach is that the length of VLC feature vectors can be variable, which never increases redundancy or intercepts information. After converting each e-mail into a corresponding VLC feature, feature vectors reflecting position-related information are obtained. At the same time, the variable-length vectors are applied into recurrent neural network (RNN) which has the ability of memory to remember and deal with e-mails' information.

8.2 Structure of Variable Length Concentration Model

The general structure of the VLC model is shown in Figure 8.1. The tokenization is just a simple step to tokenize messages into words (terms) by examining blanks or other delimiters. Terms selection, VLC calculation and RNN training are described as follows:

8.2.1 Construction of Variable Length Feature Vectors

In this section, we introduce the construction of the variable length feature vectors. Assuming that spam detective set DS_s stands for terms from spam library and legitimate detective set DS_l stands for terms from legitimate library, then with the

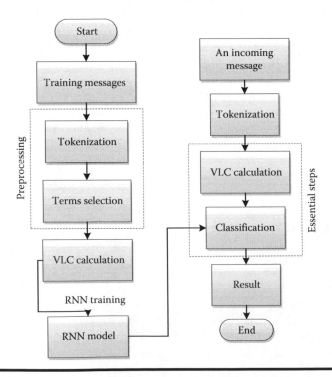

Figure 8.1   Training and classification steps of the VLC model.

Algorithm 8.1 Construction of variable length feature vectors

1: Choose ω_n, which indicates the number of terms in each sliding window;
2: Move the ω_n-term sliding window to separate each e-mail, without overlap.
3:
4: **for** each moving window **do**
5:     **for** each term in the moving window **do**
6:         calculate the matching $M(t_j, DS_s)$ between term t_j with DS_s;
7:     **end for**
8:     According to (8.1), calculate the concentration of spam terms SC_j;
9:     According to (8.2), calculate the concentration of legitimate terms LC_j;
10: **end for**
11:
12: Combine local concentration in each sliding window to construct the variable-length concentration feature vector: $\langle (SC_1, LC_1), (SC_2, LC_2), \ldots, (SC_K, LC_K) \rangle$

---

help of DS_s and DS_l, each e-mail can be converted into its corresponding feature vector. In detail, during the conversion, a sliding window is used to split each message into several locations, and then concentration is calculated in each window. Algorithm 8.1 shows procedure of the construction of variable length feature vectors. In the procedure, $M(t_j, DS_s)$ means the matching degree between term t_j and detective set DS_s. Besides, SC_j means spam concentration of window j and LC_j means legitimate concentration of window j. And N_t is the total number of terms in message t.

$$SC_j = \frac{\sum_{j=1}^{\omega_n} M(t_j, DS_s)}{N_t} = \frac{\sum_{j=1}^{\omega_n} \sum_{d_k \in DS_s} M(t_j, d_k)}{N_t} \qquad (8.1)$$

$$LC_j = \frac{\sum_{j=1}^{\omega_n} M(t_j, DS_l)}{N_t} = \frac{\sum_{j=1}^{\omega_n} \sum_{d_k \in DS_l} M(t_j, d_k)}{N_t} \qquad (8.2)$$

8.2.2 Recurrent Neural Networks

Recurrent neural networks (RNNs) are inspired by the cyclical connectivity of neurons in brain, which introduce iterative function loops to store information [80]. The difference between a multilayered perceptron (MLP) and a RNN is that a MLP maps inputs to output vectors directly, whereas a RNN can map whole previous inputs to each output. In other words, the RNNs allow a "memory" of previous inputs, which stay in the networks and have effect on the outputs.

In this section, we focus on a simple RNN containing a single, self-connected hidden layer, as shown in Figure 8.2. Although it is similar to a multilayered perceptron, there are also big improvements between them. A MLP just simply maps from

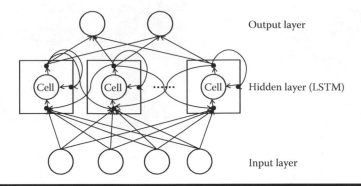

Figure 8.2 A recurrent neural network with LSTM.

input to output vectors, whereas a RNN allows a "memory" of previous inputs to stay in the network, and thereby influences the network output.

However, for standard RNN architectures, the networks' ability to hold contexts is quite limited. In other words, the influence of a given input on the hidden layer, and therefore on the network output, either decays or blows up exponentially as it cycles around the network's recurrent connections, which is referred to as the vanishing gradient problem [19,94]. As a result, in Figure 8.2, we can see that the hidden layer is composed of Long Short-Term Memories models (LSTMs), which are used to tackle the vanishing gradient problem to enhance the "memory" of the network [95].

The following function (8.3) shows that the forward pass of a RNN is similar to MLP, except that the activations arriving at the hidden layer are from both the current external input and the hidden layer activations from the previous timesteps.

$$a_h^t = \sum_{i=1}^{I} \omega_{ih} x_i^t + \sum_{h=1}^{H} \omega_{h'h} b_{h'}^{t-1} \tag{8.3}$$

$$b_h^t = \theta_h(a_h^t) \tag{8.4}$$

where
  I means input units
  H means hidden units

Let x_i^t be the value of input i at time t, and a_h^t and b_h^t be the input to unit h at time t and the activation of unit h at time t. And ω_{ih} means weights between input i and unit h, as well as $\omega_{h'h}$ means weights between unit h' and unit h. Function (8.4) shows the activation of unit h at time t.

At the beginning of training, messages have been transformed into feature vectors with different length through terms selection and VLC calculation. Then these vectors are taken as inputs of RNN, because RNN can handle input sequences with different length. What's more, RNN is an effective structure for sequence learning tasks where the data is strongly correlated along a single axis, and it has achieved good performance in the fields of speech recognition and image recognition. Similarly, an e-mail message can also be taken as a text sequence because of its content terms. As a result, RNN is taken as the classifier and experiments in the next section compares performance among RNN and other classifiers.

8.3 Experimental Parameters and Setup

In 2004, Androutsopoulos and his colleagues [13] collected and published the series of PU data sets—PU1, PU2, PU3, and PUA—which are widely used in spam detection research. Among them, PU1 and PU2 are based on English e-mails, while PU3 and PUA consist of English and non-English ones. Experiments are organized on the four data sets. To ensure objectivity, experiments are conducted with 10-cross-fold validation. In addition, recalls, precision, accuracy, and F_1 measure are used to evaluate the results. Among them, F_1 measure is taken as the comprehensive evaluation, which is the most important indicator.

8.3.1 Proportion of Terms Selection

During terms selection phase, all terms need to be filtered so as to reduce the size of gene libraries. When choosing terms, cutting off noise terms and retaining important terms should be considered. Finally only $q\%$ of the terms is preserved. In practice, this parameter can be adjusted according to the time and space complexity.

According to References [246,248], the performance of experiments achieves best on PU data sets when q is set to 50. In this way, 50% of terms are also chosen to create the gene libraries.

8.3.2 Dimension of Feature Vectors

Because of sliding window, each message is divided into several parts and converted into corresponding feature vector. The lengths of each sliding window are fixed to N, and a message containing m terms can be transformed into $\lfloor m/N \rfloor$-dimensional feature vector.

The parameter N is set to 5, 10, 15, ..., 30 to study the best feature vector dimension for the PU series corpora. Tables 8.1 through 8.4 show the performances on different lengths of sliding window. At the same time, Figures 8.3 through 8.6 show the performance comparisons between the VLC method which combines RNN with VLC (RNN-VLC), and other spam detection methods.

8.3.3 Selection of Size of Sliding Window

As mentioned earlier, LC can reflect area-correlating information about messages, which improves the performance of spam detection. However, during feature

Table 8.1 Performance of VLC on Corpus PU1

Corpus	Size of Sliding Window	Accuracy (%)	Precision (%)	F_1 (%)	Recall (%)
PU1	$N = 5$	97.36	96.98	97.56	96.46
	$N = 10$	**98.90**	97.58	**98.77**	**100**
	$N = 15$	96.38	97.03	95.81	94.72
	$N = 20$	94.48	97.82	93.42	89.61
	$N = 25$	95.41	98.27	96.81	91.25
	$N = 30$	94.70	97.64	96.13	91.16

Note: Bold values mean the best values among the different size of sliding windows for each Corpus.

Table 8.2 Performance of VLC on Corpus PU2

Corpus	Size of Sliding Window	Accuracy (%)	Precision (%)	F_1 (%)	Recall (%)
PU2	$N = 5$	**99.40**	99.09	**98.86**	**98.69**
	$N = 10$	99.01	99.33	97.38	95.71
	$N = 15$	98.17	98.62	95.00	92.14
	$N = 20$	96.23	97.76	88.99	83.17
	$N = 25$	94.96	98.85	84.72	75.24
	$N = 30$	92.25	98.89	75.03	61.43

Note: Bold values mean the best values among the different size of sliding windows for each Corpus.

construction, LC may lose some information or increase some redundancy. Consequently, VLC method is proposed to calculate variable-length feature vectors with the help of fixed length sliding window, whose length equals a certain number of terms in the window. And in the experiments, different values of the length of sliding window are set to compare their performances, just as shown in Figures 8.3 through 8.6, aiming to find the most suitable lengths of sliding window for different corpora.

8.3.4 Parameters of RNN

In the RNNs, long short-term memory (LSTM) is used to enhance the memory ability of the network. In detail, the network has only one hidden layer, which

Table 8.3 Performance of VLC on Corpus PU3

Corpus	Size of Sliding Window	Accuracy (%)	Precision (%)	F_1 (%)	Recall (%)
PU3	$N = 5$	**96.66**	**97.92**	**96.14**	**94.45**
	$N = 10$	95.37	96.87	94.64	92.55
	$N = 15$	95.04	96.23	94.26	92.42
	$N = 20$	94.65	96.64	93.74	91.15
	$N = 25$	94.94	96.91	94.09	91.51
	$N = 30$	94.43	97.23	93.43	89.97

Note: Bold values mean the best values among the different size of sliding windows for each Corpus.

Table 8.4 Performance of VLC on Corpus PUA

Corpus	Size of Sliding Window	Accuracy (%)	Precision (%)	F_1 (%)	Recall (%)
PUA	$N = 5$	89.12	87.19	89.08	91.60
	$N = 10$	94.30	94.04	94.35	94.99
	$N = 15$	**96.16**	**96.05**	**96.16**	**96.32**
	$N = 20$	94.30	93.86	94.28	94.78
	$N = 25$	94.21	93.68	94.19	94.86
	$N = 30$	91.16	91.28	91.29	91.62

Note: Bold values mean the best values among the different size of sliding windows for each Corpus.

consists of ten LSTM blocks. What's more, the learning rate of RNN is set to $1e^{-4}$ and the momentum is set to 0.9.

8.4 Experimental Results on the VLC Approach

Comparison experiments are conducted to show the effectiveness of the VLC approach. Ten-fold cross validation is adopted into these experiments to ensure objectivity. The average performance experiments are reported in Tables 8.1 through 8.4, which show different classification results on different sizes of sliding windows. Figures 8.3 through 8.6 show comparisons among our models, and other methods.

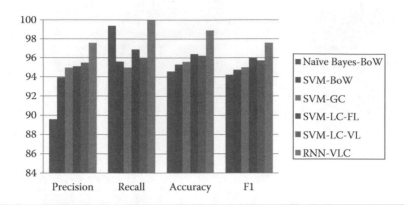

Figure 8.3   Comparison of different methods' results on corpus PU1.

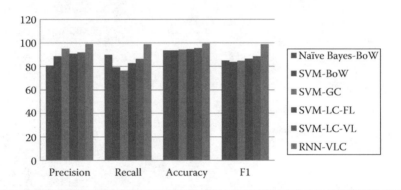

Figure 8.4   Comparison of different methods' results on corpus PU2.

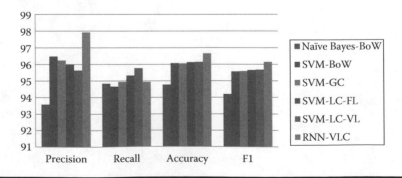

Figure 8.5   Comparison of different methods' results on corpus PU3.

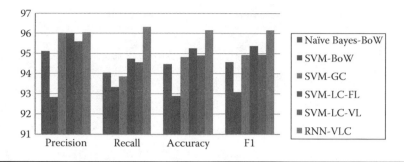

Figure 8.6   Comparison of different methods' results on corpus PUA.

8.5 Discussion

The VLC method is proposed to adaptively construct feature vectors according to different length of messages. According to the experimental results, it is obvious that the proposed method can further enhance the effectiveness of immune concentration vectors. The disadvantage of GC is information loss and the disadvantage of LC is information redundancy, which mainly results from the fixed length of feature vectors. However, compared with GC and LC, VLC can adaptively convert each message into its corresponding feature vector which reduces information loss and redundancy.

In Tables 8.1 through 8.4, we can see that different corpora have their unique best length of sliding windows. For example, for corpus PU1, accuracy, precision, recall, and F_1 measure all achieve peak values when $N = 10$, which indicates that $N = 10$ is the best length of sliding window for corpus PU1. In order to determine a common N-value on all corpora, performance results are averaged and shown in Table 8.5. From the table, we can see that when $N = 10$, accuracy and F_1 measure are both the best. As a result, $N = 10$ is determined as the common N-value. However, this is not always the most satisfying N-value. For PU3 and PUA, which contain not only English e-mails but also non-English ones, results are better when N-value isn't 10. As a result, the best N-value depends on specific dataset.

In Figures 8.3 through 8.6, best performance of RNN-VLC on the four corpora are chosen to make a comparison with other methods. It is obvious that RNN-VLC achieves better performance than Naive Bayes, SVM-GC, SVM-LC, and other methods on all the PU corpora. Considering F_1 measure, RNN-VLC even improves the experiment performance by almost 18%, which is a significant improvement.

In conclusion, different corpora have their suitable sliding window sizes and the VLC method enhances the experimental effects to achieve better classification.

Table 8.5   Average Performance of VLC on PU Corpora

Corpus	Size of Sliding Window	Accuracy (%)	Precision (%)	F_1 (%)	Recall (%)
Average on PU	$N = 5$	95.64	95.30	95.41	95.30
	$N = 10$	**96.90**	96.96	**96.29**	**95.81**
	$N = 15$	96.44	**96.98**	95.31	93.90
	$N = 20$	94.92	96.52	92.61	89.68
	$N = 25$	94.88	96.93	92.45	88.22
	$N = 30$	93.14	96.26	88.97	83.55

Note: Bold values mean the best values among the different size of sliding windows for each Corpus.

8.6 Summary

In this chapter, we introduce a new concentration vector construction method, which adaptively converts each e-mail into its corresponding feature vector. During the phase of feature extraction, IG is used to evaluate and choose important terms. Then sliding window is used to converts e-mails into their corresponding feature vectors. To deal with these variable-length feature vectors, recurrent neural network is chosen as the classifier to accomplish the final training and classification. And finally, the experimental results on PU corpora indicate that the method is more effective and promising.

Chapter 9

Parameter Optimization of Concentration-Based Feature Construction Approaches

This chapter presents a framework that can optimize the parameters of anti-spam models with heuristic swarm intelligence (SI) optimization algorithms and integrate various classifiers and feature extraction methods [225]. The related background information for proposing the framework is introduced first, as well as the knowledge of local concentration (LC)-based feature extraction approach and fireworks algorithm (FWA), which are selected as the representatives of anti-spam methods and SI optimization algorithms, respectively. The parameter optimization framework and its implementation on the selected methods are then described in detail. Finally, the experimental validation is given.

9.1 Introduction

Many approaches have been proposed to handle the spam problem, in which intelligent approaches play an increasingly important role in anti-spam in recent years for their ability of self-learning and good performance. Spam detection is seen as a two-class categorization problem in intelligent approaches, which mainly contain feature extraction and classification phases. In previous researches, parameters in the anti-spam process are set simply and manually. However, the manual setting might cause several problems. For instance, lack of prior knowledge may lead to improper parameter setting, repeated attempts of users cost a great amount of human effort, and the rigidity of the dataset-relevant parameters should also be taken into account.

To solve the problems, this chapter presents a new framework that automatically optimizing parameters in the anti-spam model with heuristic swarm intelligence (SI) optimization algorithms, and this framework could integrate various classifiers and feature extraction methods [186]. Two experimental strategies were designed to objectively reflect framework performance. Then, experiments are conducted, using the fireworks algorithm (FWA) [188,189,201] as a SI algorithm, the local concentration (LC) approach as the feature extraction method, and SVM as the classifier [225]. Experimental results demonstrate that this framework improved the performance on the corpora PU1, PU2, PU3, and PUA, and the computational efficiency is applicable in the real world.

9.2 Local Concentration-Based Feature Extraction Approach

In an anti-spam model, feature extraction is an essential step. The feature extraction method decides spatial distribution characteristics of e-mail sample points, influencing the construction of a specific e-mail classification model, and the final classification performance. An effective feature extraction method is able to extract distinguishing features of e-mails, endowing different kinds of e-mails possessing obvious spatial distribution difference. Moreover, it should be capable of reducing the complexity and difficulty of classification so as to improve overall performance of the anti-spam model. The LC approach [246,248] is proved to meet both of the requirements aforementioned. It not only greatly reduces feature dimensionality by retaining the position-correlated information of e-mails but also performs better in terms of both accuracy and measure compared to the BoW approach [13,164] and the CFC approach [155,190].

Inspired from the biological immune system, the LC feature extraction approach is able to extract position-correlated information from messages by transforming each area of a message to a corresponding LC feature effectively. Two implementation strategies of the LC approach were designed by using a fixed-length sliding window and a variable-length sliding window. To incorporate the LC approach into the whole process of spam filtering, a generic LC model is designed. In the LC model, two types of detector sets are at first generated by using terms selection methods and a well-defined tendency threshold. Then a sliding window is adopted to divide the message into individual areas. After segmentation of the message, the concentration of detectors is calculated and taken as the feature for each

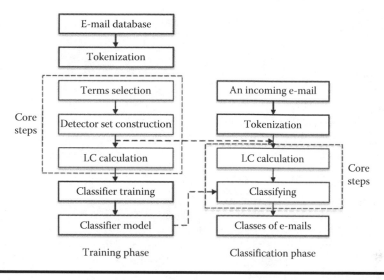

Figure 9.1   Training and classification phases of the local concentration model.

local area. Finally, all the features of local areas are combined as a feature vector of the message.

The generic structure of the LC model is shown in Figure 9.1. The tokenization is a simple step, where messages are tokenized into words (terms), while terms selection, detector set construction, and LC calculation are quite essential to the model.

In the terms selection step, terms are sorted in the order of importance and the top $m\%$ of the terms are selected to form the gene library. The terms selection rate parameter, $m\%$, decides the size of the gene library, influencing the computational complexity of the detector construction algorithm and distinguishing ability of detectors in the next step. An optimal value of $m\%$ is supposed to effectively screen out noise terms, while guaranteeing the existence of the informative terms.

In the detector construction step, the tendency of each detector—the difference between a term's posterior probability of presence in normal e-mails and that in spams—is calculated. If the tendency of a term exceeds θ, the term will be added into the detector set. This parameter, θ, as the standard of detector set construction, is capable of controlling the significance of detector matching, yet can not be set too large, so as not to cause loss of information.

In the LC calculation step, the number of sliding windows, N, no matter in fixed-length LC approach or in variable-length LC approach, is an important parameter, since it decides the size of a single sliding window and defines the local region. As a result, it has a great impact on the dimensionality of LC feature vectors, and also performance of the algorithm. The three aforementioned parameters, as well as the parameters of classifiers in the classification step, are fairly essential in LC approach. They, as a whole, heavily influence the performance of the anti-spam model.

In the previous research, these parameters in LC approach were set simply and manually. However, the manual setting might cause several problems. For instance, lack of prior knowledge may lead to improper parameter setting, repeated attempts of users cost overmuch human effort, and the inflexibility of the dataset-relevant parameters should also be taken into counting. To solve these difficulties, a parameter-optimized LC approach using FWA is proposed in this chapter.

9.3 Fireworks Algorithm

In the past two decades, swarm intelligence SI algorithms have been popular among researchers who are working on optimization problems. SI algorithms, for example, FWA [187,188,200], particle swarm optimization (PSO) [238,239], ant system, clonal selection algorithm, and swarm robotic, have advantages in solving many optimization problems. Among all the SI algorithms, FWA is one of the most popular algorithms for searching optimal locations in a D-dimensional space [182].

Like most SI algorithms, FWA is inspired by some intelligent colony behaviors in nature. Specifically, the framework of FWA is mimicking the process of setting off fireworks. The explosion process of a firework can be viewed as a search in the local space around a specific point where the parent firework is set off through the offspring sparks generated in the explosion.

Assume the population size of fireworks is N and the population size of generated spark is M. Each fireworks $i(i = 1, 2, \ldots, N)$ in a population has the following properties: a current position x_i, a current explosion amplitude A_i, and the amount of the generated sparks s_i. Each firework generates a number of sparks within a fixed explosion amplitude. In each generation, N fireworks set off within a feasible bound within explosion amplitude A_i and spark size s_i, and then the spark are generated. In addition, the FWA also takes Gaussian mutation operators to enhance local search capability.

The best firework is kept for the next generation, and the other $N - 1$ fireworks for the next generation are selected based on their distance to other fireworks or randomly as to keep the diversity in the set, which includes the N fireworks, the generated sparks, and Gaussian mutation fireworks. The FWA continues conducting these operations till the termination criteria is satisfied.

As to the optimization problem f, a point with better fitness is considered as a potential solution, which the optima locate nearby with high chance, vice versa. Suppose FWA is utilized to solve a generic optimization problem:

$$\min f(x) \in R, x \in R^n \tag{9.1}$$

where

$x = x_1, x_2, \ldots, x_d$ denotes a location in the potential space

$f(x)$ is an objective function

R^n denotes the potential space

Then the FWA is implemented to find a point $x \in R^n$, which has the minimal fitness value. This is also how the optimization of the anti-spam process is implemented.

9.4 Parameter Optimization of Local Concentration Model for Spam Detection by Using Fireworks Algorithm

The classification problem that whether an e-mail is spam or a normal e-mail is here considered as an optimization problem, that is, to achieve the lowest error rate by finding the optimal parameter vector in the potential search space.

The optimal vector $P^* = \langle F_1^*, F_2^*, \ldots, F_n^*, C_1^*, C_2^*, \ldots, C_m^* \rangle$ is composed of two parts: the first part is the feature calculation-relevant parameters $\langle F_1^*, F_2^*, \ldots, F_n^* \rangle$, and the second part is the classifier-relevant parameters $\langle C_1^*, C_2^*, \ldots, C_m^* \rangle$. Parameters $\langle F_1^*, F_2^*, \ldots, F_n^* \rangle$ determine the performance of feature construction independently, and parameters $\langle C_1^*, C_2^*, \ldots, C_m^* \rangle$ affect the performance of the specific classifier. The optimal vector P^* is the vector whose cost function $CF(P)$ associated with classification achieves the lowest value, with

$$CF(P) = Err(P) \tag{9.2}$$

where

$Err(P)$ is the classification error measured by cross validation on the training set

Input vector P consists of two parts—parameters $\langle F_1^*, F_2^*, \ldots, F_n^* \rangle$ associated with a certain feature extraction method and $\langle C_1^*, C_2^*, \ldots, C_m^* \rangle$ associated with a certain classifier

$\langle F_1^*, F_2^*, \ldots, F_n^* \rangle$ uniquely determines the performance of feature construction, while $\langle C_1^*, C_2^*, \ldots, C_m^* \rangle$ influences the performance of a certain classifier

Different feature extraction methods hold different parameters and lead to different performances. For LC approach, specifically, m, the terms selection rate helps select the top $m\%$ terms with descending importance in term set, which determines the term pool size. θ, the proclivity threshold, the minimal difference of a term's frequency in nonspam e-mails minus that in spam e-mails, has an assistant function in screening out terms with greater discrimination. N, the number of sliding windows, determines the dimensionality of the feature vector of e-mails. Different classifiers hold different parameters and also lead to different performances. Parameters associated with neural network, which determine the structure of the network, include number of layers, number of nodes within a layer, and each connection weight between two nodes. SVM-related parameters that determine the position of optimal hyperplane in feature space include cost parameter C and kernel parameters, just to name a few.

Vector P is the optimization objective whose performance is measured by $CF(P)$. Therefore, this optimization of concentrations can be formulated as follows. Finding $P^* = \langle F_1^*, F_2^*, \ldots, F_n^*, C_1^*, C_2^*, \ldots, C_m^* \rangle$, so that

$$CF\left(P^*\right) = \min_{\{F_1, F_2, \cdots, F_m, C_1, C_2, \cdots, C_m\}} CF\left(P\right) \tag{9.3}$$

Several optimization approaches not demanding an analytical expression of the objective function such as PSO and genetic algorithm can be employed for the optimization process. FWA is used to design concentrations.

Figure 9.2 shows the optimization process of parameter optimization of LC model for spam detection using FWA.

This framework utilizes the FWA to optimize parameters in the LC approach. Not only the essential parameters in the LC approach but also the classifier-relevant parameters are optimized in this framework, so that the whole anti-spam process gets optimized.

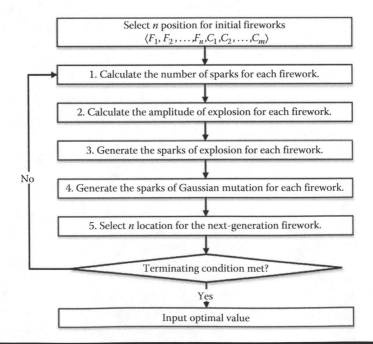

Figure 9.2   Process of the framework.

This framework optimizes anti-spam model with heuristic swarm intelligence optimization algorithms, which could integrate various classifiers and feature extraction methods.

9.5 Experimental Validation

9.5.1 Experimental Setup

All the experiments were conducted on a PC with Intel Core i5-2300 CPU and 4G RAM. The LC-based model with variable-length sliding window was optimized and the terms selection method utilized was information gain. SVM was employed as classifier and LIBSVM was applied for the implementation of the SVM. A 10-fold cross validation was utilized on each corpus. Since FWA is a stochastic algorithm, the experimental results we presented here are average results under 10 independent runs. Accuracy, recall, precision, and F1 measure were selected as evaluation criteria, in which accuracy and F1 measure are main ones since they can reflect the overall performance of spam filtering.

Experiments were conducted on four benchmark corpora PU1, PU2, PU3, and PUA, using 10-fold cross validation to verify the effectiveness of FWA-based parameter optimization of spam detection. During the experiments, the range of the terms selection rate $m\%$ is set to [0,1], the range of the tendency threshold θ is set to [0,0.5], and the sliding window number N [1,50]. SVM-related parameters $c \in (1, 100)$ and $\gamma \in (0, 20)$. Parameters involved in FWA are the same with original FWA in [201].

9.5.2 Experimental Results and Analysis

Two strategies for experiments were designed to investigate the effectiveness of the proposed optimization process of LC model. In both strategies, optimization of the LC model is conducted on the training set and finally examined on the testing set in each fold. In this case, the original training set is further divided into a new training set and a testing set for computing the fitness to evaluate the LC model that the current spark is corresponding to.

For the consideration of efficiency, the first strategy (strategy 1) is designed by defining a validation set on the original training set and making it independent from the original training set, for example, the original training set is divided into a new training set and a validation set. The fitness of each spark is independently computed on the validation set after a corresponding classifier is trained on the new training set. The optimal model corresponding to the optimal spark achieved and trained on the new training set is finally examined on the testing set in each fold. In this strategy, fitness of each spark is evaluated on an independent validation set in each fold; thus, the computational complexity is relatively low and the optimization process of the LC model could be finished quickly.

Table 9.1 Performance Comparison of Local Concentration Before and After Optimization with Strategy 1

Cor.	App.	Pre. (%)	Rec. (%)	Acc. (%)	F_1 (%)
PU1	LC	94.85	95.63	95.87	95.21
	strategy 1	96.55	95.21	**96.33**	**95.81**
PU2	LC	95.74	77.86	94.79	85.16
	strategy 1	95.15	80.71	**95.35**	**86.65**
PU3	LC	96.68	94.34	96.03	95.45
	strategy 1	95.81	95.71	**96.18**	**95.69**
PUA	LC	95.60	94.56	94.91	94.94
	strategy 1	96.63	94.56	**95.53**	**95.49**

Note: Bold values mean the better values among different approaches.

Cor., corpus; App., approach; Pre., precision; Rec., recall; Acc., accuracy.

Experiments were conducted on the original PU1, PU2, PU3, and PUA corpus to verify the effectiveness of strategy 1. Table 9.1 shows the optimization results with strategy 1 as well as the performance of the original LC model. It is clear that the performance of the LC model is improved with the optimization process defined by strategy 1, indicating that strategy 1, for example, the FWA-based optimization process, is effective to improve the performance of the original LC model. On the other hand, as shown in Table 9.1, the performance improvement of the LC model with strategy 1 is limited because the validation set cannot well reflect the data distribution of the testing set all the time.

For the consideration of robustness, the second strategy (strategy 2) is designed based on strategy 1. Different from strategy 1, the fitness of each spark in this strategy is not simply computed on an independent validation set. Instead, a 10-fold cross validation mechanism is employed in the process of computing fitness of each spark, where the original training set is divided into 10 parts and one of them is defined as the validation set and others are defined as the new training set in each fold. The current spark is evaluated by training a corresponding model on the new training set and computing fitness on the validation set 10 times. In this case, each spark is comprehensively evaluated by the performance on 10 folds. The optimal model that is corresponding to the optimal spark achieved and trained on the original training set is finally examined on the testing set. In this strategy, fitness of each spark is evaluated on the training set by a 10-fold cross validation, overcoming the shortage

Table 9.2 Performance Comparison of Local Concentration Before and After Optimization with Strategy 2

Cor.	App.	Pre. (%)	Rec. (%)	Acc. (%)	F_1 (%)
PU1s	LC	100	92.36	96.67	95.88
	Strategy 2	100	96.64	**98.57**	**98.22**
PU2s	LC	100	64.00	90.71	74.62
	strategy 2	100	94.17	**98.57**	**96.57**
PU3s	LC	97.84	91.30	95.37	94.34
	strategy 2	98.25	95.91	**97.56**	**97.02**
PUAs	LC	95.78	90.72	93.64	92.68
	strategy 2	98.75	96.44	**97.73**	**97.42**

Note: Bold values mean the better values among different approaches.

Cor., corpus; App., approach; Pre., precision; Rec., recall; Acc., accuracy.

of strategy 1 that the performance improvement of LC model is totally dependent on the consistency of data distribution in validation set and testing test. Strategy 2 enhances the robustness of the optimization process and is considered to achieve the improvements, with great performance, of the LC model.

Considering the efficiency of experiments, we randomly selected part of each corpus instead of the original corpus to investigate the effectiveness of strategy 2, for example, 20% samples of PU1, PU2, and PUA were selected to form PU1s, PU2s, and PUAs, and 10% samples of PU3 were selected to form PU3s. Table 9.2 presents the comparison of LC model before and after the optimization with strategy 2. It is notable that strategy 2 indeed brings a great improvement to the performance of the LC model, validating the effectiveness (taking the precision, recall, accuracy, and F_1 into account) of this strategy as well as the FWA-based optimization process. But the drawback of strategy 2 is that employing 10-fold cross validation in computing the fitness of sparks is time consuming. However, in fact, the usual offline training of the spam filters in the real world endows this strategy with usability.

9.6 Summary

This chapter introduces parameter optimization of the LC approach with FWA. A unique optimization framework for optimizing parameters of anti-spam models with heuristic SI optimization algorithms is presented, which could integrate various classification techniques and feature extraction methods. Different experimental strategies designed for reflecting the performance of the framework depict that performance of the anti-spam model is improved significantly by employing this optimization framework and the trade-off between performance and efficiency should be made.

Chapter 10

Immune Danger Theory-Based Ensemble Method

This chapter presents the immune danger theory-based ensemble (DTE) method for spam detection, in which signal I, danger signal, and danger zone are designed for machine learning task by mimicking the mechanism of danger theory (DT) [247]. After a brief introduction of the related background, three main steps of the DTE method—generating signals, classification using signals, and self-trigger processes—are described. Then the framework and further analysis of the DTE method are given. Finally, the experimental validation is shown.

10.1 Introduction

The development of artificial immune system (AiS) is usually promoted by the proposal of novel biological immune system (BIS) paradigms. In recent years, a novel biological paradigm—danger theory (DT), proposed by Matzinger [128], has become popular in explaining the mechanism of BIS. According to the DT, an immune response is not triggered by the detection of *nonself* but the discovery of *danger*, and immunity is controlled by an interaction between tissues and the cells of the immune system. Although there are still debates on the relation between the DT and classical viewpoints, the DT does contain enough inspiration for building a relative AIS [4]. Based on DT, novel AIS paradigms have been proposed and applied to web mining and intrusion detection. Secker et al. [166] presented a DT-based adaptive mailbox, where a high number of unread messages were defined as the source of danger. Aickelin et al. [3] shared thoughts on the way to build a next-generation intrusion detection system based on DT. In Reference [5], the development and application of two DT-based algorithms for intrusion detection—the dendritic cell algorithm and the toll-like receptor algorithm—were presented.

The immune system has the ability of detecting and responding to dangerous things, according to DT. This phenomenon implies that the immune system can discriminate between *danger* and *non-danger*. Thus, it is logical to build a DT-based learning model for a two-group classification problem. This chapter is concerned with how to transplant the three main concepts of DT—match signal I, danger signal, and danger zone—into the field of machine learning.

10.2 Generating Signals

The signal I is generated using the classifier I for each test sample in the danger theory–based ensemble (DTE) model. The process is depicted in Figure 10.1a. When the classifier I classifies a test sample as positive class (match occurs), it will send a positive signal I to the sample. Otherwise if no match occurs, it will send a negative one to the sample.

Figure 10.1b shows how a danger signal (signal II) is triggered by the classifier II. Although the generating process of a danger signal seems to be quite similar to that of the signal I, the transmission coverage of a danger signal is quite different from that of the signal I. When a signal I is triggered, it will be sent only to the specific sample, from which the signal has arisen. However, a triggered danger signal will be sent to all the test samples within the danger zone, besides the specific sample.

10.3 Classification Using Signals

This phase is the key procedure of the DTE model, which defines an immune-based interaction between the two classifiers. As shown in Figure 10.1c, a test sample is labeled only if the two signals that it received agree with each other. Otherwise, a self-trigger process is utilized to get the test sample classified.

The weighted result given by the interaction between the two classifiers is defined as Equation 10.1.

$$E(x_i) = \sum_{x_j \in D} \delta(c_1(x_i), c_2(x_j)) K(d(x_i, x_j)) \tag{10.1}$$

where
  x_i and x_j are test samples
  D denotes the test set
  $c_1(x)$ and $c_2(x)$ are the two classifier models
  $d(x_i, x_j) = \| x_i - x_j \|$ is the distance between two samples
  $K(z)$ is defined in Equation 10.2, and $\delta(y_1, y_2) = 1$, if $y_1 = y_2$, and 0 otherwise

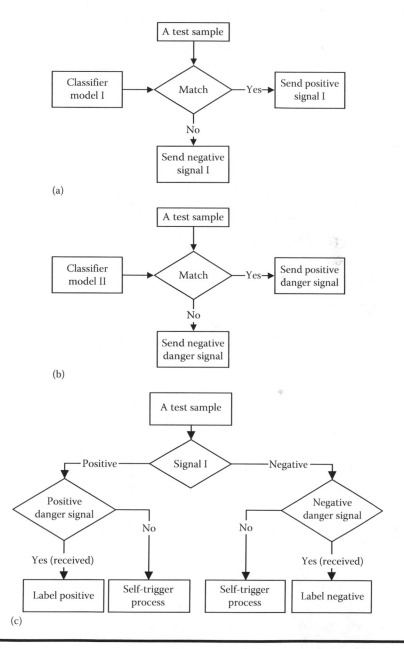

Figure 10.1 The process of classification using signals. (a) The process of generating signal I, (b) the process of generating signal II, and (c) classification process using signals.

$K(z)$ defines the effect of the danger zone as follows:

$$K(z) = \begin{cases} 1 & \text{if } z \leqslant \theta \\ 0 & \text{otherwise} \end{cases} \tag{10.2}$$

where θ is the size of the danger zone.

After obtaining the weighted result $E(x_i)$, the sample x_i can get its class label using Equation 10.3.

$$L(x_i) = \begin{cases} c_1(x_i) & \text{if } E(x_i) \geqslant 1 \\ f(x_i) & \text{otherwise} \end{cases} \tag{10.3}$$

where $f(x)$ denotes the class label given by the self-trigger process.

10.4 Self-Trigger Process

For the test samples that get conflicting results from classifiers I and II, a self-trigger process is designed. Intuitively, one should get the sample activated using its nearest neighbor (NN). Thus, the NN approach is applied in this phase [46]. In future work, we intend to incorporate other approaches for the self-trigger process into the DTE model and compare their performance.

10.5 Framework of DTE Model

Algorithm 10.1 summarizes the framework of the DTE model, in which two grounding classifiers interact through two signals. In the model, two grounding classifiers are first chosen and trained independently. Then the signal I and the danger signal, simulating the signals in the DT, are triggered upon each test sample utilizing the two classifiers. Finally, each test sample gets labeled by considering the interaction between the two classifiers.

10.6 Analysis of DTE Model

For any machine learning model, its essence is the conditional probability $P(y_k|x_i)$ of class y_k that it computes for each test sample x_i. In the DTE model, a test sample x_i gets a label y_k in two cases as follows:

■ The two grounding classifiers give a consistent label y_k to the sample x_i: Suppose the two grounding classifiers are conditionally independent, given a test sample x_i. Then the probability $P(y_k \mid x_i, case_1)$, which denotes the

---

Algorithm 10.1   Framework of the DTE model

Select two uncorrelated classifiers: classifier I, II;
Train the two classifiers respectively on train corpus;
for each sample x_i in test corpus **do**
    Trigger a signal I upon x_i using classifier I and send the signal to x_i;
    Trigger a danger signal upon x_i using classifier II and send the signal to the
test samples within the danger zone of x_i;
end for
for each sample x_i in test corpus **do**
    if x_i has received a positive signal I **then**
        if x_i has received a positive danger signal **then**
            Label x_i as positive class;
        else
            Call self-trigger process;
        end if
    else
        if x_i has received a negative danger signal **then**
            Label x_i as negative class;
        else
            Call self-trigger process;
        end if
    end if
end for

---

probability that the two grounding classifiers give consistent label y_k to the sample x_i, is computed as follows:

$$P(y_k \mid x_i, case_1)$$

$$\leqslant P(c_1(x_i) = y_k \mid x_i) \cdot \sum_{x_j \in D} P(c_2(x_j) = y_k \cap K(\| x_i - x_j \|) = 1 \mid x_i, x_j)$$

$$(10.4)$$

■ There is conflict between the two grounding classifiers, and the self-trigger process gives the label y_k to the sample x_i. The probability $P(y_k \mid x_i, case_2)$, which denotes the probability that this case may happen, is defined as follows:

$$P(y_k \mid x_i, case_2)$$

$$= P(E(x_i) = 0 \cap f(x_i) = y_k \mid x_i)$$

$$(10.5)$$

Following this analysis, the probability $P(y_k \mid x_i)$, computed by the DTE model, is presented in Equation 10.6 as follows:

$$P(y_k \mid x_i) = P(y_k \mid x_i, case_1) + P(y_k \mid x_i, case_2) \tag{10.6}$$

which can be expanded using Equations 10.4 and 10.5.

10.7 Filter Spam Using the DTE Model

At the beginning, terms are selected according to their importance for classification, which can be measured by information gain (IG) [232].

Bag-of-words (BoW) model, also referred to as vector space model, is usually utilized as the feature extraction approach for spam filtering [87]. In BoW, an e-mail is transformed into a d-dimensional vector $\langle x_1, x_2, \ldots, x_d \rangle$ by calculating the occurrence of previously selected terms. For BoW with Boolean attribute, x_i is assigned to 1 if t_i occurs in the e-mail, or it is assigned to 0 otherwise. In the experiments, 300 features were selected by using IG, and a BoW with Boolean attribute was applied to the feature extraction phase.

Support vector machine (SVM) and Naive Bayes (NB) are chosen as the two grounding classifiers of the DTE model, as they are two of the most prevalent and effective classifiers especially for spam filtering [67,156].

To validate the effectiveness of the proposed DTE model, two overall performance measures were adopted in our experiments: accuracy and F_1 measure [87]. The two components of F_1 measure are also given in the experimental results.

Experiments were conducted on four benchmark corpora PU1, PU2, PU3, and PUA [13], using 10-fold cross validation. The corpora have been preprocessed when published, by removing attachments, HTML tags, and header fields except for the subject. The details of the corpora can be found in Reference [13].

The specific interaction between the two grounding classifiers is implemented by the design of the danger zone. To some extent, the success of the DTE model lies in a proper danger zone design and an optimal size of the danger zone. In this subsection, we investigate the impact of the danger zone size on the overall performance of the DTE model. Experiments of the DTE model with different danger zone size were conducted on PU1, using 10-fold cross validation. The results are depicted in Figure 10.2a, which shows the variational performance of the DTE model, as the size of the danger zone growing larger. At initial stages, the accuracy and F_1 measure increase as the size of the danger zone is enlarged. Then, the performance of the DTE model peaks at a size of 20. After that, the performance declines as the size growing even larger.

Comparative experiments were also conducted on four benchmark corpora PU1, PU2, PU3, and PUA to validate the proposed DTE model, using 10-fold cross validation. As the four corpora have already been preprocessed when published, our experiments began at the phase of feature extraction. First, 300 discriminative words

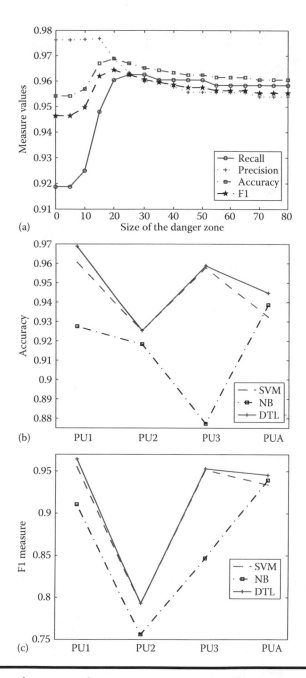

Figure 10.2 Performance of SVM, NB, and DTE on corpora PU1, PU2, PU3, and PUA. (a) Performance of the DTE model with different danger zone size, (b) accuracy of SVM, NB, and DTE on corpus PU1, PU2, PU3, and PUA, and (c) F1 measure of SVM, NB, and DTE on corpus PU1, PU2, PU3, and PUA.

Table 10.1 Performance of SVM, NB, NN, and DTE on Corpora PU1, PU2, PU3, and PUA Using 10-Fold Cross Validation

Cor.	App.	Rec. (%)	Pre. (%)	Acc. (%)	F_1 (%)	FD
PU1	SVM	95.83	95.39	96.06	95.54	300
	NB	85.00	98.30	92.75	91.06	300
	NN	84.17	94.43	90.73	88.86	300
	DTE	96.04	96.89	**96.88**	**96.44**	300
PU2	SVM	72.86	88.72	**92.54**	**79.31**	300
	NB	65.71	91.00	91.83	75.60	300
	NN	45.71	84.13	87.32	58.52	300
	DTE	72.86	88.72	**92.54**	**79.31**	300
PU3	SVM	94.45	96.04	95.79	95.19	300
	NB	77.25	94.03	87.72	84.66	300
	NN	84.51	95.38	91.33	89.57	300
	DTE	94.73	95.99	**95.88**	**95.31**	300
PUA	SVM	94.56	92.60	93.25	93.41	300
	NB	94.39	93.98	93.86	93.95	300
	NN	90.88	86.87	87.98	88.39	300
	DTE	95.44	93.93	**94.47**	**94.57**	300

Note: Bold values mean the best values among different approaches.

Cor., corpus; App., approach; Rec., recall; Pre., precision; Acc., accuracy; FD, feature dimensionality.

were selected by using the IG method. Then based on this, each e-mail was transformed to a 300-D feature vector. Finally, the two grounding classifiers were built from the feature vector set.

In the experiments, two performance measures—accuracy and F_1 measure—were adopted as mentioned in Section 1.5.1. Figure 10.2b depicts the comparison of accuracy among SVM, NB, and DTE, while Figure10.2c shows the comparison of F_1 measure among the three approaches. More details on the comparison are shown in Table 10.1, where the two components of F_1 measure—spam recall and spam precision—are also given. Besides, the performance of NN, which was utilized in self-trigger process, is also presented in the table.

On corpora PU1, PU3, and PUA, the DTE model outperforms SVM and NB in terms of both accuracy and F_1 measure. On corpus PU2, the DTE model performs equally as SVM and outperforms NB. From these results, we can draw a preliminary conclusion that the proposed DTE model can effectively improve the performance of classifiers.

Why does the DTE model perform not so outstandingly on corpus PU2 as it does on the three other corpora? To answer this, we have carried out some investigation into the details of the results given by the two grounding classifiers of the model. The investigation shows that the two grounding classifiers make more correlated errors on corpus PU2 compared to the other corpora. This reveals that the success of the DTE model lies in selection of uncorrelated grounding classifiers. Besides, the poor performance of the self-trigger process (NN) on PU2 is also a reason for the unideal performance of the DTE model.

10.8 Summary

This chapter elaborated the main concepts of DT into building an immune-based learning model. In addition, the DTE model has been successfully applied to spam detection, which is one of the typical machine learning problems. The experimental results showed that the DTE model can promote the performance of grounding classifiers considerably.

Chapter 11

Immune Danger Zone Principle-Based Dynamic Learning Method

This chapter presents the immune danger zone principle-based dynamic learning model, which defines strategies for combining global learning with local learning based on the proposed multi-objective risk minimization principles [245]. After an introduction and analysis of global learning and local learning, the necessity of building hybrid models is declared. As the foundation of the dynamic learning method, the proposed multi-objective learning principles are then stated. Afterward, strategies for combining global learning and local learning are described, as well as the analysis of local trade-off between capacity and locality. Implementations of the dynamic learning method are given. The relation of the dynamic learning method to multiple classifier combination is also analyzed. Finally, validation of the dynamic learning method is shown.

11.1 Introduction

In learning theory, there generally exist two kinds of statements [211] about the learning problem: global learning and local learning. The main difference between them lies in whether to fit a model to the entire or partial training set. According to global learning, a unique model would be built to minimize empirical errors on the entire training set, and it is assumed all the data may come from a fixed unknown distribution source. On the contrary, the local learning [26,211] assumes that data are unevenly distributed in the input space, and models (functions) are estimated in

155

the vicinity of a query. For analyzing learning models, Vapnik [211] presented two important learning principles: empirical risk minimization (ERM) and structural risk minimization (SRM). Based on the two principles, the learning process was formalized as a trade-off between capacity and locality.

When building global models, capacity of models may be tuned so as to match the numbers of examples in the training set. In the literature, many global algorithms, including naive Bayes (NB) [156], support vector machine (SVM) [67], artificial neural network [41], and decision trees [148,149] have been proposed and applied to many real-world problems. Although these algorithms build models based on different induction rules and assumptions, they all try to minimize empirical errors on the entire training set and tune their capacity through control parameter and model structure.

Local learning shares some similarities with global learning and also has mechanisms for adjusting model capacity. Nevertheless, compared to global learning, local learning has one more free parameter for tuning locality. Besides some classical local algorithms, such as k-nearest neighbors (k-NN) and radial basis function networks [116], many novel local algorithms have been proposed in recent years [26,38,39,109,237]. Most of these novel algorithms can be viewed as hybrid algorithms of k-NN and global algorithms.

The locality parameter generally differentiates local algorithms from global algorithms. With this parameter, it is theoretically possible to achieve a better compromise between capacity and locality. Nevertheless, it is not that easy to find an optimal locality for each query for a real-world problem. With a bad locality, local learning may perform worse than global learning. In addition, finding an optimal locality and building independent local models for each query would be quite time consuming [245].

11.2 Global Learning and Local Learning

Compared to global learning, local learning has one additional locality control parameter, which maintains number of examples involved in building models. The main relationship between the two mechanisms is analyzed from the following aspects:

■ *Trade-off between capacity and number of examples*: The trade-off is an important factor in the learning problem, and it affects the performance of a learning model. The best performance of a model is achieved when locality (which controls number of examples) and capacity match well. For global learning, a unified model is built over the whole training set, and thus its locality is fixed for all the data. To improve the performance of a global model, only capacity can be tuned so that the capacity can well match the number of training data.

However, both locality and capacity can be tuned for a local learning model, and they can be adjusted for each separate region.

- *Effect of data distribution*: Global learning methods build a unique model for all the data, while local learning methods build specified models for separate regions. It is natural and reasonable to build a unique model for identically distributed data. For unevenly distributed data, it is hard to approximate multiple distribution by using a single model; thus, it is more suitable to build local models for each distribution. However, the performance of local models depends on selecting an optimal locality for each region. Without information on true distribution, optimal locality is impossible to decide.

- *Utilization of information*: In building local models, partial information is utilized, and thus the local model cannot reflect the overall distribution of data but the partial distribution of the specified region. Local models may suffer from problems of overfitting in case of limited data. In contrast, global learning can make good use of all the available data and is robust of outliers.

- *Viewpoint of learning process*: Global learning studies the input space as a whole, whereas local learning utilizes multiple models and studies each separate region independently. As learning can be regarded as a process of understanding input space, global learning pays more attention to the overall characteristics of data distribution, while local learning only focuses on partial characteristics of some small regions. For instance, data may come from a Gaussian distribution, but data in a small region may satisfy uniform distribution. Combining different levels of viewpoint may help understand the input space better.

- *Complexity issues*: High computational complexity is one major problem of local learning, and thus many research groups focus on speeding up local learning algorithm. However, even with efficient implementation, local learning is still much more complex than global learning, as multiple models need to be built for separate regions in local learning.

11.3 Necessity of Building Hybrid Models

Locality control parameter may help local learning find optimal match between capacity and number of examples. However, this mechanism causes new problems to local learning. To tune locality according to data, many local models need to be built for separate regions, which is very time consuming. In addition, it is hard to choose an optimal locality for a specific problem. Bad selection of a locality may lead to overfitting problem, and small locality may cause the local model sensitive to the outliers. To solve these problems, it is necessary to study strategies of adaptively tuning locality and thus to combine global learning with local learning.

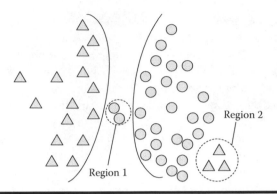

Figure 11.1   Example of pattern space with uneven distribution of data.

Figure 11.1 illustrates a pattern space with uneven distribution of data, in which a global decision boundary is also given. From this example, it can be seen that the general data distribution is well described by the global model. However, data distribution in regions 1 and 2 is quite different. Two specific local models need to be built for these two regions. In building the two models, their locality may necessarily be tuned according to the separate data distribution.

11.4 Multi-Objective Learning Principles

In literature, learning principles formulate learning problem as a process of function selection, where a single optimal approximation function is selected for a specific region (locally or globally). By using an additional locality parameter, local learning seems to be superior in minimizing empirical error on training data. Nevertheless, as the true distribution of data is unknown for real-world problems, it is impossible to decide whether a limited locality may help reduce generalization error for a specific problem. In addition, no practical criteria are available in finding an optimal value for the locality parameter. To provide mechanisms for combining learning models with varied locality, we put forward a multi-objective risk minimization (MORM) principle by combining global risk minimization (RM) and multiple local RMs:

$$R(w, b, x_0) = \begin{cases} \text{Minimize} & R_1(w, b_1, x_0) \\ \text{Minimize} & R_2(w, b_2, x_0) \\ \vdots & \vdots \\ \text{Minimize} & R_n(w, b_n, x_0) \end{cases} \tag{11.1}$$

Subject to $0 < b_1 < b_2 < \cdots < b_n$

where each R_p denotes an objective with regard to b_p,

$$R(w, b_p, x_0) = \int L(y, f(x, w)) \frac{K(x, x_0, b_p)}{\| K(x_0, b_p) \|} dP(x, y) \qquad (11.2)$$

and R_n denotes the global RM, in which $b_n \to \infty$.

Accordingly, multi-objective empirical risk minimization (MOERM) is given as an approximation to MORM, since the true distribution of $P(x, y)$ cannot be obtained:

$$E(w, b, x_0) = \begin{cases} \text{Minimize} & E_1(w, b_1, x_0) \\ \text{Minimize} & E_2(w, b_2, x_0) \\ \vdots & \vdots \\ \text{Minimize} & E_n(w, b_n, x_0) \end{cases} \qquad (11.3)$$

$$\text{Subject to } 0 < b_1 < b_2 < \cdots < b_n$$

where each E_p denotes an objective with regard to b_p,

$$E(w, b_p, x_0) = \frac{1}{l} \sum_{i=1}^{l} L(y_i, f(x_i, w)) \frac{K(x, x_0, b_p)}{\| K(x_0, b_p) \|} \qquad (11.4)$$

and E_n denotes the global ERM, in which $b_n \to \infty$.

As the parameter b does not affect capacity but only locality, the existing SRM principle can be directly applied to find an optimal element S^*, except that MOERM should be utilized in minimizing each element S_p of a structure.

11.5 Strategies for Combining Global Learning and Local Learning

According to MOERM principle, multiple models with varied locality are built, and they are combined to achieve an optimal compromise between capacity and locality. Figure 11.2 depicts a natural and direct strategy for combining global learning and local learning. Using the strategy, a global model and multiple local models with varied locality are built simultaneously. These models are then combined by evaluating how well are their capacity and locality matched.

The strategy is useful in minimizing empirical error. However, the strategy is quite time consuming, as multiple models need to be built for each query (testing instance). A cascade combination strategy is shown in Figure 11.3. By using the cascade strategy, learning models with varied locality are successively built. A successor model would be built only when the predecessor models cannot achieve good compromise between capacity and locality. To reduce computational complexity,

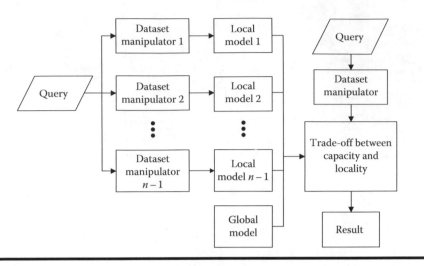

Figure 11.2   A simple strategy for combining models with varied locality.

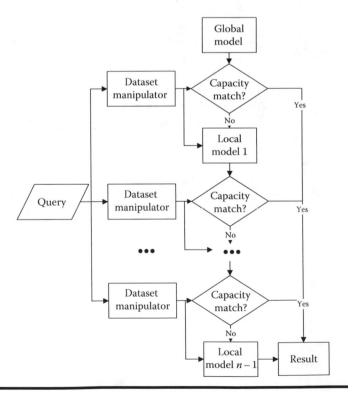

Figure 11.3   Query-based cascade strategy for adaptively tuning locality of models.

global model is built at the first stage and preferably utilized for a query, since a uniform global model can be used for all the query (test instance). When the capacity of the global model cannot well match number of examples, local models with smaller locality are necessarily built. Locality of models are adaptively adjusted based on the data distribution around a query.

11.6 Local Trade-Off between Capacity and Locality

In implementing the cascade strategy, effective evaluation mechanisms need to be adopted, so as to justify the necessity of tuning locality of models. The main purpose of tuning locality is to minimize generalization error (actual risk) of a given model, and thus generalization error is an ideal evaluation mechanism. However, it is unable to get generalization error for real-world problems. By taking inspiration from danger theory (DT), we estimate the match degree between capacity and locality based on the characteristics of local data distribution around a query.

In Reference 128, Matzinger proposed a novel biological immune paradigm, danger therapy (DT), which well explained how an immune recognition was triggered. Based on this theory, many artificial immune-based learning models were designed by mimicking the recognition (learning) process between antibody and antigen. One important principle of DT is the usage of a danger zone, which provides a way of recognition confirmation. From the perspective of machine learning, a query represents an antigen, a learning model corresponds to antibodies, and function of danger zone amounts to local estimation of the model's performance. Therefore, it is logical to design an artificial danger zone and utilize it to estimate whether the model's capacity matches locality of data. In addition, local estimation mechanisms are not only found in DT-based models but also in traditional learning approaches. In References 166 and 247, local estimation was utilized for computing weight classifiers in building multiple classifier systems (MCSs).

Based on these analyses, local estimation mechanism is applied in maintaining trade-off between capacity and locality. Two ways of local estimation may be considered. One strategy is defining a danger zone for each query on the training set. As the data in a danger zone have already been seen by a learning model, the corresponding estimation may be inaccurate and over-optimistic. To solve the problem, the other one is to divide labeled data into a training set and an independent validation set, and define danger zones on the validation set. In the following section, the effectiveness of the two strategies is investigated, and the latter strategy performs much better.

11.7 Hybrid Model for Combining Models with Varied Locality

Algorithm 11.1 demonstrates a cascade strategy for combining global learning and local learning. The labeled data are divided into two independent sets: a training set

---

Algorithm 11.1 A cascade strategy for combining global learning and local learning

---

Divide the labeled data into two set:

training set $T = \{(x_1, y_1), (x_2, y_2), \ldots, (x_n, y_n)\}$, and

validation set $V = \{(x_1, y_1), (x_2, y_2), \ldots, (x_m, y_m)\}$;

Initialize the locality parameter: $b = n$;

Build a global learning model $f_g(x, w)$ on the whole training set T, by minimizing $E(w)$;

for an instance x_0 in the testing set **do**

Select k_t samples from V with minimal $K(x, x_0)$;

Use the k_t samples to evaluate the performance of $f_g(x, w)$: $p = 1 - \frac{1}{l} \sum_{i=1}^{k_t} L(y_i, f(x_i, w)) \frac{K(x, x_0)}{\|K(x_0)\|}$;

while $p < \theta$ *and* $b - \Delta b > 0$ **do**

$b = b - \Delta b$;

Build a local learning model $f_l(x_i, w, b)$ on T, by minimizing $E(w, b, x_0)$;

Use the k_t samples to evaluate the performance of existing models:

$p = 1 - \frac{1}{l} \sum_{i=1}^{k_t} L(y_i, \sum \alpha_j f_j(x_i, w)) \frac{K(x, x_0)}{\|K(x_0)\|}$,

where α_j is the weight of $f_j(x_i, w)$;

end while

Label x_0 using existing models:

$y_0 = \sum \alpha_j f_j(x_i, w)$;

end for

---

and a validation set. The training set is utilized to build a global model and multiple local models. The independent validation set is utilized to evaluate the performance of current models and determine the necessity of tuning locality and building up suitable models. After segmentation of data set, a unique global model is built on the whole training set. In classifying test instances, the global model is first applied, and its performance is evaluated on validation set. In performance evaluation, k_t nearest neighbors to a test instance are found on the validation set, and they are utilized to estimate whether a model fits to the local distribution around the test instance. When the global model cannot fit a local distribution well, the locality parameter is gradually decreased and local models are built.

According to the algorithm, the locality parameters is gradually adjusted with a step width of δb. In implementation, the parameter δb can be either set to a fixed value or adaptively estimated based on local data around a query. Once an optimal locality is found, the test instance is classified using the optimal model or a combination of existing models. In combining a global model and multiple local models, various strategies, including best model selection, majority voting, and weighted voting, can be adopted. The effects of these strategies are investigated in Algorithm 11.2.

Algorithm 11.2 A two-phase strategy for combining global learning and local learning

---

Divide the labeled data into two set:

training set $T = \{(x_1, y_1), (x_2, y_2), \ldots, (x_n, y_n)\}$, and

validation set $V = \{(x_1, y_1), (x_2, y_2), \ldots, (x_m, y_m)\}$;

Build a global learning model $f_g(x, w)$ on the whole training set T, by minimizing $E(w)$;

for an instance x_0 in the testing set **do**

    Select k_t samples from V with minimal $K(x, x_0)$;

    Use the k_t samples to evaluate the performance of $f_g(x, w)$: $p = 1 - \frac{1}{l} \sum_{i=1}^{k_t} L(y_i, f(x_i, w)) \frac{K(x, x_0)}{\|K(x_0)\|}$;

    if $p < \theta$ **then**

        Estimate a set of suitable locality parameter $B = \{b_1, b_2, \ldots, b_l\}$, according to the global model and its current performance;

        for each $b_p \in B$ **do**

            Build a local learning model $f_l(x_i, w, b_p)$ on T, by minimizing $E(w, b_p, x_0)$;

        end for

    end if

    Label x_0 using existing models:

$y_0 = \sum \alpha_j f_j(x_i, w)$;

end for

In essence, Algorithm 11.1 presents a multistage strategy for gradually tuning locality. Although it helps achieve an optimal compromise between capacity and locality, the tuning process of the algorithm may cost much time, especially when the step width Δb is small. One alternative is to simplify this multiphase strategy into a two-phase strategy, which is shown in Algorithm 11.2. When a global model cannot work well, multiple complementary local models are built simultaneously. Locality tuning is achieved by assigning weights for these models. Preliminary empirical results show that the two-phase strategy works much faster and its performance is also as well as the multistage one.

11.8 Relation to Multiple Classifier Combination

In MCSs [227], multiple global classifiers are built on the whole training set. In contrast, in the combination of global learning and local learning (CGL), a global model and multiple local models are built according to distribution characters of separate regions. Although they all try to combine performance of multiple models, they are very different from each other in the following aspects.

■ *Induction principles*: In most MCSs, individual classifiers are built based on different induction principles. However, a unique induction principle is utilized for building global and local models in CGL.
■ *Capacity and locality*: MCS pays more attention to combining models with varied capacity, while CGL focuses on adaptively tuning locality according to local data distribution.

11.9 Validation of the Dynamic Learning Method

The effects of parameters were investigated on a small independent corpus, where 2000 instances were randomly selected from TREC07. The small corpus was partitioned into 10 stratified folds, and 10-fold cross validation was utilized. In experiments, ID3 tree was utilized as basic inducer for building models.

11.9.1 Danger Zone Size

In hybrid models, match degree between capacity and locality is estimated on danger zones, which is defined as vicinity of a query on the validation set. In addition, the parameter controls the compromise between global learning and local learning.

Figure 11.4 depicts the performance of the hybrid model under different sizes of danger zone. The size value denotes the ratio of validation set, which is utilized in estimation. It can be seen that the model performs better with small danger zone and the performance declines slightly when the danger zone becomes large. As the

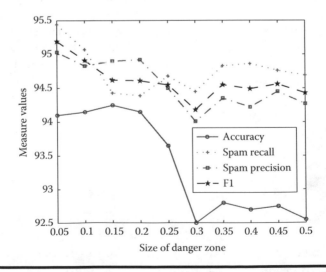

Figure 11.4 Performance of the hybrid model with varied danger zone size.

main function of danger zone is to estimate local distribution around a query, it is reasonable to use small danger zone in applications.

11.9.2 Effects of Threshold

The threshold θ works as a knob for combining global and local models. With larger θ, local models are built with higher probability, and more instances will be classified using a combination of multilocalities. Figure 11.5 shows the complexity of the hybrid model on a different threshold θ. With the growth of θ, the computational complexity gradually increases. However, even with a large θ, the hybrid model still performs faster than local learning. A preliminary conclusion can be drawn that the complexity of the hybrid models lies between the complexity of global learning and local learning. In real-world applications, the threshold may be tuned according to limitation of complexity, and it endows the hybrid models with high scalability. In Section 11.9.3, experimental results show that the hybrid models achieve better accuracy than both global and local models.

11.9.3 Comparison Results

The hybrid models were compared to global and local models on five corpora using 10-fold cross validation, and NB, C4.5, ID3, and SVM were utilized as basic inducers. In the experiments, performance of models with varied locality was fully investigated, so as to show that optimal locality may depend on data distribution of a specific corpus.

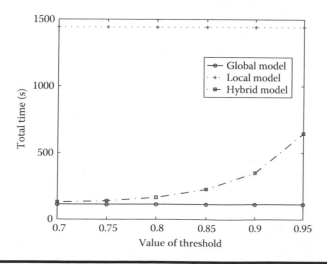

Figure 11.5 Complexity of the hybrid model with varied threshold θ.

Tables 11.1 through 11.4 show the accuracy of global and local models on the five spam corpora. In the table, the parameter b controls the locality, and n denotes the number of examples on the training set. From the results, an optimal locality depends on both data distribution and capacity of models. Good performance is achieved for NB with small locality b; medium locality b is suitable for decision tree C4.5 and ID3, while large locality should be chosen for SVM. As data distributions are different in each corpus, optimal localities are also different on these corpora. For instance, NB with $b = 0.1n$ performs best on PU3 and TREC, whereas NB with $b = 0.4n$ achieves highest accuracy on the other three corpora. It is impossible to find a unique optimal locality for all the corpora and classifiers. Thus, locality should be tuned according to local data distribution and the match degree between locality and capacity.

In Tables 11.5 through 11.8, the accuracy of hybrid models on the corpora is given, and the average performance of models in Tables 11.1 through 11.4 is taken

Table 11.1 Performance of Global and Local Models with Naive Bayes Under Settings of Different Locality on Spam Corpora (%)

	Corpus				
Approach	*PU1*	*PU2*	*PU3*	*PUA*	*TREC*
Global model ($b = n$)	91.47	90.70	87.72	94.65	86.15
Local model ($b = 0.7n$)	96.61	89.44	93.61	94.82	86.05
Local model ($b = 0.4n$)	97.61	93.38	94.50	95.53	84.12
Local model ($b = 0.1n$)	97.34	93.10	95.08	94.30	90.03
Average	95.76	91.66	92.73	94.83	86.59

Table 11.2 Performance of Global and Local Models with C4.5 Under Settings of Different Locality on Spam Corpora (%)

	Corpus				
Approach	*PU1*	*PU2*	*PU3*	*PUA*	*TREC*
Global model ($b = n$)	91.28	89.72	92.25	88.68	95.74
Local model ($b = 0.7n$)	91.28	90.42	92.42	87.89	95.52
Local model ($b = 0.4n$)	91.38	88.31	92.47	86.93	95.57
Local model ($b = 0.1n$)	87.80	88.31	91.26	87.81	95.14
Average	90.44	89.19	92.10	87.83	95.49

Table 11.3   Performance of Global and Local Models with Id3 Under Settings of Different Locality on Spam Corpora (%)

Approach	Corpus				
	PU1	*PU2*	*PU3*	*PUA*	*TREC*
Global model ($b = n$)	92.39	88.73	92.18	88.16	94.84
Local model ($b = 0.7n$)	92.94	88.87	92.03	88.42	95.27
Local model ($b = 0.4n$)	91.65	90.00	92.20	88.86	95.59
Local model ($b = 0.1n$)	89.36	86.76	91.50	89.56	95.70
Average	91.59	88.59	91.98	88.75	95.35

Table 11.4   Performance of Global and Local Models with Support Vector Machine Under Settings of Different Locality on Spam Corpora (%)

Approach	Corpus				
	PU1	*PU2*	*PU3*	*PUA*	*TREC*
Global model ($b = n$)	96.33	94.08	95.33	92.63	96.90
Local model ($b = 0.7n$)	96.33	93.24	95.42	92.02	96.89
Local model ($b = 0.4n$)	95.96	92.82	95.59	92.11	96.73
Local model ($b = 0.1n$)	94.59	91.83	94.04	91.58	95.62
Average	95.80	92.99	95.10	92.09	96.54

Table 11.5   Performance of Hybrid Models That Combine Global Learning and Local Learning of Naive Bayes on Spam Corpora (%)

Approach	Corpus				
	PU1	*PU2*	*PU3*	*PUA*	*TREC*
Baseline	95.76	91.66	92.73	94.83	86.59
Global + unilocal($b = 0.7n$)	98.35	94.65	93.75	95.26	88.23
Global + unilocal($b = 0.4n$)	99.08	94.51	94.87	96.84	88.02
Global + unilocal($b = 0.1n$)	98.44	93.66	95.57	94.91	90.08
Global + multilocal 1	99.36	94.51	95.01	97.02	88.88
Global + multilocal 2	99.08	95.07	94.87	97.19	87.17

Table 11.6   Performance of Hybrid Models That Combine Global Learning and Local Learning of C4.5 on Spam Corpora (%)

	Corpus				
Approach	PU1	PU2	PU3	PUA	TREC
Baseline	90.44	89.19	92.10	87.83	95.49
Global + unilocal($b = 0.7n$)	93.30	92.96	92.78	87.72	95.61
Global + unilocal($b = 0.4n$)	93.58	91.83	93.08	89.30	95.82
Global + unilocal($b = 0.1n$)	93.12	92.54	92.93	88.51	95.59
Global + multilocal 1	93.03	92.68	93.20	88.86	95.87
Global + multilocal 2	93.76	93.24	93.39	88.33	96.01

Table 11.7   Performance of Hybrid Models That Combine Global Learning and Local Learning of Id3 on Spam Corpora (%)

	Corpus				
Approach	PU1	PU2	PU3	PUA	TREC
Baseline	91.59	88.59	91.98	88.75	95.35
Global + unilocal($b = 0.7n$)	93.85	90.70	92.54	89.12	95.87
Global + unilocal($b = 0.4n$)	94.77	91.83	92.91	89.47	95.79
Global + unilocal($b = 0.1n$)	93.67	91.41	92.06	88.77	95.89
Global + multilocal 1	94.40	92.25	93.08	90.79	96.48
Global + multilocal 2	94.50	92.39	93.39	90.79	96.25

as baseline. Two general strategies of combination are fully investigated. One is to combine a global model with a single local model (global+unilocal), and the other is to combine a global model with multiple local models (global+multilocal). In global+multilocal 1, a global model is combined with multiple models, and the locality parameters of these local models are, respectively, $0.7n$, $0.4n$, and $0.1n$. In global+multilocal 2, the locality parameters of those local models are, respectively, $0.7n$, $0.5n$, and $0.3n$.

The experimental results in Tables 11.5 through 11.8 well demonstrate that hybrid models can effectively achieve better performance, compared to global and local models. In most cases, global+multilocal strategy outperforms the global+unilocal strategy. For SVM, global+unilocal with $b = 0.7n$ gives the best performance. In general, both the strategies can improve performance of models,

Table 11.8   Performance of Hybrid Models That Combine Global Learning and Local Learning of Support Vector Machine on Spam Corpora (%)

Approach	Corpus				
	PU1	PU2	PU3	PUA	TREC
Baseline	95.80	92.99	95.10	92.09	96.54
Global + unilocal($b = 0.7n$)	96.88	93.52	96.08	93.42	96.87
Global + unilocal($b = 0.4n$)	96.70	93.52	95.81	93.60	96.83
Global + unilocal($b = 0.1n$)	96.33	93.52	95.54	92.63	96.77
Global + multilocal 1	96.97	88.73	94.77	93.51	95.79
Global + multilocal 2	96.97	88.73	94.70	93.25	95.81

and the improvements result from the mechanism of adaptively tuning locality. Better performance can be expected, when the two strategies are unified in a cascade framework. In addition, the results also verify the reasonability of multi-objective learning principles.

11.10 Summary

In this chapter, learning is formalized as a MORM problem, and it is pointed out that risk should be minimized with regard to multiple localities. By combining global and local models, hybrid models are proposed for adaptively tuning locality according to local distribution around a query. The different essence between hybrid models and MCS is well demonstrated. In the experiments, the performance of hybrid models was investigated on five real-world spam corpora, and results shew that hybrid models outperforms both global and local models. The success of the hybrid models lies in a good compromise between capacity and locality.

Chapter 12

Immune-Based Dynamic Updating Algorithm

This chapter presents the immune based dynamic updating algorithm using support vector machine (SVM) and artificial immune system (AIS) as the basis for uninterrupted detection approaches for spam filtering [194]. The first three sections introduce the background knowledge, including exceeding margin update (EM-update) principle and sliding window, which are two of the core strategies employed in the strategies. After description of the primary and secondary responses in BIS, overview of the dynamic updating algorithm is given by mimicking some of the mechanisms or functions in BIS. We then give the whole implementation process and related factors of the dynamic updating algorithm in detail, including message representation, dimension reduction, initialization of the window, classification criterion, update of the classifier, and purge of out-of-date knowledge. Finally, experimental validation and discussion are shown.

12.1 Introduction

Support Vector Machine (SVM) has already proved its superiority in pattern recognition for its generalization performance. Natural immune system has some desirable properties for spam detection, including pattern recognition, dynamically changing coverage and noise tolerance, etc. Those properties are considerably desirable for our task of anti-spam.

SVM is a classification algorithm based on the Structural Risk Minimization principle from statistical learning theory formulated by Vapnik [66,209,210]. The goal of SVM is to find an optimal hyperplane for which the lowest true error can be guaranteed.

Artificial Immune Systems (AIS), inspired by the mammalian immune system have become an increasingly popular computational intelligence paradigm in recent years. AIS seeks to use the immune components and processes of mammalian immune system as metaphors to produce artificial systems that encapsulate desirable properties of the natural immune system. These AIS are then applied to solve complex problems in a wide variety of domains [57].

This chapter introduces the algorithm using SVM and AIS as the basis for uninterrupted detection approaches for stopping spam. The support vectors of the trained SVM are used to generate naïve detectors for the proposed AIS-based approaches. The naïve detectors frequently used for classification are promoted to be memory cells. For the purpose of tracing the dynamic changing property of the content of e-mails and user's interests, a window is used to hold several classifiers, each one classifies the incoming e-mail independently and then the window labels the e-mail through majority voting. The exceeding margin update technique is used to dynamically update the classifier, the detector set, and the memory set. The messages that exceed the margin are used to update the classifier. A sliding window is used to purge the out-of-date knowledge. When new batch arrives, the "oldest" classifier in the window will be removed from the window and the remaining classifiers slide a position to right. The "youngest" classifier is generated from the previous batch of data. Thus, the proposed approaches are able to trace the changing content of e-mails and user's interests in a continuous way.

Several approaches—including Hamming Distance (with and without mutation), Included Angle, SVM, and Weighted Voting, which can be regarded as different implementations to the uninterrupted detection of e-mail stream—are developed here. Furthermore, experiments on two public benchmark corpora PU1 and Ling are conducted to verify the performance of the approaches. Finally, a performance comparison between the different approaches is made for accuracy, precision, recall, miss rate, and speed.

12.2 Backgrounds of SVM and AIS

In this section, some basic backgrounds of SVM and AIS are briefly introduced. The focus is on the parts pertinent to the algorithms to be presented. For a complete review of them, interested readers refer to literature [66,96,209,210].

12.2.1 Support Vector Machine

Support Vector Machine is a classification algorithm based on the Structural Risk Minimization principle in statistical learning theory. Assume there are two classes, $y_i \in \{-1, 1\}$, and N labeled training examples: $\{x_1, y_1\}, \ldots, \{x_N, y_N\}, x \in \mathbb{R}^d$ where d is the dimension of the vector x.

If the two classes are linearly separable, one can find an optimal weight vector w^* such that $\|w^*\|^2$ is minimum, subjected to

$$y_i(w^* \cdot x_i - b) \geq 1 \tag{12.1}$$

The training examples satisfying the equality in Equation 12.1 are termed support vectors. Support vectors define two hyperplanes in feature space to separate the two classes. The distance between the two hyperplanes defines a margin which is maximized when the norm of the weight vector $\|w^*\|$ is minimum. An intuitive illustration of the margin is shown in Figure 12.1. It has been shown that the minimization of $\|w^*\|$ can be carried out by maximizing the following function with respect to the variables α_j.

$$W(\alpha) = \sum_{i=1}^{N} \alpha_i - 0.5 \sum_{i=1}^{N} \sum_{j=1}^{N} \alpha_i \alpha_j (x_i \cdot x_j) y_i y_j s.t. \quad \alpha_j \geq 0 \tag{12.2}$$

where
  symbol · represents the dot product
  x_j with positive α_j is called as a support vector

To classify a newly incoming unknown vector x_j, one can find

$$F(x_j) = \text{sign}\{w^* \cdot x_j - b\} \tag{12.3}$$

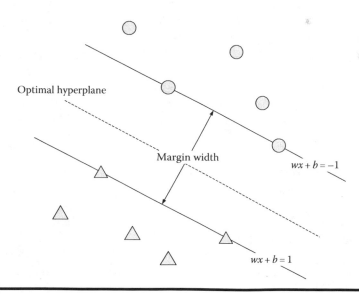

Figure 12.1 **The optimal hyperplane and margin in feature space, $wx + b = 1$ and $wx + b = -1$ represent separating hyperplanes where support vectors locate, respectively.**

where

$$w^* = \sum_{i=1}^{r} \alpha_i y_i x_i \tag{12.4}$$

where r is the number of support vectors whose α's are nonzero.

If the two classes are linearly nonseparable, training errors are allowed, instead we should minimize

$$\|w^*\|^2 + C \sum_{i=1}^{N} \xi_i \text{s.t.} \quad y_i(w^* \cdot x_i - b) \leq 1 - \xi, \qquad \xi > 0 \tag{12.5}$$

where
ξ is a slack variable

In this case, we allow training examples to exist between the two hyperplanes that go through the support vectors of two classes. We can equivalently minimize $W(\alpha)$ subject to $0 \leq \alpha_i \leq C$ instead of $\alpha_j \geq 0$. Maximizing $W(\alpha)$ can be carried out by using quadratic programming techniques, some of which are particular to SVM [143,144].

12.2.2 Artificial Immune System

The main goal of human immune system (HIS) is to distinguish self from nonself such as bacteria, viruses, fungi, etc. For this purpose, HIS uses the specialized white blood cells, for example, B and T *lymphocytes*. On the surface of each lymphocyte there are *receptors*. The lymphocyte can be activated by binding the receptor to the patterns presented on the surface of *antigens*. The binding process is schematically shown in Figure 12.2a.

Lymphocytes are created in the bone marrow. The match between a receptor and an antigen may not be exact, so a single lymphocyte may recognize a number of antigenic patterns, which brings HIS the nature of noise tolerance. Generally, the similarity between receptor and antigen is measured by *affinity*. When the binding of the receptor to antigens takes place, the binding stimulates an immune response of *clone selection*. In this process, the cloning takes place with a rate proportional to the affinity, while the mutation rate is inversely proportional to the affinity [57,183]. The binding receptor making a correct decision, that is, the matched antigen is real pathogenic, is promoted to be a memory cell for an immune memory of the encountered antigen. It takes longer for HIS to mount a response to an antigen for the first time when a new pathogen is encountered, for example, the process of *Primary Response*. Yet, when the same pathogen or its likeness appears again, the HIS can respond very quickly because of the memory cells and their mutants, for example, the process of *Secondary Response*. Figure 12.2b depicts the immune response processes in HIS.

Over the last few years, a novel paradigm of computational intelligence called Artificial Immune System (AIS) has received extensive attention from researchers.

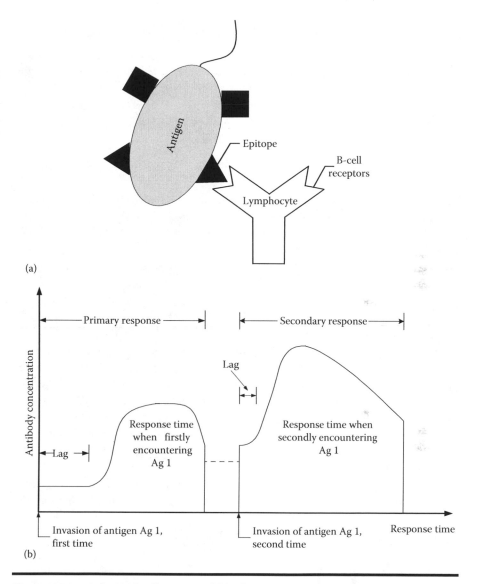

Figure 12.2 Schematic diagrams of binding and immune response processes of biological immune system. (a) Binding of the receptor to patterns presented on the antigen and (b) primary response and secondary response in HIS.

Inspired by the human immune system, AIS seeks to use the observed immune components and processes as metaphors to build artificial systems to encapsulate the desirable properties of HIS. The AIS has already been applied to a wide variety of domains, including: machine learning, pattern recognition, optimization, data mining, and computer security [55,57,183].

12.3 Principles of EM-Update and Sliding Window

In this section, the three main principles employed in the algorithms to be presented are elaborated: exceeding margin update (EM-Update) technique, sliding window technique and immune response process of HIS.

12.3.1 EM-Update

In pattern recognition, one would like to consider more data or examples simultaneously to estimate the underlying class distribution as accurately as possible. However, for spam detection, there is a very small amount of training data available. Furthermore, data of e-mails are in stream mode and arrive successively. Thus incremental techniques are required to update of the stream data.

SVMs have been successfully used as a classification tool in a large variety of practical domains. The representation of the data is given by the set of support vectors along with corresponding weights. The number of support vectors in a SVM is much smaller than the total number of training examples, therefore, the support vectors provide a compact representation of the data [64]. At each incremental step, the support vectors which describe the essential class boundary information together with the new incoming data, are used as training set for the SVM update.

There are several techniques for the incremental learning of SVM, including: *Error-driven technique (ED)*, *Fixed-partition technique (FP)*, *Exceeding-margin technique (EM)*, and *Exceeding-margin+error technique (EM+E)* [134,176]. The experimental results on Large-noisy-crossed-norm data and real data set Pima taken from UCI Machine Learning Repository, show that *EM* technique achieves similar error rate compared to the other three techniques, yet, the number of support vectors is small by comparison [176]. Therefore, *Exceeding-margin technique (EM)* is adopted to update the SVMs in algorithm.

Given the model SVM_t at time t, the algorithm checks if new data (x_i, y_i) exceeds the margin defined by SVM_t, that is, $y_i(w^* \cdot x_i - b) \leq 1$. If the condition is satisfied the data point is kept, otherwise it is discarded. Once a given fixed number n_e of data which exceed the margin is collected, the update of SVM_t takes place, that is, the support vectors of SVM_t, together with the n_e data points, are used as training data to obtain a new model SVM_{t+1} at time $t + 1$.

12.3.2 Work Process of Sliding Window

On one hand, the EM technique is employed to construct the incremental learning algorithm. On the other hand, data points which are no longer effective or usable have to be purged. The characteristic of the data in stream mode changes rapidly with time, and historical data may not be a good predictor for future data points. Here, a *sliding window* is used to purge the out-of-date knowledge [64].

We consider the incoming data in batches with size b, and maintain w models to represent the previous $1, 2, \ldots, w$ batches in the window simultaneously.

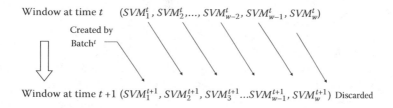

Figure 12.3 The slide process of the window with size w.

Thus, the window holds W ($=wb$) data points. The w models are updated incrementally and independently according to the EM technique once data become available. Let us denote the w models, at time t, as SVM_1^t, SVM_2^t, ..., SVM_w^t, respectively. When a new batch of data arrives at time $t + 1$, SVM_w^t is discarded, meanwhile, the remaining $SVM_1^t, \ldots, SVM_{w-1}^t$ become $SVM_2^{t+1}, \ldots, SVM_w^{t+1}$, sequentially. SVM_1^{t+1} is newly created by only using the data of the previous batch. This process can be formulated as

$$SVM_{i+1}^{t+1} = \begin{cases} SVM_i^t & 1 \leq i \leq w - 1 \\ \text{created by batch at time } t & i = 0 \end{cases} \qquad (12.6)$$

where
w is the size of the window

Figure 12.3 depicts an intuitive illustration of this process of the sliding window.

Each SVM in the window represents the recent batches of data seen so far. Specifically, SVM_1^t represents the latest batch of data while SVM_w^t represents the previous w batches of data. When a new data point arrives, each SVM in the *window* classifies the data independently and has an equal weight. The label of the data is decided by the strategy of majority voting. Here, SVMs in the window can be considered as "experts" with different knowledge and work together to give out the final decision for the new data.

A more complicated strategy of voting, weighted majority voting, could be adopted to weight each SVM in the window. The weight could be set at different values according to the feature of the data and could be adjusted dynamically. When the characteristic of the data stream drifts dramatically, we can increase the weights of "younger" classifiers such as SVM_1^t, SVM_2^t, to reflect the immediate change of the data. On the contrary, when the variation of the data is slight, it will benefit from increasing the weights of "older" classifiers because they have seen more data and have more amount of knowledge. In practice, the changing trend may be smooth or not, therefore, the update of weights of SVMs must be a dynamic process.

12.3.3 Primary Response and Secondary Response

The HIS takes longer time to mount a response to a pathogen encountered for the first time. This process is called *Primary Response*. The detectors that detect the pathogens successfully undergo the immune response of clone selection. They are promoted to be a long-lived memory cell to memorize the encountered pathogen. After a primary response, the HIS can react immediately when a similar pathogen intrudes again. This process is called the *Secondary Response*. The concept of a memory cell is used as a metaphor in algorithm. The purpose is to recognize the previously met spam. There are three ways to generate initial detector set. First, use a negative selection algorithm. Second, use a positive selection algorithm. Third, use a positive–negative selection algorithm. The negative selection algorithm constructs the initial detector set from negative samples. Some of representative samples and their mutants can directly serve as detectors. The positive selection algorithm only uses the positive samples for this purpose. The positive–negative selection algorithm is a combination of the two ways mentioned previously. Both positive samples and negative samples are used to generate detectors. The size of positive detector set relative to the size of the negative set is set according to the real application.

12.4 Implementation of Algorithms

12.4.1 Overview of Dynamic Updating Algorithm

We consider HIS and SVM as inspiration because their properties are particularly suitable for developing a spam filter. The similarities between the immune system and a spam detection system are:

1. *Pattern recognition*: The goal of spam detection is to distinguish spam mails from non-spam mails while HIS differentiates self from potentially dangerous nonself.
2. *Dynamical change*: The formats of the e-mail vary, and the content of e-mail and user's interest are always changing. Tracing these changes is also the goal of spam detection. Similarly, HIS is capable of recognizing a variety of invaders dynamically.
3. *Noise tolerance*: A desirable feature in pattern recognition is noise tolerance, while the immune system is capable of recognizing different mutants of pathogens.

SVM is a prominent classifier with a solid theoretical foundation of statistical learning and superior generalization of performance. Moreover, there are many successful applications based on AIS and SVM techniques. Thus, the proposed algorithms in this chapter employ the incremental SVM technique and the concepts of detectors, as well as, memory cells for uninterrupted spam detection.

The incoming e-mails arrive successively in a stream mode. For the processing of this kind of data, an incremental update technique is required for the incorporation of new knowledge from the data stream. Since the content of the user's e-mail and interest constantly drift, we have to forget the data points that are no longer in active. The key idea of algorithm is to employ a sliding window to hold several classifiers simultaneously, meanwhile, each classifier in the window updates independently through the EM technique. When a new e-mail arrives, it is classified independently through the classification criterion, which will be presented in details in Section 12.4.5. The label of the new e-mail is determined by majority voting. The out-of-date knowledge is purged when a new batch of e-mail arrives. The "oldest" classifier, the one farthest right, is removed from the window while the remaining classifiers slide to the right. The "youngest" classifier, the one farthest left, is newly created by using the previous batch. The window must be initialized to start the work. Each e-mail needs to be transformed to a feature vector before it is classified. The overview of the algorithm is presented in Algorithm 12.1, each step of it is described in detail in the following sections.

Algorithm 12.1 Algorithm for spam detection

Preprocess each message in the *Training Set*
Initialize the window, namely generate the *classifier*$_1$

while Algorithm is running **do**
   if *message* is received **then**
      for each *classifier* in the window **do**
         classify the *message* independently
         if the *message* exceeds the margin **then**
            the *message* is kept
         else
            the *message* is discarded
         end if
         if a given number of messages exceeding the margin is collected **then**
            update the *classifier*
         end if
      end for

      the label of the *message* is given by *classifiers* in the window in terms of voting
      if the received *message* is the last message of current batch **then**
         Slide the window
         generate the *classifier*$_1$ by current batch only
      end if
   end if
end while

12.4.2 Message Representation

The first stage of pattern recognition is the preprocessing of the data. The problem of e-mail classification is how to represent the message. A word in the message is defined as a feature, and the message can be easily represented as a feature vector through a bag of words that is formed by analyzing a set of training samples. There are several methods to construct a feature vector, such as, TF (Term Frequency), TF-IDF (Term Frequency–Inverse Document Frequency), and binary representation. Drucker et al. showed that SVM with binary features outperforms other methods [67]. Here, we adopt the binary representation of a message in algorithm. When we use w_i to represent a word, the message can be expressed as

$$\text{message} = (w_1, w_2, \ldots, w_m) \tag{12.7}$$

where
  m is the number of words in the bag
  $w_i, (i = 1, 2, \ldots, m)$ takes binary value of 1 or 0 to indicate whether it occurs in this message or not

12.4.3 Dimension Reduction

If we extract each word appearing in a message to form a dictionary, the size of this dictionary will be too large. Thus, a dimension reduction of the feature space is required to avoid the curse of dimension. According to Reference [250], the features that appear in most of the documents are not relevant to the separation, because all the classes contain those same features. On the contrary, the words used rarely also give us few information during classification either. Therefore, for simplification, we adopt the processing method in Reference [21], which discards the features that appear less than 5% and more than 95% in all messages of the corpus.

12.4.4 Initialization of the Window

At the beginning, the window is empty. The initialization of the window is to generate the *classifier*₁. For each classification criterion, there is a different construction of the classifier. The different initialization processes correspond to specific classification criteria described in the following paragraphs. Here, some parts of the corpus are used as training samples to generate the *classifier*₁.

For the classification criteria of *Hamming Distance* and *Included Angle*, the classifier is comprised of *Detector Set* and *Memory Set*. At first, each mail is transformed into a binary vector in the previously mentioned way. After preprocessing, the training vectors are used to train the SVM. The *support vectors* of the trained SVM are used as *naïve detectors* to form the *Detector Set*.

The *Memory Set* is a set of *memory cells* that have better performance. The *Detector Set* is used to classify the training samples according to the classification criterion of

---

Algorithm 12.2 Generation of detector set and memory set

Detector Set ⇐ φ
Memory Set ⇐ φ
Convert each message in the *Training Set* to a binary vector
Use the preprocessed *Training Set* to train the SVM
Detector Set ⇐ *Support Vectors* of the trained SVM

for each *msg* ∈ *Training Set* **do**
    Use *Detector Set* to classify *msg* in terms of certain criterion
    for each *naïve detector* participating in decision making and judging correctly **do**
        Increment the number of correctly classified messages of *naïve detector*
    end for
end for

for each *naïve detector* ∈ *Detector Set* **do**
    if the number of correctly classified messages exceeds the threshold n_m **then**
        Assign a *lifespan* to this *naïve detector*
        Memory Set ⇐ *Memory Set* ∪ {*naïve detector*}
    end if
end for

Detector Set ⇐ *Detector Set* − *Memory Set*

Hamming Distance or Included Angle. The *naïve detector* is promoted to a memory cell when the number of its correctly classified messages exceeds the preset threshold n_m, and it is then removed from current *Detector Set*. Each member of *Detector Set* and *Memory Set* is labeled identically with its corresponding *support vector*. Each memory cell is assigned a *lifespan*. There are two sorts of support vectors, one sort represents non-spam and the other sort represents spam. The way of the generation of detectors adopted here is an implementation of a positive–negative selection algorithm. An overview of the generation process of *Detector Set* and *Memory Set* is described in Algorithm 12.2.

For classification criterion of *SVM*, there are no *Detector Set* and *Memory Set*. We just need to train the SVM by using the samples only.

12.4.5 Classification Criterion

Four kinds of classification criteria are developed as uninterrupted detection for spam. There are detailed performance comparisons made in the experiments. The criteria are described as follows.

1. *Hamming distance*: This approach calculates the *Hamming Distance* between the message to be classified and each *naïve detector* and each *memory cell*. Each one that meets the minimum distance is added to a set called the *Committee*. Each member of the *Committee* votes through its label. The final label of the message is determined by majority vote of the *Committee*. In circumstances where the votes of the two sides are equal, the message is classified as non-spam. This action is taken because misclassifying a non-spam as a spam is much more serious than the opposite. Under the circumstance of using the binary representation of the feature vector, the minimum *Hamming Distance* is equivalent to the minimum *Euclidean Distance*. Thus, this decision making is equivalent to *Nearest Neighbor* (NN). Also, there is an optional procedure called *mutation*, in which each member in the *Committee* can be mutated. The committee member that makes one correct decision is mutated to get closer to the message in the feature space. The committee member that makes a mistake is moved farther away from the message. This idea is implemented by changing some entries of the vector to be identical with or different from the corresponding entries of the message. The number of mutated entries is proportional to the mutation *rate* which is preset in advance. The procedure of classification using *Hamming Distance* with mutation is outlined in Algorithm 12.3.
2. *Included angle*: In this approach, the included angle is used as the measure of classification. We compute the cosine value of included angle between the message to be classified and each *naïve detector* and each *memory cell*. The one with maximum cosine value is added to the *Committee* set. The following process is just the same as *Hamming Distance* without mutation procedure.
3. *SVM*: This method directly uses SVM to classify the message. It locates and classifies the message on the *optimal hyperplane* as shown in Figure 12.1.
4. *Weighted voting*: This method is a combination of *Hamming Distance*, *Included Angle*, and *SVM*. For *Hamming Distance* and *Included Angle*, *Committee* voting can be considered voting at the first level. *SVM* is regarded as the voting of *support vectors* in Equation 12.3. The idea of weighted voting is to use the results of above three to vote at the second level, while the weight of each single method can be preset in advance and updated dynamically according to its performance. Specifically, the approach that performs best can be weighted higher the others lower.

12.4.6 Update of the Classifier

The task of on-line e-mail classification is actually to process data in stream mode. The content of e-mails and user's interests change constantly, and a classifier built from previous data may not always be suitable for future data. Therefore, *EM technique* is adopted for incremental update of the classifier.

Given a model *classifier$_t$* at time t, once the number of messages exceeding the margin is equal to or greater than n_e, the update of *classifier$_t$* takes place.

Algorithm 12.3 Classification using hamming distance with mutation

---

Input: The message waiting for classification.
Output: The label of the message.

for each *detector* ∈ (*Detector Set* ∪ *Memory Set*) **do**
    Compute the *hamming distance* between *detector* and *message*
    Elements_Iden ⇐ positions of entries identical with *message*
    Elements_Diff ⇐ positions of entries different from *message*
end for

Add the ones with minimum *hamming distance* to set *Committee*

if Number of detectors with non-spam label ≥ those with spam label **then**
    labelofMsg ⇐ non-spam
else
    labelofMsg ⇐ spam
end if
                ▷ The following is the process of mutation, it is optional
for each *detector* ∈ *Committee* **do**
    if *detector* correctly classifies the *message* **then**
        num_mutate ⇐ ⌈ *size of Elements_Diff* ∗ *ratio* ⌉
        repeat
            pos ⇐ Randomly pick up a position not picked previously from
Elements_Diff
            Take NOT operation to the entry of vector of *detector* at *pos*
        until num_mutate times
    else
        num_mutate ⇐ ⌈ *size of Elements_Iden* ∗ *ratio* ⌉
        repeat
            pos ⇐ Randomly pick up a position not picked previously from
Elements_Iden
            Take NOT operation to the entry of vector of *detector* at *pos*
        until num_mutate times
    end if
end for

For classification criteria of *Hamming Distance* and *Included Angle*, the *Detector Set* and *Memory Set* of *classifier_t*, together with n_e messages, are used as training data to obtain a new model *classifier_{t+1}*. The *memory cells* with positive *lifespan* are reserved during each update, regardless whether the memory cells are the newly derived support vectors or not. When SVM is used as the classification criterion, we only need

---

Algorithm 12.4 Update of the *classifier$_t$*

Input: *classifier$_t$*
Output: *classifier$_{t+1}$*

DetectorSet$_{t+1}$ $\Leftarrow \phi$
IncrementalMem $\Leftarrow \phi$
MemorySet$_{t+1}$ $\Leftarrow$ memory cells in *MemorySet$_t$* whose *lifespan* > 0
Training Set $\Leftarrow$ *DetectorSet$_t$* $\cup$ *MemorySet$_t$* $\cup$ {n_e *messages*}
SVM$_{t+1}$ $\Leftarrow$ SVM constructed from *Training Set*
DetectorSet$_{t+1}$ $\Leftarrow$ *Support Vectors* derived from SVM$_{t+1}$

for each *msg* $\in$ *Training Set* **do**
    Use *DetectorSet$_{t+1}$* to classify *msg* in terms of certain criterion
    for each *naïve detector* participating in decision making and judging
correctly **do**
        Increment the number of correctly classified messages of *naïve detector*
    end for
end for

for each *naïve detector* $\in$ *DetectorSet$_{t+1}$* **do**
    if the number of correctly classified messages exceeds the threshold n_m **then**
        IncrementalMem $\Leftarrow$ *IncrementalMem* $\cup$ {*naïve detector*}
    end if
end for

MemorySet$_{t+1}$ $\Leftarrow$ *MemorySet$_{t+1}$* $\cup$ *IncrementalMem*
Assign a *lifespan* to each member of *MemorySet$_{t+1}$*
DetectorSet$_{t+1}$ $\Leftarrow$ *DetectorSet$_{t+1}$* $-$ *IncrementalMem*

---

to construct the SVM$_{t+1}$ of *classifier$_{t+1}$*, by using the *support vectors* of SVM$_t$ and n_e messages as training data, because there are no *Detector Set* and *Memory Set* in this case. Algorithm 12.4 lists this process in details.

Through the duration of two successive EM updates, there will be some slight updates for the *Detector* and *Memory Sets*. The number of its correctly classified messages is increased one when *naïve detector* makes a correct classification. The one whose number of correctly classified messages exceeds the threshold n_m is added to *Memory Set* immediately. The lifespan of each memory cell decreases one after each classification. Therefore, slight updates are not needed for SVM classification criterion.

12.4.7 Purge of Out-of-Date Knowledge

As sliding window is used for tracing the changes in the content of e-mail, user's interests, and purging knowledge no longer in active use. In this chapter, the incoming e-mail stream is considered batches with a given size of b. A window includes w classifiers which are built by the previous $1, 2, \ldots, w$ batches, respectively. Each classifier in the window has a corresponding weight, which denotes the relative importance. Each classifier updates independently according to EM technique when the number of messages exceeding the margin is equal to or greater than n_e. When a new e-mail arrives, each classifier classifies it independently using some criterion described in Section 12.4.5 and gives a label to this e-mail accordingly. The final label of the e-mail is determined by a strategy of majority voting. To purge of out-of-date knowledge, when a new batch arrives, the "oldest" classifier, the *classifier$_w$*, is removed from the window while remaining classifiers move one step to the right. The "youngest" classifier, the *classifier$_1$*, is newly generated by using the data of previous batch only.

12.5 Filtering Spam Using the Dynamic Updating Algorithms

The parameters of algorithm and its values used in the following experiments are all shown in Table 12.1. A legal range for each parameter is also given. The values of these parameters are obtained by trial and error during the initial verification. A range of values for each parameter is tested in the initial experiments. The values of these parameters shown in Table 12.1 are the ones that work well in the initialization, which then are adopted in the experiments in this chapter. The initial experiments

Table 12.1 Parameters and Its Values of Proposed Approaches

Parameter	Val.	Ran.
w (size of the window)	3 or 5	≥ 1
b (size of the batch)	60	≥ 1
n_e (number of messages exceeding the margin)	30	≥ 1
n_m (threshold of promotion for a naïve detector)	5	≥ 1
Lifespan (lifespan of the memory cell)	60	≥ 1
Ratio (the ratio for mutation)	5%	[0, 1]

Val., value; Ran., range; Met., method; Acc., accuracy; Pre., precision; Rec., recall; MR, miss rate.

of parameters with different values led to some differences in performance. Thus, a certain analysis is given for the influence of each parameter on the performance.

The size of the window is set to be odd to avoid an equal number of votes one each side. When the size of the window is larger than some threshold, the computational speed will decrease because the update of the classifiers consumes more CPU time (because there are more classifiers held in the window), yet the performance does not improve on noticeably or even gets worse. Therefore, a window with good performance and fast speed is desirable. A relatively small window (with window size 3 or 5) is adopted with competent performance in the experiments.

The size of the batch should be set based on the characteristics of the data stream. When the data changes dramatically, the size of the batch should be small to purge of out-of-data knowledge (i.e., the slide process of the window) can be carried out in time. A large batch size can be adopted for a smooth data stream. The variations of the corpus PU1 and Ling used in the experiments are not big and obvious, therefore, a relatively large batch size (i.e., 60) is adopted in the experiments.

The number of messages exceeding the margin (n_e) should not be too small or too large. When n_e is too small, noises will cause vibration and the frequent update of the classifiers is too time consuming. When n_e is too big, the classifier can not be updated in time to reflect or capture the novel data distribution. The vibration and the delayed update degrade the performance severely. Therefore a proper n_e should be chosen for the experiments. A ne of 30 balances the frequency of classifier update and the vibration. Thus, $ne = 30$ is used in all experiments.

Similar to n_e, the threshold of promotion for a naive detector (n_m) should be set properly. When n_m is too small, it is very easy for a naive detector to satisfy the threshold, but many of the promoted naive detectors are not representative (those matching only a small amount of messages). This fact lowers the effectiveness of the memory set. When n_m is too large, it will be too difficult for a naive detector to become a memory cell, in turn, the size of the memory may be zero. The goal is to maintain an efficient memory set with relatively small size. Testing showed the value 5 meets this requirement well.

The lifespan of the memory cell Lifespan controls the aging process of memory cells. This value should not be too small, otherwise, memory cells will make no contribution to the classification because they have been purged before matching with similar messages. If the lifespan is too long, the useless memory cells can not be expelled in time. The value of lifespan and batch size are set to be same in these experiments. This fact implies that a memory cell correctly classifying only one piece of e-mail in a batch can survive.

Furthermore, the ratio for mutation must be set properly in experiments. A ratio that is too small will lead to the coverage of a mutant nearly the same as the mutated one, which only increases the space used without any improvement in performance. Yet, the mutants generated in too large of a ratio may be dramatically different from the original one but still have the same label. This fact leads to a wrong e-mail classification. The ratio is set at 5% in these experiments.

LIBSVM software package is used for the implementation of the SVM [34]. The linear kernel, polynomial kernel, RBF kernel, and sigmoid kernel are tested in the initial experiments. The difference in the performances of different kernels is slight. The included angle classification criterion is only feasible on linear kernel, in turn, the linear kernel is adopted in the experiments. The parameter C of SVM is determined as follows. The range of the parameter C for the test is in the integer interval [1,65]. C is picked where it achieves the highest classification accuracy on the training samples as the final C value. The accuracy on the training samples is measured by 10-fold validation.

The weights of classifiers in the window are set to be identical. All experiments are conducted on a PC with CPU of AMD Athlon 3200+ and 448M RAM. The experiments compare the different classification criteria described in Section 12.4.5. The eight methods to be compared in the experiments are listed in Table 12.2.

The SVM on the farthest right of the window only (M5) is the approach mentioned in Reference [212]. A *window* is maintained and each *classifier* in the *window* updates independently according to EM technique. Yet, only the *classifier*$_w^t$ is used to predict the label of the new coming e-mail.

The SVM without a window (M6) can be regarded as a special case because the *window* size is 1. The classification is performed successively by the unique SVM classifier, which updates itself according to EM technique.

The SVM with 90% Support Vectors without window (M7) is a method which makes a trade-off between performance and the speed of execution. The *support vectors* are sorted in descending order according to the corresponding coefficients, which indicate the relative importance of the *support vectors*. The 10% of *support vectors* at the rear of the sorted queue are discarded and the other 90% support vectors are used to compute w^* by Equation 12.4. The other processes are just the same as M6.

Table 12.2 Eight Methods with Different Classification Criterion for Comparison in the Experiments

Met.	Description
M1	The hamming as classification criterion without mutation
M2	The hamming as classification criterion with mutation
M3	The included angle as classification criterion
M4	The SVM as criterion
M5	The SVM on the farthest right of the window only
M6	The SVM without a window
M7	The SVM with 90% support vectors without window
M8	The weighted voting as classification criterion

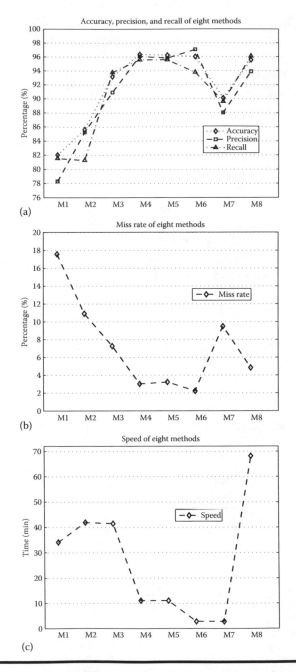

Figure 12.4 Accuracy, precision, recall, miss rate, and speed on testing set of partitions 3–10 (880 messages), using partitions 1–2 (219 messages) as training set with window size 5, on corpus PU1. (a) Accuracy, precision, recall (b) Miss rate, and (c) speed.

We choose different combinations of partitions in each corpus to construct training set and testing set, the window size is 3 or 5, respectively. Figure 12.4 shows the accuracy, precision, recall, miss rate, and speed of the eight methods on PU1. Partitions 1–2(219 messages) are used as training set. The partitions 3–10(880 messages) are used as testing set, and 5 is used as the window size. Figure 12.5 shows the performance measures of the eight methods on Ling. The partitions 9–10(580 messages) are used as training set. Partitions 1–8(2313 messages) are used as testing set, and 3 is used as the window size. The performances of the experiments are averaged on different combinations of partitions of corpus and are listed in Tables 12.3 through 12.6.

Figure 12.6a shows the variations of classifier's *Detector Set* and *Memory Set* during its lifetime from initially generated by batch 1 to being removed from *window* on PU1. The *included angle* is used as classification criterion and 5 as window size. Figure 12.6b shows, for SVM classification criterion, the variation of classifier's *support vectors* during its lifetime from initially generated by batch 1 to removed from the *window*. Abscissa 1 denotes the generation of the classifier and other abscissas indicate each time when the *EM-Update* technique is used to update the classifier.

Tables 12.7 and 12.8 show the performances of Naïve Bayesian, Linger-V, and SVM-IG on corpus PU1 and Ling reported in References 11,14,41, and 112. Linger-V is a NN-based system for automatic e-mail classification. The Naïve Bayesian, the original version of corpus is adopted, while Linger-V and SVM-IG use stemming version. All these results are obtained by using 10-fold validation. In References 11,14,41, and 112, the authors only report the accuracy, precision, and recall, the miss rate given here is derived by the given three indexes.

12.6 Discussion

In this section, we analyze the experimental results in detail and give explanations for them. The eight methods are divided into three groups as shown in Table 12.9.

Each method in AIS group has a *Detector Set* and a *Memory Set*, which is the inspiration for the HIS. Methods in SVM group use SVM as the basic classification tool. The Weighted Voting (WV) group contains the M8 approach, which combines the classification criteria of *Hamming distance, included angle*, and *SVM*.

The results on corpus PU1 show that methods M4, M5, and M6 in SVM group obtain a good performance on accuracy, precision, recall, and a miss rate below 5%. Performance of M7 degrades dramatically compared to M6, while an advantage in speed is not obvious. A possible explanation for this fact is that the number of *support vectors* is small as shown (Figure 12.6b). As a result, the number of the 10% small support vectors is also small, the absolute number of *support vectors* is not reduced remarkably, therefore, there is no improvement in speed. When the number of *support vectors* is tremendously large, the advantage in speed may be increased.

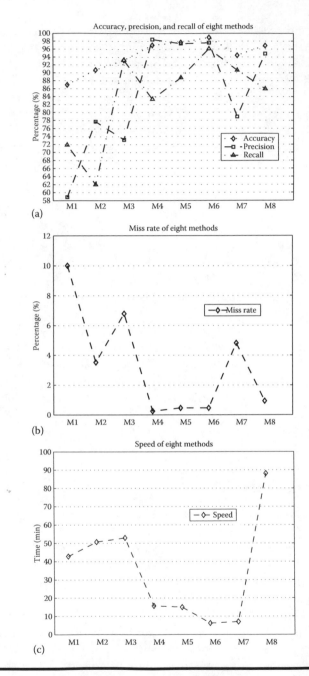

Figure 12.5 Accuracy, precision, recall, miss rate, and speed on testing set of partitions 1–8 (2313 messages), using partitions 9–10 (580 messages) as training set with window size 3, on corpus Ling. (a) Accuracy, precision, recall, (b) Miss rate, and (c) speed.

Table 12.3   Performances of Eight Methods on Corpus PU1 with Window Size 3

Met.	Acc. (%)	Pre. (%)	Rec. (%)	MR (%)
M1	80.758	77.2524	79.471	18.239
M2	83.4483	82.8473	78.4758	12.6785
M3	91.0182	88.1228	91.8624	9.6393
M4	95.7811	95.4235	94.9131	3.5426
M5	95.7345	95.0696	95.1905	3.8418
M6	96.2926	96.5779	94.9422	2.6567
M7	92.9538	90.646	93.7673	7.6819
M8	94.3057	93.309	93.7322	5.2467

Met., method; Acc., accuracy; Pre., precision; Rec., recall; MR, miss rate.

Table 12.4   Performances of Eight Methods on Corpus PU1 with Window Size 5

Met.	Acc. (%)	Pre. (%)	Rec. (%)	MR (%)
M1	81.5696	79.2014	78.5389	16.0689
M2	86.2257	87.3313	80.2468	9.1166
M3	91.6421	89.4713	91.6916	8.397
M4	96.1644	96.3969	94.7746	2.7533
M5	96.3495	95.9985	95.708	3.1519
M6	96.2926	96.5779	94.9422	2.6567
M7	92.9538	90.646	93.7673	7.6819
M8	95.2396	95.2084	93.8697	3.6927

Met., method; Acc., accuracy; Pre., precision; Rec., recall; MR, miss rate.

The strategy of using classifiers in the *window* to vote (M4) does not show in advantage when compared to M5 and M6. This fact suggests that changes to the contents and user's interests do not present problem, or the variation of samples is too little in the PU1 corpus. When there are notable drifts (e.g., a healthy person might have no interests on pharmaceutical at first, but he changes his interests on

Table 12.5 Performances of Eight Methods on Corpus Ling with Window Size 3

Met.	Acc. (%)	Pre. (%)	Rec. (%)	MR (%)
M1	86.0903	56.4391	77.309	12.1604
M2	90.8851	77.0192	64.3103	3.8227
M3	92.4888	71.1464	93.1514	7.643
M4	97.0434	97.5746	84.2888	0.4167
M5	97.7805	96.4355	90.7653	0.657
M6	98.7186	96.0549	96.2479	0.7897
M7	96.3315	84.6912	95.5456	3.5119
M8	96.6121	91.5655	87.9770	1.6677

Met., method; Acc., accuracy; Pre., precision; Rec., recall; MR, miss rate.

Table 12.6 Performances of Eight Methods on Corpus Ling with Window Size 5

Met.	Acc. (%)	Pre. (%)	Rec. (%)	MR (%)
M1	87.0358	59.1022	77.9555	11.1557
M2	92.2556	83.6818	66.1891	2.5532
M3	92.8725	72.0113	94.0351	7.3591
M4	97.6485	97.0959	88.483	0.5264
M5	98.0584	95.4202	92.7775	0.8865
M6	98.7186	96.0549	96.2479	0.7897
M7	96.3315	84.6912	95.5456	3.5119
M8	97.1328	91.9936	90.7708	1.6

Met., method; Acc., accuracy; Pre., precision; Rec., recall; MR, miss rate.

the pharmaceutical when he faces a health problem), the "younger" experts with latest knowledge, such as *classifier*$_1^t$, *classifier*$_2^t$, can reflect the immediate variation. Thus the drift can be tracked and a good performance can be achieved when a sliding window is used.

SVM group outperforms the other groups in performance and speed. The method for SVM M6 is the best one for performance and speed.

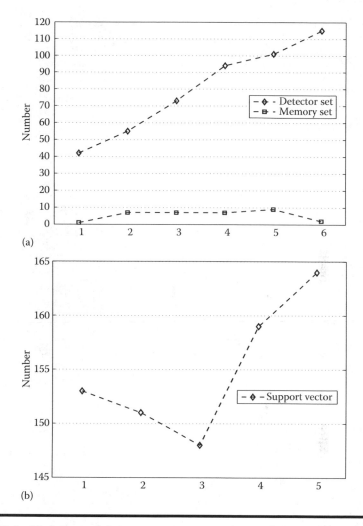

Figure 12.6   Variation of detector set, memory set, and support vectors, using partitions 1–5 (549 messages) as training set, partitions 6–10 (550 messages) as testing set, on corpus PU1. (a) Detector set, memory set and (b) Support vector.

The performance of AIS group has been unsatisfactory. This is especially true for the *Hamming Distance* method. The original intention to construct a *Detector Set* and a *Memory Set* via SVM is to utilize the "representative" feature of *support vectors*. The *detectors* would be regraded as "boundary detectors" and the size of the set would be relatively small. When using *Hamming Distance* as the classification criterion, using minimum distance to label the e-mail (Nearest Neighbor) may not reflect the distribution of two classes as the optimal hyperplane in SVM does. Performance of *Included Angle* is superior to that of *Hamming Distance*. The limitation of this

Table 12.7   Performances of Naïve Bayesian
(NB), Linger-V, and SVM-IG on Corpus PU1,
Using 10-Fold Cross Validation

Met.	Acc. (%)	Pre. (%)	Rec. (%)	MR (%)
NB	91.076	95.11	83.98	3.4
Linger-V	93.45	96.46	88.36	2.588
SVM-IG	93.18	95.7	88.4	3.1

Table 12.8   Performances of Naïve Bayesian
(NB), Linger-V, and SVM-IG on Corpus Ling,
Using 10-Fold Cross Validation

Met.	Acc. (%)	Pre. (%)	Rec. (%)	MR (%)
NB	96.408	96.85	81.10	0.539
Linger-V	98.2	95.62	93.56	0.875
SVM-IG	96.85	99	81.9	0.17

Table 12.9   Groups of Methods Compared in
Experiments

Group	Methods
AIS	M1, M2, M3
SVM	M4, M5, M6, M7
WV	M8

method is that only linear kernel can be used for SVM, otherwise, the cosine value cannot be computed for the included angle between two vectors. Another characteristic of AIS group is to have a *Memory Set*. Figure 12.6a shows that the size of the *Memory Set* is small and stable. The number of *memory cells* is proportional to the presetting threshold. The lower the threshold, the more *memory cells*. The value of lifespan and batch size are set to be same, which implies that a *memory cell* correctly classifying only one piece of mail in a batch can survive. The intention introducing a *Memory Set* is to maintain those "outstanding" *memory cells*, which are not updated according to EM-Update. Also lifespan is introduced to age and purge those *memory cells* no longer in active use. The curve depicting the size of *Detector Set* in

Figure 12.6a shows the number of *detectors* increases after each EM-Update since the classifier is initially generated from batch 1. The explanation is based on the more data the classifier used, the more knowledge that is being accumulated, and more *detectors* are generated. Figure 12.6b shows the variation of *support vectors* for illustration. The curve drops then goes up. The reason is that SVM has the chance to use relatively more examples (549 messages) in the training stage, therefore, more *support vectors* can be generated. The first time the EM-Update, the number of *support vectors* together with messages exceeding the margin is relatively smaller than the training examples. Thus, the number of newly generated *support vectors* decreases accordingly. During the filtering process of the spam, the amount of the data increases, and the number of *support vectors* will increase as the data come in.

The M8 method in WV group is not better than M4 in SVM group. The reason for this is that the performance of the *Hamming Distance* and the *Included Angle* is not in accordance with SVM.

When the size of *window* increases from 3 to 5, the performance of AIS group and WV group rises, while the improvement of performance is not noticeable for the SVM group. Augmentation of the *window* makes the classifiers at the right of the window (the "older" experts) have more data. Furthermore, the bigger the size of the window, the more the data that can be used. As a result, if the content of the data does not drift dramatically, a considerable improvement of performance can be achieved.

In corpus Ling there is an unbalance between the numbers of negative examples and positive examples. As a consequence, the results on Ling differ from that on PU1 in several aspects. Each method gets higher accuracy and lower miss rate on Ling than on PU1. In particular, SVM group has lower than 1% miss rate. As the spam rate of Ling is only 16.63%, misclassifying a spam to legitimate mail has much more negative influence on precision and recall than that on accuracy.

Methods of AIS group do not give a better balance between accuracy, precision and recall as shown in Figure 12.5a.

The presented algorithms show competent performances compared to current methods listed in Tables 12.7 and 12.8. It is noticeable that the reported results of Naïve Bayesian, Linger-V, and SVM are all obtained by using 10-fold cross validation. In each iteration, 90% of the data is used for training while the other 10% is used for its test. Therefore, the classifiers can estimate the underlying class distribution as accurately as possible. This action will achieve better performance. However, these methods may not work in practice because the data available for training is limited and only accounts for a very small percentage of the data. As shown in Figures 12.4 and 12.5, when using only 20% of the data of the corpus for training, the performance of proposed methods is promising. Moreover, the proposed methods in this chapter are dynamic, the update of the classifier and the slide of the window are carrying out constantly throughout the total running process. Therefore, these methods are remarkably suitable for most of the real applications of anti-spam programs.

12.7 Summary

In this chapter, immune based dynamic updating algorithm based on incremental SVM and AIS for uninterrupted detection of spam in the e-mail stream is introduced. A sliding window is used to label e-mail and trace the dynamic change of the content of e-mail and user's interests. The final label of a new e-mail is given by majority voting. The EM-update technique is also used for dynamic update of classifiers in the window. The sliding window is employed to purge of out-of-date knowledge. Eight methods for the uninterrupted detection are developed, these include: Hamming Distance (with or without mutation), Included Angle, SVM, and Weighted Voting. Extensive experimental results show that the proposed approaches give promising performances and will be effective and efficient tools in many practical applications for spam detection.

Chapter 13

AIS-Based Spam Filtering System and Implementation

This chapter presents the Artificial Immune System (AIS) based spam filtering system and its implementation way in the real world [194]. After a brief introduction, the integral framework of the AIS-based spam filtering model is described, which is mainly constituted by feature construction, e-mail classification, and classifier updating with the techniques introduced in the previous Chapters 4–6 and 11–12. Then we give an overall cognitive of the Postfix e-mail server based implementation way. The detailed implementation factor are then described one by one, including design of milter-plugin, maildrop-based local filter, user interests–based parameter design, and user interaction. Finally, the test and results analysis are displayed.

13.1 Introduction

Artificial Immune System (AIS) is an inter-discipline research area [205] that aims to build computational intelligence models [42,71] by taking inspiration from Biological Immune System (BIS). BIS is an adaptive natural system [54], which possesses several interesting properties [58,204] such as distributed detection, noise tolerance, and reinforcement learning. It can detect and react to invading pathogens based on signals and interaction among immune cells. Taking immune processes as good metaphors, many AIS models [54] have been proposed to solve engineering problems. Some prevalent ones are negative selection, clonal selection, immune network model, and danger theory algorithm. These models have been applied to a number of real-world problems [4,56,99] such as pattern recognition, data mining, spam filtering [247], and computer security [70].

Spam filtering is an important and typical pattern recognition problem, as spams cause many problems to our daily-communication life. In solving the problem, both classical statistical methods and AIS methods have been presented, and most of them focus on studying feature extraction methods and design of classifiers. The main function of feature extraction is to extract discriminative information from messages, and transform messages into feature vectors. The statistical feature extraction methods try to collect and analyze numerical characteristics of messages, such as term frequencies, and relation between terms, and e-mail categories. Some prevalent ones are Bag-of-Words (BoW) [13], Sparse Binary Polynomial Hashing (SBPH), and Orthogonal Sparse Bigrams (OSB) [170]. Different from the statistical ones, the AIS methods [139] construct feature vectors by mimicking the process of antibody creation in BIS. In design of classifiers, classical pattern recognition methods, for example, Naive Bayes (NB) [40,156], Support Vector Machine (SVM) [67], *k*-Nearest Neighbor (*k*-NN) [12,157], and Artificial Neural Network (ANN) [41,228] were proposed on the basis of statistical theory. In contrast, AIS models were inspired by natural functions and mechanisms of BIS [88,139].

These statistical methods and AIS ones are quite different in terms of both origins and principles, which endow them with quite distinct properties. Combining the strength of statistical approaches with the AIS ones may help achieve better performance. In this chapter, we introduce and discuss several recent works of our laboratory [154,155,190,194,246−248], which applied mixed principles to feature attraction, classifier combination, and classifier updating, so as to demonstrate the rationality of combining statistical and AIS methods for spam filtering. In addition, we present a generic framework of an immune based model for spam filtering, and online implementation strategies are given to demonstrate how to build an immune based intelligent e-mail server.

13.2 Framework of AIS-Based Spam Filtering Model

There exist many explanations about the mechanisms of BIS. An explanation may be superior for analyzing some specific immune phenomena, but less persuasive for some other aspects. For AIS practitioners, it is not quite necessary to find which theory is better in explaining immune mechanisms. What matters most is the heuristic principles behind these explanations. By taking inspiration from two prevalent immune theories, we proposed several immune based spam filtering methods [154,155,190,194,246−248], in which statistical information is also well considered [193].

According to Self-Non-Self (SNS) theory [201], two typical immune processes play important roles in the BIS: the primary response and the secondary response. The primary response occurs when a type of pathogen appears in the body for the first time. As the BIS is not familiar with the pathogen, the antibodies with affinity to the pathogen are produced slowly. However, when the same pathogen is encountered next time, the secondary response is aroused, and the concentration of relevant antibodies increases rapidly. It is worth of noticing that the concentration of antibodies is a key point in recognizing the corresponding pathogen. A high concentration of antibodies reflects that the BIS detects the pathogen with high confidence. From another perspective, concentrations of antibodies characterize the detection of pathogens in BIS. Based on this observation, we proposed immune concentration based feature extraction methods for spam filtering: global concentration based methods [155,190] and local concentration based methods [246,248].

Danger Theory (DT), proposed by Matzinger [128], is a novel biological paradigm for explaining mechanisms of BIS. According to DT, the cells of the body interact with each other through match signals, danger signals, and danger zones. In BIS, antibodies bind to (match) antigens when the affinity between them is higher than a certain threshold. However, the antigens would not be culled from the body until the antibodies receive a danger signal from distressed cells. Danger signals indicate that the distressed cells are infected to death, and the cells release the signals to antibodies nearby (within the danger zone) just to activate immune response. Thus, the danger signals can be regarded as a confirmation of the match signals between antibodies and antigens. The interaction using the signals ensures the robustness of BIS. We find that the signals are quite helpful in combining classifiers, and design a DT-based Ensemble (DTE) method [247] in the classification phase of spam filtering.

Besides detecting antigens, dynamics of immune cells is also one of the most important properties possessed by BIS. Antibodies can evolve to recognize emerging antigens, and the recognition memory will be preserved to detect antigens more effectively next time. In addition, there are some ways in measuring the importance of antibodies, such as lifespan and weights. The dynamic change of lifespan and weights ensures that the existing antibodies give the best protection to the body. Mimicking the mechanism, we presented dynamic strategies for classifier updating in [154,194].

Based on these previous works, we present a generic framework of an immune based spam filtering model, as depicted in Figure 13.1. According to the model, concentration based feature vectors are extracted from messages by computing match concentration of detections. Classifiers are then built on the concentration vectors of training corpus. Finally, incoming messages can be classified by using the DTE method. In addition, classifiers are updated at all times based on the drift of messages and classification performance. In the following subsections, we briefly introduce and discuss the principles of these methods, and analyze the rationality of combining statistical principles with AIS ones.

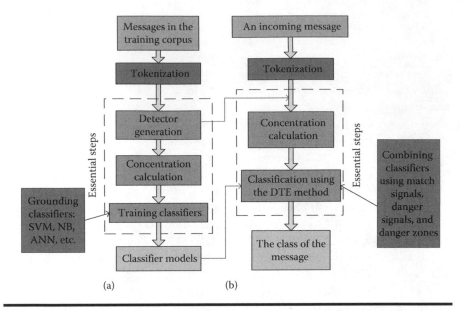

(a)   (b)

Figure 13.1 Training and classification phases of the immune-based model. (a) Training phase of the model and (b) classification phase of the model.

13.3 Postfix-Based Implementation

Postfix is an efficient e-mail server system developed by a well-known security expert from IBM, whose name is Wietse Venema, to replace Sendmail. It uses a modular design way and a large number of excellent techniques to achieve security purpose. Now, Postfix has been developed into an outstanding Mail Transfer Agent (MTA) with rich functionality, good scalability, and strong security. Meanwhile, there remain active developments on the Postfix system, making it suitable for systems with high traffic and large load.

The main process of Postfix processing e-mails is shown in Figure 13.2: e-mails are transferred to the Postfix system through the Simple Mail Transfer Protocol (SMTP)

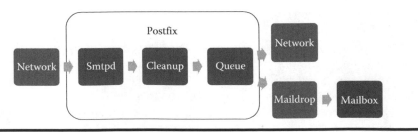

Figure 13.2 E-mail processing of Postfix.

from the Internet; the "Smtpd" process of the system is responsible for receiving e-mails and the e-mails are passed to the "Cleanup" process through the pipeline for processing; the processed e-mails are put in the queue "Queue"; the system takes the processed e-mails out the queue by a certain time, and if an e-mail is sent to a local mailbox, it will be passed to the program "maildrop" and put into the local user's mail directory, while if an e-mail is sent to other domains, the system will connect other e-mail server through the SMTP protocol and send it out.

The Postfix e-mail server system has provided three ways to implement spam filtering: (1) implement the "milter" interface and build a filter plug-in, which interacts with the "Smtpd" process and scans the e-mails coming into Postfix in real time; (2) establish a filter program where the e-mails are first transferred into the program for filtering before passed to the "Cleanup" process; and (3) establish a filter program where the e-mails which should be put into the local directory are first transferred to the program for filtering by the MTA (the "maildrop" program) and then put into the appropriate directory.

In real-world application, we use Postfix as e-mail server, and apply the immune based model as a plug-in unit for spam filtering. Two strategies can be adopted, either by using the milter interface or the maildrop interface. Figure 13.3a and b respectively depict the two strategies. The immune-based model is implemented

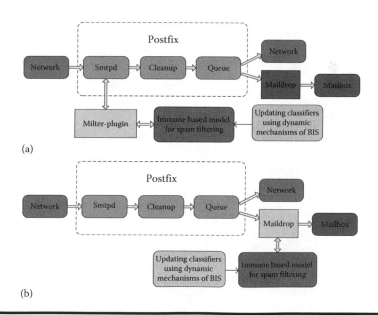

(a)

(b)

Figure 13.3 Implementation of hybrid intelligent methods on Postfix server. (a) Implementation by using milter interface and (b) implementation by using maildrop interface.

as an intelligent filter in the processing e-mails. Besides, immune based dynamic updating strategies are adopted in order to build an adaptive system [193].

13.3.1 Design of Milter-Plugin

Study of the Milter interface is important, which is a plug-in agreement of Sendmail, the widely used e-mail server system under UNIX systems. In order to reuse the Milter-plugin left by the Sendmail system, the Postfix system has agreement to support Sendmail restrictively. The interaction between Milter-based plug-in and Postfix can be seen in Figure 13.3a. Postfix simulates the e-mail processing way of Sendmail. It receives e-mails by SMTP and sends the segmented e-mail content (header and body) to the plug-in. The plug-in reads the e-mail part by part and scans the content. It will make some appropriate modifications (such as the mark of whether the e-mail is Spam) and finally give a conclusion of accepting or rejecting this e-mail. Postfix will immediately accept or reject the e-mail according to the results given by the plug-in. During the process of receiving e-mails, Postfix also interacts with the Milter plug-in, while the speed of scanning e-mails is low (for you need to decode mime and determine whether an e-mail is spam). Thus, large number of concurrent e-mails will affect the efficiency of the system. In addition, all the e-mails received from the Internet by SMTP will go through the plug-in, while there may be missing for dealing with local e-mails as well as dealing with e-mails of nonlocal domains.

13.3.2 Maildrop-Based Local Filter

Maildrop is a MDA (Mail Deliver Agent) software that is used with MTA under Linux. As the e-mail delivery program, Maildrop supports Maildir mailbox (i.e., catalog form mailbox, which is more flexible than single-file form mailbox), user-defined scripts, rule based delivery, customized filters, etc. System that incorporates the filter with Maildrop and Postfix is shown in Figure 13.3b. Maildrop receives the e-mails sent by Postfix and then uses xfilter command to send e-mails to the filter. The filter scans and analyzes the e-mail and adds a mark of whether the e-mail is spam (X-SPAMCHECK). When Maildrop finds that an e-mail is marked as spam, it will put the e-mail into the specified directory, otherwise the e-mail will be placed into the normal directory of the user.

13.4 User Interests–Based Parameter Design

The spam filter should be trained according to the user feedback to better adapt to the new situations. However, when the number of users increases, the conflict of interest between different users could not be ignored. It is difficult to reconcile this contradiction for filters that use the global parameters under such conditions, and even it is possible for an e-mail to be used for repeated training. Thus, if the filter uses different parameters for different users, this kind of problem can be well handled.

The general algorithm uses a single set of parameters for all e-mails. In order to reflect the interests of different users, different recipients need to use different sets of parameters to classify e-mails. At the same time, different parameter sets are also used for different e-mails senders according to the possibility that different e-mails senders may lead to different interests of users. A parameter set corresponds to a desired set of parameters that the original algorithm needs, including the parameters that the SVM model, detecting sets and the sliding window of SVMs needs (as shown in Chapter 12). Changes of user interests could be well tracked by tracking the changes in these parameters, especially changes of the keywords in the detecting sets.

Meanwhile, two global arrays for saving the addresses of recipients and senders need to be added, in order to find the corresponding parameters according to the recipient and sender addresses when to select the parameters.

13.4.1 Generation and Storage of Parameters

The parameter set of the system is stored in a form of table (class of the form used in the program is $std :: map < std :: pair < int, int >, \ldots >$) as shown in Figure 13.4. The row and column numbered 0 are used as the default parameter sets for comparison. For example, the parameter set corresponding to $(0, 0)$ is the global parameter set used by the basic algorithm, and $(0, ex)$ and $(re, 0)$ correspond to the corresponding parameter sets of some sender or recipient.

Sender No. \ Recipient No.	0	1	2	......
0	Parameter	Parameter	Parameter	
1	Parameter	Parameter	Parameter	......
2	Parameter	Parameter	Parameter	
......		......		......

Figure 13.4   Storage of parameter set.

All the parameter sets are initialized and trained on the same training set. Thus all the parameter sets are originally the same. Differences between the parameter sets will gradually occur with the continuous training of new e-mails, reflecting the differences of interests between different users and the differences between different senders.

New parameters need to be added when a new recipient or sender appears during running of the server. In this case, the corresponding global parameter are selected for initialization. For example, when a new recipient is added, its parameters are initialized as the global parameters recipients by copying the contents of the column $(0, ex)$. The purpose of this action is to consider the information of current recipient or sender the same as the global, reflecting the compromise of all users' interests on the current server. On this basis, parameters of this user will change according to the user's interests when e-mails of this recipient or sender enter.

13.4.2 Selection of Parameters

When receiving a new e-mail or retraining on an e-mail, the program will set the parameter set currently used in accordance with the information of the sender and recipients of the e-mail. The program first parses the e-mail addresses of the recipient and the sender, and then finds the corresponding numbers of the recipient and sender. In the test, in order to compare the differences between the different parameter sets, four parameter sets are selected for the same e-mail to conduct classification or training operations, as shown in Figure 13.5. The four parameter sets are global

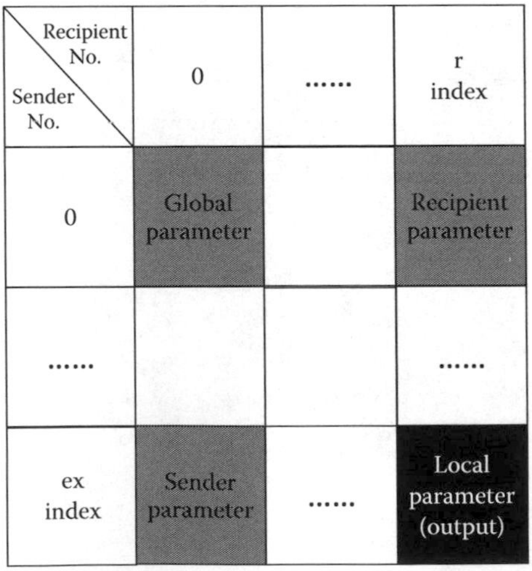

Figure 13.5   Selection of parameter set.

parameter set, recipient parameter set, sender parameter set, and local parameter set respectively.

The operations on each parameter set are exactly the same and the local parameters are selected as output. The other three sets of parameters are taken as comparison parameters, and all the results of the four sets of parameters are saved in the log for comparison and analysis.

13.5 User Interaction

Interaction with users is necessary in the use of e-mail server system. Since this system supports the POP3 (Post Office Protocol - Version 3) protocol, we can use Outlook and other softwares to operate the mailboxes, or use the web client "Extmail" (access http://mail.cil.pku.edu.cn/extmail/cgi/index.cgi). The previous two methods can both send and receive e-mails, and the server system will automatically call the filter spam to classify e-mails.

In daily use of the system, e-mail classification errors occur inevitably. There are two ways for the users to submit error messages. One method is forwarding the spam that is not filtered successfully to spammail.cil.pku.edu.cn, submitting this spam to the system for training. This method is suitable for the users who view e-mails by using POP3, for POP3 will automatically delete the e-mails downloaded in the inbox. Since POP3 will not download the filtered spam, users need to use the web client to view the spam. If there were filtered normal e-mails, the next method should be used to submit the error message.

The other method is the customized user interaction pages (http://mail.cil.pku.edu.cn/spam/feedback.cgi) as shown in Figure 13.6a. The incorrectly classified e-mails could be selected in the inbox or spam page for the retraining submission to the system, as shown in Figure 13.6b. Specifically, select the corresponding check boxes in front of e-mails and click the "This is not Spam" or "This is Spam" buttons to submit training information. This operation can submit e-mail samples for training to the program and move the e-mails to appropriate directories meanwhile.

13.6 Test and Analysis

13.6.1 Testing Method

Testing method defined for the system is as follows: The data set is divided into three parts: the training set, correction set, and testing set. The classification model is first trained on the training set, and then corrected on the correction set (retraining on the incorrectly classified e-mails in the correction set) in order to reflect the changing process of user interests. The testing set is finally used to test the accuracy of e-mail classification. Since changing of user interests is a continuous process, the correction and testing procedures are conducted repeatedly.

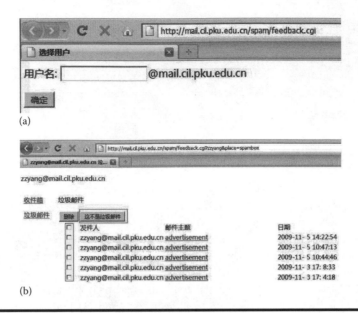

Figure 13.6 Redefined user interface. (a) Login interface and (b) submit error interface.

Performance of the model tracking user interests is verified in accordance with the accuracy curve.

In the test, the training set used is Linglemm, while the correction and testing sets are from dataset Enron. Enron has totally six parts, each of which corresponds to a user's e-mails. Test on each user is conducted individually. 10%, 30%, 50%, and 80% of the total e-mails of each user are selected to form the correction set respectively (holding the ratio of normal e-mails and spam), and the reserved part of each user is as the testing set. The correction procedure is repeated for 15 times and four tests are conducted with six users.

13.6.2 Testing Results

Figures of the testing results can be divided into two parts: one contains the accuracy changing curves of different users (Enron1 to 6) under a certain correction rate, as shown in shown in Figure 13.7a and b; the other one contains the accuracy changing curves of a certain user under different correction rates, see Figures 13.8 through 13.13. In the figures, the horizontal axis is the time axis, where accuracy of time 0 indicates that the testing accuracy before correction and accuracy of time 1 represents the testing accuracy after the first correction and so forth. The vertical axis is the accuracy axis.

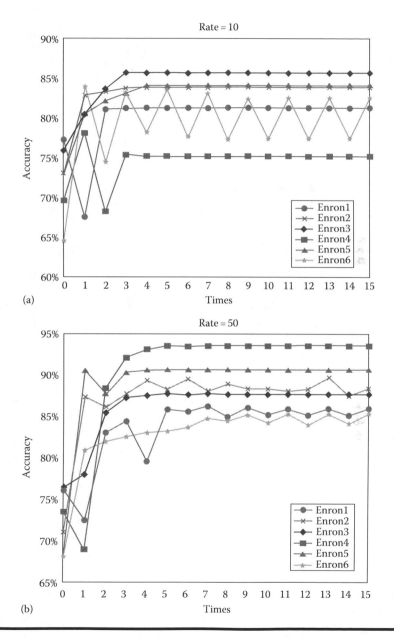

Figure 13.7   Accuracy of different users under certain correction rate. (a) Correction rate = 10 and (b) correction rate = 50.

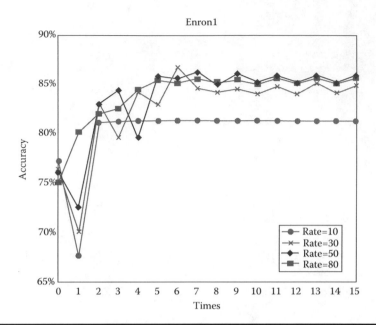

Figure 13.8   Accuracy of different correction rates of user Enron1.

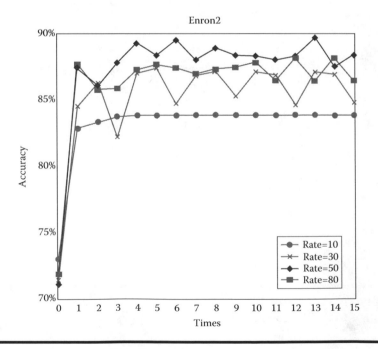

Figure 13.9   Accuracy of different correction rates of user Enron2.

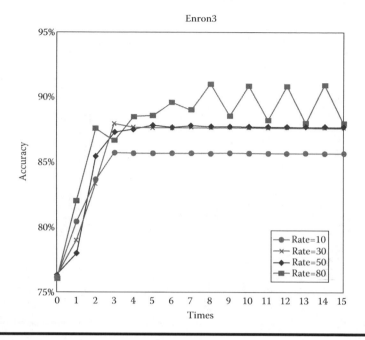

Figure 13.10   Accuracy of different correction rates of user Enron3.

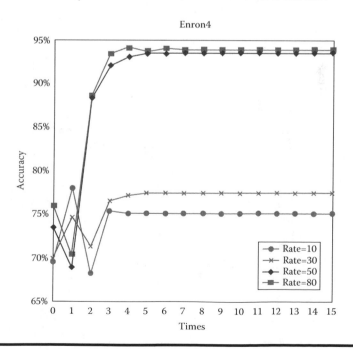

Figure 13.11   Accuracy of different correction rates of user Enron4.

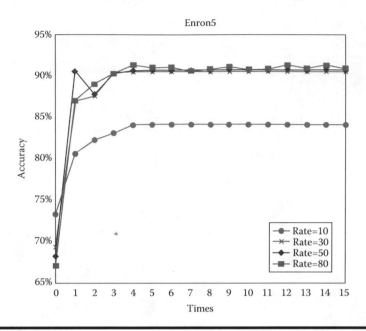

Figure 13.12   Accuracy of different correction rates of user Enron5.

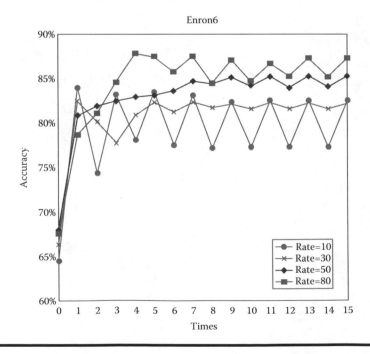

Figure 13.13   Accuracy of different correction rates of user Enron6.

13.6.3 Results Analysis

As can be seen, the testing accuracy is rising of an overall trend as the correction is performed continuously. Generally, there is a remarkable result rising from 65%~70% to 80%~90%, and the model gets stable after trained for two to three times, making it applicable for daily use. The testing accuracy curves go in two ways, one is unchanged and the other goes with sustained concussions. This depends on the property of the correction set. The former situation is that the correction set is completely separable and there is no change after each correction, resulting in stable testing accuracy. The later situation is that the correction set is not completely separable and each correction tends to normal e-mails or spam, resulting in changes of e-mail classification and the concussions of curves, but the extent of the concussions is generally small.

13.7 Summary

In this chapter, we briefly introduced our recent advances in immune based spam filtering methods, and put emphasis on combining immune theory with statistical methods. It is shown that combining immune ideas with classical statistical methods can effectively improve the performance of a spam filter. In addition, we presented a framework of an immune based spam filtering model, which demonstrates how to utilize these methods in real-world applications. In the model, immune mechanisms are brought in different phases of spam filtering model. First, concentration concept is utilized for extracting feature vectors from messages, and it is demonstrated that the concentration method is more robust and accurate than the prevalent BoW method. Mechanisms of DT are then shown to be effective in combining classifiers. Besides, dynamic mechanisms of BIS are adopted to updating classifiers of the spam filter. Finally, implementation strategies of an immune based intelligent e-mail server based on Postfix were also given. The immune based-model is built by borrowing some ideas from mechanisms of BIS. The effect of the model is not limited by the implementation details. Thus, it is natural and easy to extend the model using different implementation strategies.

References

1. A. Abi-Haidar and L. Rocha. Adaptive spam detection inspired by a cross-regulation model of immune dynamics: A study of concept drift. *Proceedings of the Seventh International Conference, ICARIS 2008, Artificial Immune Systems*, pp. 36–47, Volume 5132 of the series Lecture Notes in Computer Science, Phuket, Thailand, August 2008.

2. U. Aickelin and S. Cayzer. The danger theory and its application to artificial immune systems. In *Proceedings of the First International Conference on Artificial Immune Systems*, pp. 141–148, Canterbury, U.K., 2002.

3. U. Aickelin, P. Bentley, S. Cayzer, J. Kim, and J. McLeod. Danger theory: The link between ais and ids? In *Artificial Immune Systems*, pp. 147–155. Springer, New York, 2003.

4. U. Aickelin and S. Cayzer. The danger theory and its application to artificial immune systems. *arXiv preprint arXiv:0801.3549*, 2008.

5. U. Aickelin and J. Greensmith. Sensing danger: Innate immunology for intrusion detection. *Information Security Technical Report*, 12(4):218–227, 2007.

6. O. Al-Jarrah, I. Khater, and B. Al-Duwairi. Identifying potentially useful email header features for email spam filtering. In *ICDS 2012, The Sixth International Conference on Digital Society*, pp. 140–145, Valencia, Spain, 2012.

7. O. Amayri and N. Bouguila. Online spam filtering using support vector machines. In *IEEE Symposium on Computers and Communications, 2009. ISCC 2009.* pp. 337–340. IEEE, Sousse, Tunisia, 2009.

8. D.S. Anderson, C. Fleizach, S. Savage, and G.M. Voelker. Spamscatter: Characterizing internet scam hosting infrastructure. In *Proceedings of 16th USENIX Security Symposium on USENIX Security Symposium*, pp. 1–10. USENIX Association, 2007.

9. J. Andreas and Y. Tan. Swarm intelligence for non-negative matrix factorization. *International Journal of Swarm Intelligence Research*, 2(4):12–34, 2011.

10. J. Andreas and Y. Tan. Efficient euclidean distance transform algorithm of binary images in arbitrary dimensions. *Pattern Recognition*, 46(1):230–242, 2013.

11. I. Androutsopoulos, J. Koutsias, K.V. Chandrinos, G. Paliouras, and C.D. Spyropoulos. An evaluation of naive bayesian anti-spam filtering. In *11th European Conference on Machine Learning (ECML 2000)*, pp. 9–17. Barcelona, Spain, 2000.

12. I. Androutsopoulos, G. Paliouras, V. Karkaletsis, G. Sakkis, C.D. Spyropoulos, and P. Stamatopoulos. Learning to filter spam e-mail: A comparison of a naive bayesian

and a memory-based approach. In *4th European Conference on Principles and Practice of Knowledge Discovery in Databases*, pp. 1–13. Lyon, France, 2000.

13. I. Androutsopoulos, G. Paliouras, and E. Michelakis. Learning to filter unsolicited commercial e-mail. Technical report, Demokritos, National Center for Scientific Research, Athens, Greece, 2004.

14. I. Androutsopoulos, J. Koutsias, K. V. Chandrinos, and Constantine D. Spyropoulos. An experimental comparison of naive bayesian and keyword-based anti-spam filtering with personal e-mail messages. In *Proceedings of the 23rd Annual International ACM SIGIR Conference on Research and Development in Information Retrieval*, pp. 160–167. ACM, 2000.

15. H.B. Aradhye, G.K. Myers, and J.A. Herson. Image analysis for efficient categorization of image-based spam e-mail. In *Document Analysis and Recognition, 2005. Proceedings. Eighth International Conference on*, pp. 914–918. IEEE, 2005.

16. A. Attar, R.M. Rad, and R.E. Atani. A survey of image spamming and filtering techniques. *Artificial Intelligence Review*, 40(1):71–105, 2011.

17. S. Balachandran, D. Dasgupta, F. Nino, and D. Garrett. A framework for evolving multi-shaped detectors in negative selection. In *Foundations of Computational Intelligence, 2007. FOCI 2007. IEEE Symposium on*, pp. 401–408. IEEE, 2007.

18. J. Balthrop, F. Esponda, S. Forrest, and M. Glickman. Coverage and generalization in an artificial immune system. In *Proceedings of the Genetic and Evolutionary Computation Conference*, pp. 3–10. Citeseer, 2002.

19. Yoshua Bengio, Patrice Simard, and Paolo Frasconi. Learning long-term dependencies with gradient descent is difficult. *IEEE Transactions on, Neural Networks*, 5(2): 157–166, 1994.

20. D.J. Bernstein. Internet mail 2000. http://cr.yp.to/im2000.html, accessed: 2012.

21. G. B. Bezerra, T. V. Barra, H. M. Ferreira, H. Knidel, L. N. de Castro, and F. J. Von Zuben. An immunological filter for spam. In *Artificial Immune Systems*, pp. 446–458. Springer, New York, 2006.

22. S. Bickel and T. Scheffer. Dirichlet-enhanced spam filtering based on biased samples. *Advances in Neural Information Processing Systems*, 19:161, 2007.

23. B. Biggio, G. Fumera, I. Pillai, and F. Roli. Image spam filtering using visual information. In *Image Analysis and Processing, 2007. ICIAP 2007. 14th International Conference on*, pp. 105–110. IEEE, 2007.

24. B. Biggio, G. Fumera, I. Pillai, and F. Roli. A survey and experimental evaluation of image spam filtering techniques. *Pattern Recognition Letters*, 32(10):1436–1446, 2011.

25. E. Blanzieri and A. Bryl. A survey of learning-based techniques of email spam filtering. *Artificial Intelligence Review*, 29(1):63–92, 2008.

26. L. Bottou and V. Vapnik. Local learning algorithms. *Neural Computation*, 4(6): 888–900, 1992.

27. P.O. Boykin and V.P. Roychowdhury. Leveraging social networks to fight spam. *Computer*, 38(4):61–68, 2005.

28. J. Brownlee. Clonal selection algorithms. Technical report, Complex Intelligent Systems Laboratory (CIS), Centre for Information Technology Research (CITR), Faculty

of Information and Communication Technologies (ICT), Swinburne University of Technology, Victoria, Australia, Technical Report ID: 070209A, 2007.

29. F.M. Burnet. Clonal selection and after. *Theoretical Immunology*, 63:85, 1978.

30. Sir F. M. Burnet et al. *The Clonal Selection Theory of Acquired Immunity*. Vanderbilt University Press, Nashville, TN, 1959.

31. B. Byun, C.H. Lee, S. Webb, and C. Pu. A discriminative classifier learning approach to image modeling and spam image identification. In *Proceedings of the 4th Conference on Email and Anti-Spam*. Citeseer, 2007.

32. J. Carpinter and R. Hunt. Tightening the net: A review of current and next generation spam filtering tools. *Computers & Security*, 25(8):566–578, 2006.

33. X. Carreras and L. Marquez. Boosting trees for anti-spam email filtering. In *4th International Conference on Recent Advances in Natural Language Processing*, pp. 1–8. Tzigov Chark, BG, 2001.

34. C.-C. Chang and C.-J. Lin. Libsvm: A library for support vector machines. *ACM Transactions on Intelligent Systems and Technology (TIST)*, 2(3):27, 2011.

35. R. Chao and Y. Tan. A virus detection system based on artificial immune system. In *Computational Intelligence and Security, 2009. CIS'09. International Conference on*, Vol. 1, pp. 6–10. IEEE, Beijing, China, 2009.

36. Y. Chao, L. Yiwen, and L. Aolin. The danger sensed method by feature changes. *Energy Procedia*, 13:4429–4437, 2011.

37. M. Walport, C. A. Janeway, Jr, P. Travers, and Mark. J. Shlomchik. *Immunobiology: The Immune System in Health and Disease*. Number 2 in Immunobiology: The Immune System in Health and Disease. New York: Garland Science, 2005.

38. H. Cheng, P.-N. Tan, and R. Jin. Localized support vector machine and its efficient algorithm. In *SDM*, pp. 461–466. SIAM, 2007.

39. H. Cheng, P.-N. Tan, and R. Jin. Efficient algorithm for localized support vector machine. *Knowledge and Data Engineering, IEEE Transactions on*, 22(4):537–549, 2010.

40. A. Ciltik and T. Gungor. Time-efficient spam e-mail filtering using n-gram models. *Pattern Recognition Letters*, 29(1):19–33, 2008.

41. J. Clark, I. Koprinska, and J. Poon. A neural network based approach to automated e-mail classification. In *Web Intelligence, 2003. WI 2003. Proceedings. IEEE/WIC International Conference on*, pp. 702–705. IEEE, 2003.

42. I. R. Cohen. Real and artificial immune systems: Computing the state of the body. *Nature Reviews Immunology*, 7(7):569–574, 2007.

43. W.W. Cohen. Fast effective rule induction. In *Proceedings of 12th International Conference on Machine Learning*, pp. 115–123. San Mateo, CA: Morgan Kaufmann, 1995.

44. Commtouch. Internet threats trend report-April 2012. Technical report, Commtouch, Netanya, Israel, 2012.

45. G.V. Cormack. Email spam filtering: A systematic review. *Foundations and Trends in Information Retrieval*, 1(4):335–455, 2007.

46. T. Cover and P. Hart. Nearest neighbor pattern classification. *Information Theory, IEEE Transactions on*, 13(1):21–27, 1967.

47. L.F. Cranor and B.A. LaMacchia. Spam! *Communications of the ACM*, 41(8):74–83, 1998.

48. M. Crispin. Rfc2060: Internet message access protocol-Version 4rev1. http://www.ietf. org/rfc/rfc2060.txt, accessed: 2012.

49. N. Cruz-Cortés, D. Trejo-Pérez, and C. Coello. Handling constraints in global optimization using an artificial immune system. *Artificial Immune Systems*, Springer, 234–247, 2005.

50. V. Cutello and G. Nicosia. Multiple learning using immune algorithms. In *Proceedings of 4th International Conference on Recent Advances in Soft Computing, RASC*, pp. 102–107, 2002.

51. D. Dasgupta and F. González. An immunity-based technique to characterize intrusions in computer networks. *Evolutionary Computation, IEEE Transactions on*, 6(3):281–291, 2002.

52. D. Dasgupta, S. Yu, and N. Majumdar. Mila¡ªmultilevel immune learning algorithm. In *Genetic and Evolutionary Computation¡ªGECCO 2003*, pp. 183–194. Springer, Berlin, Germany, 2003.

53. D. Dasgupta, S. Yu, and F. Nino. Recent advances in artificial immune systems: Models and applications. *Applied Soft Computing*, 11(2):1574–1587, 2011.

54. D. Dasgupta. Advances in artificial immune systems. *Computational Intelligence Magazine, IEEE*, 1(4):40–49, 2006.

55. D. Dasgupta and N. Attoh-Okine. Immunity-based systems: A survey. In *Systems, Man, and Cybernetics, 1997. Computational Cybernetics and Simulation., 1997 IEEE International Conference on*, Vol. 1, pp. 369–374. IEEE, Orlando, FL, 1997.

56. L. Nunes de Castro and J. Timmis. An artificial immune network for multimodal function optimization. In *Evolutionary Computation, 2002. CEC'02. Proceedings of the 2002 Congress on*, Vol. 1, pp. 699–704. IEEE, Honolulu, HI, 2002.

57. L. Nunes De Castro and J. Timmis. *Artificial Immune Systems: A new Computational Intelligence Approach*. Springer, Berlin, Germany, 2002.

58. L. Nunes De Castro and F. J. Von Zuben. Artificial immune systems: Part *i*–Basic theory and applications. *Universidade Estadual de Campinas, Dezembro de, Technical Report*, 210, 1999.

59. L.N. De Castro and F.J. Von Zuben. The clonal selection algorithm with engineering applications. In *Proceedings of GECCO*, Vol. 2000, pp. 36–39, Las Vegas, NV, 2000.

60. L.N. de Castro and F.J. Von Zuben. ainet: An artificial immune network for data analysis. *Data Mining: A Heuristic Approach*, 1:231–259, 2001.

61. L.N. De Castro and F.J. Von Zuben. Learning and optimization using the clonal selection principle. *Evolutionary Computation, IEEE Transactions on*, 6(3):239–251, 2002.

62. P.A.D. de Castro and F.J. Von Zuben. Bais: A bayesian artificial immune system for the effective handling of building blocks. *Information Sciences*, 179(10):1426–1440, 2009.

63. D. DeBarr and H. Wechsler. Using social network analysis for spam detection. Third International Conference on Social Computing - 2010, *Advances in Social Computing*, Springer, 62–69, 2010.

64. C. Domeniconi and D. Gunopulos. Incremental support vector machine construction. In *Proceedings of the IEEE International Conference on Data Mining (ICDM'01)*, pp. 589–592, San Jose, CA, December 2001.

65. M. Dredze, R. Gevaryahu, and A. Elias-Bachrach. Learning fast classifiers for image spam. In *Proceedings of the Conference on Email and Anti-Spam (CEAS)*, 2007.

66. H. Drucker, C. J. C. Burges, L. Kauffman, A. Smola, and V. N. Vapnik. Support vector regression machines. In Michael C. Mozer, Michael I. Jordan, and Thomas Petsche, editors, *Advances in Neural Information Processing System (NIPS)*, Vol. 9, pp. 155–161. MIT Press, Cambridge, MA, 1997.

67. Harris Drucker, S Wu, and Vladimir N Vapnik. Support vector machines for spam categorization. *Neural Networks, IEEE Transactions on*, 10(5):1048–1054, 1999.

68. Z. Duan, Y. Dong, and K. Gopalan. Dmtp: Controlling spam through message delivery differentiation. *Computer Networks*, 51(10):2616–2630, 2007.

69. Z. Duan, K. Gopalan, and X. Yuan. An empirical study of behavioral characteristics of spammers: Findings and implications. *Computer Communications*, 34:1764–1776, 2011.

70. S. Forrest, A.S. Perelson, L. Allen, and R. Cherukuri. Self-nonself discrimination in a computer. In *Research in Security and Privacy, 1994. Proceedings, 1994 IEEE Computer Society Symposium on*, pp. 202–212. IEEE, 1994.

71. A. A. Freitas and J. Timmis. Revisiting the foundations of artificial immune systems for data mining. *Evolutionary Computation, IEEE Transactions on*, 11(4):521–540, 2007.

72. G. Fumera, I. Pillai, and F. Roli. Spam filtering based on the analysis of text information embedded into images. *The Journal of Machine Learning Research*, 7:2699–2720, 2006.

73. J.C. Galeano, A. Veloza-Suan, and F.A. González. A comparative analysis of artificial immune network models. In *Proceedings of the 2005 Conference on Genetic and Evolutionary Computation*, pp. 361–368. ACM, 2005.

74. W. Gansterer, M. Ilger, P. Lechner, R. Neumayer, and J. Strauß. Anti-spam methods—state of the art. Institute of Distributed and Multimedia Systems, University of Vienna, 2005.

75. Y. Gao, A. Choudhary, and G. Hua. A comprehensive approach to image spam detection: From server to client solution. *IEEE Transactions on Information Forensics and Security*, 5(4):826–836, Evanston, IL, 2010.

76. Y. Gao, M. Yang, X. Zhao, B. Pardo, Y. Wu, T.N. Pappas, and A. Choudhary. Image spam hunter. In *Acoustics, Speech and Signal Processing, 2008. ICASSP 2008. IEEE International Conference on*, pp. 1765–1768. IEEE, 2008.

77. Y. Gao, G. Mi, and Y. Tan. An adaptive concentraton selection model for spam detection. In *The Fifth International Conference on Swarm Intelligence (ICSI 2014)*, pp. 223–233. Springer, New York, 2014.

78. S. Garrett. A paratope is not an epitope: Implications for immune network models and clonal selection. *Artificial Immune Systems*, 217–228, Springer, 2003.

79. F. González, D. Dasgupta, and J. Gómez. The effect of binary matching rules in negative selection. In *Genetic and Evolutionary Computation GECCO 2003*, pp. 195–206. Springer, New York, 2003.

80. A. Graves. *Supervised Sequence Labelling with Recurrent Neural Networks*, vol 385. Springer, Berlin, Germany, 2012.

81. G.A. Grimes. Compliance with the can-spam act of 2003. *Communications of the ACM*, 50(2):56–62, 2007.

82. S. Gu, Y. Tan, and X. He. Discriminant analysis via support vectors. *Neurocomputing*, 73(10–12):1669–1675, 2010.

83. S. Gu, Y. Tan, and X. He. Laplacian smoothing transform for face recognition. *Science China (Information Science)*, 53(12):2415–2428, 2010.

84. S. Gu, Y. Tan, and X. He. Recent-biased learning for time series forecast. *Information Science*, 237(10):29–38, 2013.

85. Z. Guo, Z. Liu, and Y. Tan. Detector generating algorithm based on hyper-sphere. *Journal of Chinese Computer Systems*, 26(12):1641–1645, 2005.

86. Z. Guo, Z. Liu, and Y. Tan. An NN-based malicious executables detection algorithm based on immune principles. In *Advances in Neural Networks-ISNN 2004*, pp. 675–680. Springer, New York, 2004.

87. T. S. Guzella and W. M. Caminhas. A review of machine learning approaches to spam filtering. *Expert Systems with Applications*, 36(7):10206–10222, 2009.

88. T. S Guzella, T. A Mota-Santos, J. Q. Uchôa, and W. M. Caminhas. Identification of spam messages using an approach inspired on the immune system. *Biosystems*, 92(3):215–225, 2008.

89. M. Hall, E. Frank, G. Holmes, B. Pfahringer, P. Reutemann, and I. H. Witten. The weka data mining software: an update. *ACM SIGKDD Explorations Newsletter*, 11(1):10–18, 2009.

90. J. He and B. Thiesson. Asymmetric gradient boosting with application to spam filtering. In *Proceedings of Fourth Conference on Email and Anti-Spam CEAS*, pp. 1–8. California, 2007.

91. P. He, X. Wen, and W. Zheng. A simple method for filtering image spam. In *Computer and Information Science, 2009. ICIS 2009. Eighth IEEE/ACIS International Conference on*, pp. 910–913. IEEE, 2009.

92. S. Heron. Technologies for spam detection. *Network Security*, 2009(1):11–15, 2009.

93. S. Hershkop. Behavior-based email analysis with application to spam detection. PhD thesis, Columbia University, 2006.

94. S. Hochreiter. Untersuchungen zu dynamischen neuronalen netzen. Master's thesis, Institut fur Informatik, Technische Universitat, Munchen, Germany, 1991.

95. S. Hochreiter and J. Schmidhuber. Long short-term memory. *Neural Computation*, 9(8):1735–1780, 1997.

96. S.A. Hofmeyr and S. Forrest. Architecture for an artificial immune system. *Evolutionary Computation*, 8(4):443–473, 2000.

97. F. Huamin, Y. Xinghua, L. Biao, and J. Chao. A spam filtering method based on multi-modal features fusion. In *Computational Intelligence and Security (CIS), 2011 Seventh International Conference on*, pp. 421–426. IEEE, 2011.

98. X. Huang, Y. Tan, and X. He. An intelligent multi-feature statistical approach for discrimination of driving conditions of hybrid electric vehicle. *IEEE Transactions on Intelligent Transportation Systems*, 12(2):453–465, 2011.

99. J. Hunt, J. Timmis, D. Cooke et al. Jisys: Development of an artificial immune system for real world applicaitions, *Artificial Immune Systems and Their Applications*, Dasgupta, D. (ed.). Springer-Verlag, Berlin, Germany, 1998.

100. J.E. Hunt and D.E. Cooke. Learning using an artificial immune system. *Journal of Network and Computer Applications*, 19(2):189–212, 1996.

101. J. Ioannidis. Fighting spam by encapsulating policy in email addresses. In *Proceedings of NDSS*, pp. 1–8, San Diego, CA, 2003.

102. A. Janecek and Y. Tan. Iterative improvement of the multiplicative update nmf algorithm using nature-inspired optimization. In *Natural Computation (ICNC), 2011 Seventh International Conference on*, Vol. 3, pp. 1668–1672. IEEE, Shanghai, China, 2011.

103. N.K. Jerne. Towards a network theory of the immune system. *Annales D'Immunologie*, Vol. 125, pp. 373–389, 1974.

104. Z. Ji and D. Dasgupta. Real-valued negative selection algorithm with variable-sized detectors. In *Genetic and Evolutionary Computation–GECCO 2004*, pp. 287–298. Springer, New York, 2004.

105. Z. Ji and D. Dasgupta. Revisiting negative selection algorithms. *Evolutionary Computation*, 15(2):223–251, 2007.

106. L. Jiao and H. Du. Development and prospect of the artificial immune system. In Chinese. *Acta Electronica Sinica*, 31(10):1540–1548, 2003.

107. X. Liu, J. Wang, and X. Wang. Artificial immune system and analysis of its models. (In Chineses). *Computer Technology and Development*, 16(7):105–107, 2006.

108. I. Kanaris, K. Kanaris, I. Houvardas, and E. Stamatatos. Words versus character n-grams for anti-spam filtering. *International Journal on Artificial Intelligence Tools*, 16(06):1047–1067, 2007.

109. V. Kecman and J. Paul Brooks. Locally linear support vector machines and other local models. In *Neural Networks (IJCNN), The 2010 International Joint Conference on*, pp. 1–6. IEEE, 2010.

110. J. Klensin. Rfc2821: Simple mail transfer protocol. http://www.ietf.org/rfc/rfc2821.txt, accessed: 2012.

111. M. Kokkodis and M. Faloutsos. Spamming botnets: Are we losing the war. In *The 6th Conference on Email and Anti-Spam (CEAS)*, pp. 1–3. Mountain View, CA, 2009.

112. I. Koprinska, J. Poon, J. Clark, and J. Chan. Learning to classify e-mail. *Information Sciences*, 177(10):2167–2187, 2007.

113. S.B. Kotsiantis. Supervised machine learning: A review of classification techniques. *Informatica*, 31:249–268, 2007.

114. S. Krasser, Y. Tang, J. Gould, D. Alperovitch, and P. Judge. Identifying image spam based on header and file properties using c4. 5 decision trees and support vector machine learning. In *Information Assurance and Security Workshop, 2007. IAW'07. IEEE SMC*, pp. 255–261. IEEE, 2007.

115. H.Y. Lam and D.Y. Yeung. A learning approach to spam detection based on social networks. In *Proceedings of Fourth Conference on Email and Anti-Spam*, pp. 1–9. CA, 2007.

116. Y. Lee. Handwritten digit recognition using k nearest-neighbor, radial-basis function, and backpropagation neural networks. *Neural Computation*, 3(3):440–449, 1991.

117. F. Li and M.H. Hsieh. An empirical study of clustering behavior of spammers and group-based anti-spam strategies. In *CEAS 2006: Proceedings of the 3rd Conference on Email and Anti-Spam*, 2006.

118. P. Li, H. Yan, G. Cui, and Y. Du. Integration of local and global features for image spam filtering. *Journal of Computational Information Systems*, 8(2):779–789, 2012.

119. Y. Li, B. Fang, L. Guo, and S. Wang. Research of a novel anti-spam technique based on users's feedback and improved naive bayesian approach. In *Networking and Services, 2006. ICNS'06. International Conference on*, pp. 86–86. IEEE, 2006.

120. Z. Li and H. Shen. Soap: A social network aided personalized and effective spam filter to clean your e-mail box. In *INFOCOM, 2011 Proceedings IEEE*, pp. 1835–1843. IEEE, 2011.

121. Z. Li, Y. Zhang, and H.Z. Tan. An efficient artificial immune network with elite-learning. In *Natural Computation, 2007. ICNC 2007. Third International Conference on*, Vol. 4, pp. 213–217. IEEE, Haikou, China, 2007.

122. Q. Liu, Z. Qin, H. Cheng, and M. Wan. Efficient modeling of spam images. In *Intelligent Information Technology and Security Informatics (IITSI), 2010 Third International Symposium on*, pp. 663–666. IEEE, 2010.

123. Q. Luo, B. Liu, J. Yan, and Z. He. Research of a spam filtering algorithm based on naive bayes and ais. In *Computational and Information Sciences (ICCIS), 2010 International Conference on*, pp. 152–155. IEEE, 2010.

124. W. Luo, Y. Tan, and X. Wang. A novel negative selection algorithm with an array of partial matching lengths for each detector. In *PPSN 2006*, pp. 112–121. Springer, New York, 2006.

125. W. Ma, D. Tran, and D. Sharma. A novel spam email detection system based on negative selection. In *Computer Sciences and Convergence Information Technology, 2009. ICCIT'09. Fourth International Conference on*, pp. 987–992. IEEE, 2009.

126. M.N. Marsono. Towards improving e-mail content classification for spam control: Architecture, abstraction, and strategies. PhD thesis, University of Victoria, 2007.

127. P. Matzinger. Essay 1: The danger model in its historical context. *Scandinavian Journal of Immunology*, 54(1–2):4–9, 2001.

128. P. Matzinger. The danger model: A renewed sense of self. *Science*, 296(5566):301–305, 2002.

129. B. Medlock. An adaptive, semi-structured language model approach to spam filtering on a new corpus. In *CEAS*, 2006.

130. B. Mehta, S. Nangia, M. Gupta, and W. Nejdl. Detecting image spam using visual features and near duplicate detection. In *Proceedings of the 17th International Conference on World Wide Web*, pp. 497–506. ACM, 2008.

131. V. Metsis, I. Androutsopoulos, and G. Paliouras. Spam filtering with naive bayes-which naive bayes? In *CEAS*, pp. 27–28, 2006.

132. G. Mi, P. Zhang, and Y. Tan. Feature construction approach for email categorization based on term space partition. In *Neural Networks (IJCNN), The 2013 International Joint Conference on*, pp. 1–8. IEEE, 2013.

133. G. Mi, P. Zhang, and Y. Tan. A multi-resolution-concentration based feature construction approach for spam filtering. In *Neural Networks (IJCNN), The 2013 International Joint Conference on*, pp. 1–8. IEEE, 2013.

134. P. Mitra, C.A. Murthy, and S.K. Pal. Data condensation in large databases by incremental learning with support vector machines. In *Proceedings of the IEEE International Conference on Pattern Recognition*, Vol. 2, pp. 708–711, Barcelona, Spain, September 2000.

135. H. Mo and H. Jin. Application of artificial immune system to computer security in Chinese. *Journal of Harbin Engineering University*, 24(3):278–282, 2003.

136. J. Myers and M. Rose. Rfc1939: Post office protocol—Version3. http://www.ietf.org/rfc/rfc1939.txt, accessed: 2012.

137. O. Nasaroui, F. Gonzalez, and D. Dasgupta. The fuzzy artificial immune system: Motivations, basic concepts, and application to clustering and web profiling. In *Fuzzy Systems, 2002. FUZZ-IEEE'02. Proceedings of the 2002 IEEE International Conference on*, Vol. 1, pp. 711–716. IEEE, Honolulu, HI, 2002.

138. M. Neal. An artificial immune system for continuous analysis of time-varying data. In *Proceedings of the 1st International Conference on Artificial Immune Systems (ICARIS)*, Vol. 1, pp. 76–85, Canterbury, U.K., 2002.

139. T. Oda and T. White. Developing an immunity to spam. In *Genetic and Evolutionary Computation GECCO 2003*, pp. 231–242. Springer, New York, 2003.

140. T. Oda and T. White. Immunity from spam: An analysis of an artificial immune system for junk email detection. In *Artificial Immune Systems*, pp. 276–289. Springer, New York, 2005.

141. T. Oda. Spam detection using an artificial immune system. ACM *Crossroads Magazine*, November 2004 edition.

142. Bill on Telecommunication. Tkg 2003. Technical report, https://www.rtr.at/de/tk/TKG2003, accessed: 2009.

143. E. Osuna, R. Freund, and F. Girosi. An improved training algorithm for support vector machines. In *Proceedings of IEEE Workshop on Neural Networks for Signal Processing (NNSP'97)*, pp. 276–285, September 1997.

144. J.C. Platt. Sequential minimal optimization: A fast algorithm for training support vector machines. In Bernhard Scholkopf, Christopher J. C. Burges, and Alexander J. Smola, editors, *Advances in Kernel Method: Support Vector Learning*, pp. 185–208. MIT Press, Cambridge, MA, 1998.

145. J.B. Postel. Rfc821: Simple mail transfer protocol. http://www.ietf.org/rfc/rfc0821.txt, accessed: 2012.

146. C.E. Prieto, F. Nino, and G. Quintana. A goalkeeper strategy in robot soccer based on danger theory. In *Evolutionary Computation, 2008. CEC 2008.(IEEE World Congress on Computational Intelligence). IEEE Congress on*, pp. 3443–3447. IEEE, 2008.

147. J. Qing, R. Mao, R. Bie, and X.Z. Gao. An ais-based e-mail classification method. *Emerging Intelligent Computing Technology and Applications. With Aspects of Artificial Intelligence*, pp. 492–499, 2009.

148. J. Ross Quinlan. Induction of decision trees. *Machine Learning*, 1(1):81–106, 1986.

149. John Ross Quinlan. *C4. 5: Programs for Machine Learning*, vol. 1. Morgan Kaufmann, San Francisco, CA, 1993.

150. A. Ramachandran and N. Feamster. Understanding the network-level behavior of spammers. In *ACM SIGCOMM Computer Communication Review*, Vol. 36, pp. 291–302. ACM, 2006.

151. A. Ramachandran, N. Feamster, and S. Vempala. Filtering spam with behavioral blacklisting. In *Proceedings of the 14th ACM Conference on Computer and Communications Security*, pp. 342–351. ACM, 2007.

152. A.V. Ramachandran. Mitigating spam using network-level features. PhD thesis, Georgia Institute of Technology, August 2011.

153. F. Research. Spam, spammers, and spam conrol: A white paper by ferris research. Technical report, 2009.

154. G. Ruan and Y. Tan. Intelligent detection approaches for spam. In *Natural Computation, 2007. ICNC 2007. Third International Conference on*, Vol. 3, pp. 672–676. IEEE, Haikou, China, 2007.

155. G. Ruan and Y. Tan. A three-layer back-propagation neural network for spam detection using artificial immune concentration. *Soft Computing*, 14(2):139–150, 2010.

156. M. Sahami, S. Dumais, D. Heckerman, and E. Horvitz. A bayesian approach to filtering junk e-mail. In *Learning for Text Categorization: Papers from the 1998 Workshop*, Vol. 62, pp. 98–105, Madison, WI, 1998.

157. G. Sakkis, I. Androutsopoulos, G. Paliouras, V. Karkaletsis, C. D. Spyropoulos, and P. Stamatopoulos. A memory-based approach to anti-spam filtering for mailing lists. *Information Retrieval*, 6(1):49–73, 2003.

158. S. Salehi and A. Selamat. Hybrid simple artificial immune system (sais) and particle swarm optimization (pso) for spam detection. In *Software Engineering (MySEC), 2011 5th Malaysian Conference in*, pp. 124–129. IEEE, 2011.

159. E.P. Sanz, J.M. Gomez Hidalgo, and J.C. Cortizo Perez. Email spam filtering. *Advances in Computers*, 74:45–114, 2008.

160. S. Sarafijanovic and J.Y. Le Boudec. Artificial immune system for collaborative spam filtering. *Nature Inspired Cooperative Strategies for Optimization (NICSO 2007)*, pp. 39–51, 2008.

161. M. Sasaki Spam detection using text clustering. In *Proceedings of International Conference on Cyberworlds*, pp. 316–319, 2005.

162. R.E. Schapire Boostexter: A boosting-based system for text categorization. *Machine Learning*, 39(2):135–168, 2000.

163. R.E. Schapire Singer and Y. Boosting and rocchio applied to text filtering. In *Proceedings of 21st Annual International Conference Information Retrieval, SIGIR*, 1998.

164. K.M. Schneider. A comparison of event models for naive bayes anti-spam e-mail filtering. In *Proceedings of the Tenth Conference on European Chapter of the Association for Computational Linguistics*, pp. 307–314. Association for Computational Linguistics, Madrid, Spain, 2003.

165. D. Sculley. Advances in online learning-based spam filtering. PhD thesis, Tufts University, 2008.

166. A. Secker, A. A. Freitas, and J. Timmis. A danger theory inspired approach to web mining. In *Artificial Immune Systems*, pp. 156–167. Springer, Edinburgh, U.K., 2003.

167. A. Secker, A. A. Freitas, and J. Timmis. Aisec: An artificial immune system for e-mail classification. In *Evolutionary Computation, 2003. CEC'03. The 2003 Congress on*, Vol. 1, pp. 131–138. IEEE, Canberra, Australian Capital Territory, Australia, 2003.

168. R. Segal. Combining global and personal anti-spam filtering. In *CEAS*, 2007.

169. R. Shrestha and Y. Lin. Improved bayesian spam filtering based on co-weighted multi-area information. In *Advances in Knowledge Discovery and Data Mining*, pp. 650–660. Springer, New York, 2005.

170. C. Siefkes, F. Assis, S. Chhabra, and W. Yerazunis. Combining winnow and orthogonal sparse bigrams for incremental spam filtering. In *Knowledge Discovery in Databases: PKDD 2004*, pp. 410–421. Springer, New York, 2004.

171. B. Sirisanyalak and O. Sornil. An artificial immunity-based spam detection system. In *Evolutionary Computation, 2007. CEC 2007. IEEE Congress on*, pp. 3392–3398. IEEE, 2007.

172. Sophos. Security threat report 2012. Sophos Technical report, Sophos, Oxford, U.K., 2012.

173. Anti spam Center of ISC. 2008 4q anti-spam investigation report. Technical report. http://www.12321.org.cn/pdf/2008_4_dc.pdf, accessed: 2009.

174. T. Subramaniam, H.A. Jalab, and A.Y. Taqa. Overview of textual antispam filtering techniques. *International Journal of the Physical Sciences*, 5(12):1869–1882, 2010.

175. Z. Sun and W. Wei. Artificial immune system and its application. in chinese. *Computer Engineering*, 29(15), 2003.

176. N.A. Syed, H. Liu, and K.K. Sung. Incremental learning with support vector machines. In *Proceedings of the International Joint Conference on Artificial Intelligence (IJCAI'99)*, Stockholm, Sweden, 1999.

177. Symantec. Symantec intelligence report: January 2012. Technical report, 2012.

178. Mail Abuse Prevention Systems. Definition of spam. http://www.mail-abuse.com, accessed: 2012.

179. T. Joachims. A probabilistic analysis of the rocchio algorithm with tfidf for text categorization. In *Proceedings of 14th International Conference Machine Learning*. Morgan Kaufman, Miami, FL, 1997.

180. Nicholas T. Using adaboost and decision stumps to identify spam e-mail. Technical report. http://nlp.stanford.edu/courses/cs224n/2003/fp/, accessed: 2009.

181. Y. Tan. Particle swarm optimization algorithms inspired by immunity-clonal mechanism and their applications to spam detection. *International Journal of Swarm Intelligence Research (IJSIR)*, 1(1):64–86, 2010.

182. Y. Tan and J. Wang. Nonlinear blind separation using higher-order statistics and a genetic algorithm. *IEEE Transaction on Evolutionary Computation*, 5(6):600–612, 2001.

183. Y. Tan and Z.M. Xiao. Clonal particle swarm optimization and its applications. In *Evolutionary Computation, 2007. CEC 2007. IEEE Congress on*, pp. 2303–2309. IEEE, 2007.

184. Y. Tan. Swarm robotics: Collective behavior inspired by nature. *Journal of Computer Science and System Biology (JCSB)*, 6:e106, 2013.

185. Y. Tan. Neural network design approach of cosine-modulated fir filter bank and compactly supported wavelets with almost pr property. *Signal Processing*, 69(1):29–48, 1998.

186. Y. Tan. Editorial: Special issue on advances in swarm intelligence for neural networks. *Neurocomputing*, 148(1):1–2, 2014.

187. Y. Tan. *Fireworks Algorithms: A Swarm Intelligence Optimization Method*. Springer, New York, 2015.

188. Y. Tan. *Introduction to Fireworks Algorithms*. Science Press, (In Chinese) 2015.

189. Y. Tan and C. Deng. Solving for a quadratic programming with a quadratic constraint based on a neural network frame. *Neurocomputing*, 30:117–128, 2000.

190. Y. Tan, C. Deng, and G. Ruan. Concentration based feature construction approach for spam detection. In *Neural Networks, 2009. IJCNN 2009. International Joint Conference on*, pp. 3088–3093. IEEE, 2009.

191. Y. Tan and Z. Guo. Algorithms of non-self detector by negative selection principle in artificial immune system. In *Advances in Natural Computation*, pp. 867–875. Springer, New York, 2005.

192. Y. Tan and Z. Liu. On matrix eigendecomposition by neural networks. *Neural Network World, International Journal on Neural and Mass-Parallel Computing and Information Systems*, 8(3):337–352, 1998.

193. Y. Tan, G. Mi, Y. Zhu, and C. Deng. Artificial immune system based methods for spam filtering. In *2013 IEEE International Symposium on Circuits and Systems (ISCAS 2013)*, pp. 2484–2488. IEEE, 2013.

194. Y. Tan and G. Ruan. Uninterrupted approaches for spam detection based on svm and ais. *International Journal of Computational Intelligence*, 1(1):1–26, 2014.

195. Y. Tan and J. Wang. A support vector machine with a hybrid kernel and minimal vapnik-chervonenkis dimension. *Knowledge and Data Engineering, IEEE Transactions on*, 16(4):385–395, 2004.

196. Y. Tan and J. Wang. A support vector network with hybrid kernel and minimal vapnik-chervonenkis dimension. *IEEE Transaction on Knowledge and Data Engineering*, 26(2):385–395, 2004.

197. Y. Tan and J. Wang. Recent advances in finger vein based biometrics techniques. *CAAI Transactions on Intelligent Systems*, 6(6):471–482, 2011.

198. Y. Tan, J. Wang, and J.M. Zurada. Nonlinear blind source separation using radial basis function networks. *IEEE Transaction on Neural Networks*, 12(1):124–134, 2001.

199. Y. Tan and Y. Zhu. Advances in anti-spam techniques. *CAAI Transactions on Intelligent Systems*, 5(3):189–201, 2010.

200. Y. Tan and Y. Zhu. Fireworks algorithm for optimization. In *Advances in Swarm Intelligence*, pp. 355–364. Springer, New York, 2010.

201. J. Timmis. Artificial immune systems: A novel data analysis technique inspired by the immune network theory. PhD thesis, Department of Computer Science, 2000.

202. J. Timmis, A. Hone, T. Stibor, and E. Clark. Theoretical advances in artificial immune systems. *Theoretical Computer Science*, 403(1):11–32, 2008.

203. J. Timmis and M. Neal. A resource limited artificial immune system for data analysis. *Knowledge-Based Systems*, 14(3):121–130, 2001.

204. J. Timmis. Artificial immune systems—Today and tomorrow. *Natural Computing*, 6(1):1–18, 2007.

205. J. Timmis, P. Andrews, N. Owens, and E. Clark. An interdisciplinary perspective on artificial immune systems. *Evolutionary Intelligence*, 1(1):5–26, 2008.

206. L.S. Tseng and C.H. Wu. Detection of spain e-mails by analyzing the distributing behaviors of e-mail servers. In *Design and Application of Hybrid Intelligent Systems*, pp. 1024–1033. IOS Press, 2003.

207. M. Uemura and T. Tabata. Design and evaluation of a bayesian-filter-based image spam filtering method. In *Information Security and Assurance, 2008. ISA 2008. International Conference on*, pp. 46–51. IEEE, 2008.

208. Carnegie Mellon University. Completely automated public turing test to tell computers and humans apart. http://www.captcha.net/, accessed: 2012.

209. V. Vapnik. *The Nature of Statistical Learning Theory*. Springer, New York, 2000.

210. V. N. Vapnik and S. Kotz. *Estimation of Dependences Based on Empirical Data*, Vol. 40 Springer-Verlag, New York, 1982.

211. V.N. Vapnik. Principles of risk minimization for learning theory. In *Advances in Neural Information Processing Systems*, Vol. 4, pp. 831–838, Denver, CO, 1992.

212. L. von Ahn, M. Blum, and J. Langford. Telling humans and computers apart automatically. *Communications of the ACM*, 47(2):56–60, February 2004.

213. M. Wan, F. Zhang, H. Cheng, and Q. Liu. Text localization in spam image using edge features. In *Communications, Circuits and Systems, 2008. ICCCAS 2008. International Conference on*, pp. 838–842. IEEE, 2008.

214. C. Wang, F. Zhang, F. Li, and Q. Liu. Image spam classification based on low-level image features. In *Communications, Circuits and Systems (ICCCAS), 2010 International Conference on*, pp. 290–293. IEEE, 2010.

215. F. Wang, Z. You, and L. Man. Immune-based peer-to-peer model for anti-spam. In *Computational Intelligence and Bioinformatics*, pp. 660–671. Springer, New York, 2006.

216. L. Wang, S. Ma, and X. Hei. Research on an immune mechanism based intelligent spam filter. In *Computer Science and Software Engineering, 2008 International Conference on*, Vol. 3, pp. 673–676. IEEE, Wuhan, China, 2008.

217. W. Wang, S. Gao, and Z. Tang. A complex artificial immune system. In *Natural Computation, 2008. ICNC'08. Fourth International Conference on*, Vol. 6, pp. 597–601. IEEE, Jinan, China, 2008.

218. W. Wang, P. Zhang, Y. Tan, and X. He. A feature extraction method of computer viruses based on artificial immune and code relevance. *Chinese Journal of Computer*, 34(2):204–215, 2011.

219. W. Wang, P. Zhang, Y. Tan, and X. He. An immune local concentration based virus detection approach. *Journal of Zhejiang University SCIENCE C*, 12(6):443–454, 2011.

220. W. Wang, P. Zhang, and Y. Tan. An immune concentration based virus detection approach using particle swarm optimization. In *Advances in Swarm Intelligence*, pp. 347–354. Springer, New York, 2010.

221. W. Wang, P. Zhang, Y. Tan, and X. He. A hierarchical artificial immune model for virus detection. In *Computational Intelligence and Security, 2009. CIS'09. International Conference on*, Vol. 1, pp. 1–5. IEEE, Beijing, China, 2009.

222. Z. Wang, W. Josephson, Q. Lv, M. Charikar, and K. Li. Filtering image spam with near-duplicate detection. In *Proceedings of CEAS*, 2007.

223. A. Watkins, X. Bi, and A. Phadke. Parallelizing an immune-inspired algorithm for efficient pattern recognition. *Intelligent Engineering Systems through Artificial Neural Networks: Smart Engineering System Design: Neural Networks, Fuzzy Logic, Evolutionary Programming, Complex Systems and Artificial Life*, 13:225–230, 2003.

224. B. Watson. Beyond identity: Addressing problems that persist in an electronic mail system with reliable sender identification. In *CEAS 2004: First Conference on Email and Anti-Spam*, pp. 1–8. CA, 2004.

225. Wenrui He, Guyue Mi, and Ying Tan. Parameter optimization of local-concentration model for spam detection by using fireworks algorithm. In *Proceedings of the fourth International Conferencce on Swarm Intelligence (ICSI 2013)*, pp. 439–450, 2013.

226. A.G. West, A.J. Aviv, J. Chang, and I. Lee. Mitigating spam using spatio-temporal reputation. Technical report, University of Pennsylvania, 2010.

227. Kevin Woods, Kevin Bowyer, and W. Philip Kegelmeyer Jr. Combination of multiple classifiers using local accuracy estimates. In *Computer Vision and Pattern Recognition, 1996. Proceedings CVPR'96, 1996 IEEE Computer Society Conference on*, pp. 391–396. IEEE, 1996.

228. Chih-Hung Wu. Behavior-based spam detection using a hybrid method of rule-based techniques and neural networks. *Expert Systems with Applications*, 36(3):4321–4330, 2009.

229. C.T. Wu, K.T. Cheng, Q. Zhu, and Y.L. Wu. Using visual features for anti-spam filtering. In *Image Processing, 2005. ICIP 2005. IEEE International Conference on*, Vol. 3, pp. 509–512. IEEE, Genoa, Italy, 2005.

230. Y. Xie, F. Yu, K. Achan, E. Gillum, M. Goldszmidt, and T. Wobber. How dynamic are ip addresses? In *ACM SIGCOMM Computer Communication Review*, Vol. 37, pp. 301–312. ACM, 2007.

231. Y. Yang. Noise reduction in a statistical approach to text categorization. In *Proceedings of the 18th Annual International ACM SIGIR Conference on Research and Development in Information Retrieval*, pp. 256–263. ACM, 1995.

232. Y. Yang and J.O. Pedersen. A comparative study on feature selection in text categorization. In *Proceedings of International Conference on Machine Learning*, pp. 412–420. Morgan Kaufmann Publishers, 1997.

233. Chi-Yuan Yeh, Chih-Hung Wu, and Shing-Hwang Doong. Effective spam classification based on meta-heuristics. In *Systems, Man and Cybernetics, 2005 IEEE International Conference on*, Vol. 4, pp. 3872–3877. IEEE, Waikoloa, HI, 2005.

234. William. S. Yerazunis. Sparse binary polynomial hashing and the crm114 discriminator. In *2003 Cambridge Spam Conference Proceedings*, vol. 1, Cambridge, U.K., 2003.

235. X. Yue, A. Abraham, Z.X. Chi, Y.Y. Hao, and H. Mo. Artificial immune system inspired behavior-based anti-spam filter. *Soft Computing-A Fusion of Foundations, Methodologies and Applications*, 11(8):729–740, 2007.

236. C. Zhang and Z. Yi. A danger theory inspired artificial immune algorithm for on-line supervised two-class classification problem. *Neurocomputing*, 73(7–9): 1244–1255, 2010.

237. Hao Zhang, Alexander C Berg, Michael Maire, and Jitendra Malik. Svm-knn: Discriminative nearest neighbor classification for visual category recognition. In *Computer Vision and Pattern Recognition, 2006 IEEE Computer Society Conference on*, Vol. 2, pp. 2126–2136. IEEE, New York, 2006.

238. Junqi Zhang, Ying Tan, Lina Ni, Chen Xie, and Zheng Tang. Amt-pso: An adaptive magnification transformation based particle swarm optimizer. *IEICE Transactions on Fundamentals of Electronics, Communications and Computer Sciences*, E94-D(4):786–797, 2011.

239. Junqi Zhang, Ying Tan, Lina Ni, Chen Xie, and Zheng Tang. Hybrid uniform distribution of particle swarm optimizer. *IEICE Transactions on Fundamentals of Electronics, Communications and Computer Sciences*, E93-A(10):1782–1791, 2010.

240. Le Zhang, Jingbo Zhu, and Tianshun Yao. An evaluation of statistical spam filtering techniques. *ACM Transactions on Asian Language Information Processing (TALIP)*, 3(4):243–269, 2004.

241. Pengtao Zhang and Ying Tan. Immune cooperation mechanism based learning framework. *Neurocomputing*, 148(1):158–166, 2014.

242. Xiangrong Zhang and Licheng Jiao. Feature selection based on immune clonal selection algorithm. in chinese. *Journal of Fudan University (Natural Science)*, 43(5):926–929, 2004.

243. Xiaolian Zhang. *Viral Immunology* (In Chinese), Vol. 1. Science Press, Beijing, China, 2010.

244. Y. Zhang and C. Hou. A clone selection algorithm with niching strategy inspiring by biological immune principles for change detection. In *Intelligent Control. 2003 IEEE International Symposium on*, pp. 1000–1005. IEEE, 2003.

245. Yuanchun Zhu, Guyue Mi, and Ying Tan. Query based hybrid learning models for adaptively adjusting locality. In *IEEE World Conference on Computational Intelligence (WCCI 2012) - IJCNN2012*, pp. 429–436. IEEE, 2012.

246. Yuanchun Zhu and Ying Tan. Extracting discriminative information from e-mail for spam detection inspired by immune system. In *Evolutionary Computation (CEC), 2010 IEEE Congress on*, pp. 1–7. IEEE, 2010.

247. Yuanchun Zhu and Ying Tan. A danger theory inspired learning model and its application to spam detection. In *Advances in Swarm Intelligence*, pp. 382–389. Springer, New York, 2011.

248. Yuanchun Zhu and Ying Tan. A local-concentration-based feature extraction approach for spam filtering. *Information Forensics and Security, IEEE Transactions on*, 6(2):486–497, 2011.

249. R.A. Zitar and A. Hamdan. Genetic optimized artificial immune system in spam detection: A review and a model. *Artificial Intelligence Review*, pp. 1–73, 2011.

250. Márcio Henrique Zuchini. *Aplicações de mapas auto-organizáveis em mineração de dados e recuperação de informação*. PhD thesis, Universidade São Francisco, 2003.

Index

229